Kazuo Ishiguro

Twenty-First-Century Perspectives

Series Editors: Kristian Shaw and Sara Upstone

Kazuo Ishiguro

Edited by

Kristian Shaw and Peter Sloane

MANCHESTER UNIVERSITY PRESS

Copyright © Manchester University Press 2023

While copyright in the volume as a whole is vested in Manchester University Press, copyright in individual chapters belongs to their respective authors, and no chapter may be reproduced wholly or in part without the express permission in writing of both author and publisher.

Published by Manchester University Press
Oxford Road, Manchester M13 9PL

www.manchesteruniversitypress.co.uk

British Library Cataloguing-in-Publication Data
A catalogue record for this book is available from the British Library

ISBN 978 1 5261 5763 9 hardback
ISBN 978 1 5261 8255 5 paperback

First published 2023
Paperback published 2024

The publisher has no responsibility for the persistence or accuracy of URLs for any external or third-party internet websites referred to in this book, and does not guarantee that any content on such websites is, or will remain, accurate or appropriate.

Typeset
by New Best-set Typesetters Ltd

For Faye

Contents

List of contributors	ix
Series editors' preface	xii
Acknowledgements	xiv
List of abbreviations	xv

	Introduction: 'This is the way it feels to me': the writings of Kazuo Ishiguro – Kristian Shaw and Peter Sloane	1
1	Diaspora, trauma, spectrality and world literary writing in *A Pale View of Hills* – Emily Horton	17
2	Eloquence and empathy in *A Pale View of Hills* and *An Artist of the Floating World* – Cynthia F. Wong	40
3	Ishiguro's tempered presentational realism and practice – Rebecca Karni	61
4	'An inevitable course': political responsibility in *The Remains of the Day* – Sara Upstone	84
5	Klara in the junkyard: on loneliness in *The Unconsoled* – Bruce Robbins	107
6	Novel dysfunction in *When We Were Orphans* – Andrew Bennett	126
7	Empathy and the ethics of posthuman reading in *Never Let Me Go* – Peter Sloane	146
8	*Nocturnes*, hope and 'that croony nostalgia music' – Yugin Teo	170
9	Disinterring the English sublime: haunted atmospherics in *The Buried Giant* – Kristian Shaw	188
10	Klara and the humans: agency, Hannah Arendt and forgiveness – Robert Eaglestone	212

11 Kazuo Ishiguro's film and television scriptwriting
  – Anni Shen   227

Index   248

Contributors

Andrew Bennett is Professor of English at the University of Bristol. He is editor of *The Cambridge Companion to Kazuo Ishiguro* (Cambridge University Press, 2023) and co-author, with Nicholas Royle, of *An Introduction to Literature, Criticism and Theory* (Routledge, 6th edn, 2023) and *This Thing Called Literature: Reading, Thinking, Writing* (Routledge, 2015). His other books include *Suicide Century: Literature and Suicide from James Joyce to David Foster Wallace* (Cambridge University Press, 2017), *Ignorance: Literature and Agnoiology* (Manchester University Press, 2009), and *The Author* (Routledge, 2005).

Robert Eaglestone is Professor of Contemporary Literature and Thought at Royal Holloway, University of London. He works on contemporary literature and philosophy. He is the author of eight books including *The Broken Voice: Reading Post-Holocaust Literature* (Oxford University Press, 2017) and *Truth and Wonder: A Literary Introduction to Plato and Aristotle* (Routledge, 2022) and the editor or co-editor of ten more, including *The Routledge Companion to Twenty First Century Literary Fiction* (Routledge, 2018). His work has been translated into seven languages. He co-founded the British Association for Contemporary Literary Studies.

Emily Horton is a Senior Lecturer in English Literature at Brunel University. Her research interests include contemporary world literature, popular fiction and fictional explorations of trauma and affect. Her first monograph, *Contemporary Crisis Fictions*, was published with Palgrave Macmillan in 2014. She has also co-edited two volumes: *The 1980s: A Decade in Contemporary British Fiction*, with Philip Tew and Leigh Wilson (Continuum, 2014); and *Ali Smith*, with Monica Germanà (Continuum, 2013).

Rebecca Karni is a Lecturer in the Department of Literary Arts and Studies at the Rhode Island School of Design. Her research interests are in twentieth- and twenty-first-century global Anglophone, world, British, American, Asian British and Asian American, and Japanese literatures; the novel and narrative theory; global film; aesthetics and ethics; and translation studies. Her publications include articles on Kazuo Ishiguro, among them 'Made in Translation: Language, "Japaneseness", "Englishness", and "Global Culture" in Ishiguro' in *Comparative Literature Studies*, and a chapter in the forthcoming *Cambridge Companion to Kazuo Ishiguro*.

Bruce Robbins is Old Dominion Foundation Professor in the Humanities at Columbia University. He previously taught at the universities of Geneva and Lausanne as well as Rutgers University. His most recent books are *Criticism and Politics: A Polemical Introduction* (Stanford University Press, 2022), *The Beneficiary* (Duke University Press, 2017) and *Cosmopolitanisms*, co-edited with Paulo Horta (New York University Press, 2017). He is the director of two documentaries, "Some of My Best Friends Are Zionists" and "What Kind of Jew Is Shlomo Sand?"

Kristian Shaw is Associate Professor in English Literature at the University of Lincoln. He is the author of *Cosmopolitanism in Twenty-First Century Fiction* (Palgrave, 2017) and *Brexlit: British Literature and the European Project* (Bloomsbury, 2021). He is the co-editor of *Hari Kunzru: Twenty-First Century Perspectives* (Manchester University Press, 2022).

Anni Shen is an associate professor of English currently teaching at the College of Foreign Languages and Cultures, Xiamen University. She has a PhD in English from Peking University and has worked as a postdoctoral fellow at Yale University affiliated with the Department of Comparative Literature and the Department of Film and Media Studies. Her first monograph in Chinese, *Transmedia Aesthetic Modernity: Kazuo Ishiguro's Three Novels in Relation to Film*, was published by China Social Sciences Press in 2020. Her essays have appeared in *Adaptation* and *CLIO*, and another is forthcoming in *Critique: Studies in Contemporary Fiction*.

Peter Sloane is Senior Lecturer in English at the University of Buckingham. He is the author of *David Foster Wallace and the Body* (Routledge, 2019) and *Kazuo Ishiguro's Gestural Poetics*

(Bloomsbury, 2021). He is also the editor of the forthcoming *ReFocus: The Films of Claire Denis* (Edinburgh University Press, 2023).

Yugin Teo is Senior Lecturer in Communications & English at Bournemouth University. He has previously taught literature and film at the University of Brighton and the University of Sussex where he completed his doctorate. His research on the representation of memory in literature and film has been published in the journals *Critique*, *Medical Humanities* and *Science Fiction Film and Television*. His research monograph *Kazuo Ishiguro and Memory* was published by Palgrave Macmillan in 2014.

Sara Upstone is Professor of Contemporary Literature and Faculty Director of Postgraduate Research at Kingston School of Art, Kingston University. Her publications include *Rethinking Race and Identity in Contemporary British Fiction* (Routledge, 2017), *British Asian Fiction: Twenty-First-Century Voices* (Manchester University Press, 2011) and *Spatial Politics in the Postcolonial Novel* (Ashgate, 2010). She is the co-editor of *Postmodern Literature and Race* (Cambridge University Press, 2015), *Researching and Representing Mobilities: Transdisciplinary Encounters* (Palgrave, 2014), *Postcolonial Spaces: The Politics of Place in Contemporary Culture* (Palgrave, 2011) and (with Peter Ely) the forthcoming *Community in Contemporary British Fiction* (Bloomsbury, 2022).

Cynthia F. Wong is Professor in the Department of English at the University of Colorado, Denver, where she teaches modern and contemporary world literature. She is author of *Writers and Their Work: Kazuo Ishiguro* (3rd edn, Northcote House, 2019), co-editor with Brian Shaffer of *Conversations with Kazuo Ishiguro* (University Press of Mississippi, 2008) and with Hülya Yıldız of *Kazuo Ishiguro in a Global Context* (Routledge, 2015). She has published essays on Asian American authors Jhumpa Lahiri, Karen Tei Yamashita, Joy Kogawa and Julie Otsuka.

Series editors' preface

Kristian Shaw and Sara Upstone

The twenty-first century exists as a site of social, cultural and political precarity. Captured in calls for social, political and environmental justice, shaped by war and pandemic, it demands a planetary consciousness with the vitality to imagine what might emerge beyond the uncertainties of the current moment.

Twenty-First-Century Perspectives offers a series of edited collections that examine the ways in which contemporary writers have responded to these global challenges, as a clamorous presence that has served to reignite the role of writer as public intellectual and the literary text as an agent of change. The series captures how contemporary literatures are producing striking works of political and ethical power, radically revising metanarratives of nation and identity while searching for original avenues of meaning in order to navigate these uncertain times. It examines the role of texts as daring reappraisals of literary tradition and innovations in form, acting as forces of transformation that – in their interrogations of the past, questioning of the present, and dreams of the future – demand a new critical vocabulary.

Through collections that feature an international range of voices, including some of the most notable literary scholars of the contemporary, the series identifies the key writers at the centre of this cultural moment. Focusing on distinctive individual voices, the series captures the writers in prose, poetry and dramatic writing whose bodies of work are already establishing them as the defining voices of a century. It also offers first collections on writers who have made their mark in the decades of the current century, alongside new studies of writers whose careers began in the twentieth century, critically appraising earlier texts in the context of contemporary debates to situate them within a specifically twenty-first-century aesthetic. Across the series the dual focus on socio-political contexts and formal invention builds a larger picture regarding emergent developments in contemporary literary culture. What emerges will be a lasting archive – a library of voices speaking in dialogue to the creation of a revolutionary imagination.

Acknowledgements

Special thanks go to Manchester University Press for commissioning this collection of essays and for being encouraging of the project from its inception. The editorial and production teams have been exemplary – their careful guidance and endless assistance was much appreciated. Our sincere thanks must go to Paul Clarke for his advice in developing a new *Twenty-First-Century Perspectives* series and support in bringing this collection into being.

The contributors in this collection demonstrated clear professionalism and dedication during the unprecedented difficulties of a global pandemic – it has not been forgotten.

Our greatest debts – as ever – are to our families.

Abbreviations

AW	*An Artist of the Floating World* (London: Faber & Faber, 1986)
BG	*The Buried Giant* (London: Faber & Faber, 2015)
KS	*Klara and the Sun* (London: Faber & Faber, 2021)
N	*Nocturnes* (London: Faber & Faber, 2009)
NLMG	*Never Let Me Go* (London: Faber & Faber, 2005)
PVH	*A Pale View of Hills* (London: Faber & Faber, 1982)
RD	*The Remains of the Day* (London: Faber & Faber, 1989)
U	*The Unconsoled* (London: Faber & Faber, 1995)
WWWO	*When We Were Orphans* (London: Faber & Faber, 2000)

Introduction
'This is the way it feels to me': the writings of Kazuo Ishiguro

Kristian Shaw and Peter Sloane

Arguably the leading voice in contemporary British literature, during a four-decade career Sir Kazuo Ishiguro has also established himself as an artist of international reputation. Indeed, he enjoys a rather remarkable position as a critically acclaimed author of formally innovative literary fiction who also tops bestseller charts across the world and whose new releases are anticipated with the relish usually reserved for more 'popular' writers. Beyond the text: Merchant Ivory's 1993 film adaptation of *The Remains of the Day* was nominated for eight Academy awards; Alex Garland's 2010 adaptation of *Never Let Me Go* (published in 2005) was critically lauded; and the film rights to *Klara and the Sun* (2021), possibly his most intentionally filmable work, have recently been acquired by Sony and 3000 Pictures. As an author who has settled, rather comfortably, into the traditions of English literature – pushing the boundaries of British canon-formation in the process – it is important to consider the literary stature and potential legacy of Ishiguro's writing. Despite being the recipient of (increasingly) prestigious literary prizes throughout his career, including the Winifred Holtby Prize from the Royal Society of Literature for his debut novel and 1989 Booker Prize for *The Remains of the Day*, Ishiguro's literary star is still very much on the rise. In 2017 he became the first British recipient of the Nobel Prize for Literature since Doris Lessing in 2007, the committee positioning him as a prescient and judicious writer 'who, in novels of great emotional force, has uncovered the abyss beneath our illusory sense of connection with the world' (Ishiguro, 2017). Paradoxically, of course, it is precisely this abyss (between, for example, Axl and Beatrice, Kathy and her cruel world, Mr Stevens and Miss Kenton,

Klara and her (in)human(e) creators), which encourages our empathy for his often existentially adrift protagonists.

Ishiguro was born in Nagasaki, Japan, on 8 November 1954, before his father, an oceanographer, relocated the family to Guildford, Surrey, in 1960. In conversation with the fellow Nobel-Prize-winning author Kenzaburo Oe (on Ishiguro's first visit to Japan since his relocation to England), Ishiguro admits that, although only a child at the time, he retained and nurtured a personal memory of Japan's cultural imaginary and turned to writing novels 'because I wished to recreate this Japan' (Oe and Ishiguro, 1991: 110). Appropriately, Ishiguro's first two novels, *A Pale View of Hills* (1982) and *An Artist of the Floating World* (1986), are embedded in Japanese socio-cultural and geographical landscapes, leading critics initially to read his work largely as an expression of his cultural heritage. However, he still cites his early migration to Great Britain – a trip echoed by Etsuko in *A Pale View of Hills* and Christopher Banks in *When We Were Orphans* (2000) – as a major life event which would go on to influence the texture, settings and thematic sensibilities of his later writings. Ishiguro's most critically acclaimed novel, *The Remains of the Day*, though retaining certain stylistic qualities associated with Japanese literature and an authorial fascination with the ongoing personal, familial, national and global legacies of the Second World War, signalled a move away from the imaginary of his birth nation and an engagement with quintessential, even parodic English attitudes, traditions and behaviours.

Nevertheless, as is often the case for novelists (or even poets, painters, filmmakers) working in the contemporary period, the proliferation of digitally available interviews and the growing number of living-author archives facilitate a temptation to read from biography into fiction in ways which, post-Barthes but pre-internet, had become intellectually unfashionable. Ishiguro scholarship has not been resistant to such readings, leading critics, reviewers and readers to emphasise the perceived 'Japaneseness' of his work. Ishiguro confesses that he exploited the 'Japanese side' of his transnational identity as he honed his craft. Recalling his time at the University of East Anglia while working toward his MA in Creative Writing (under the tutelage of Malcolm Bradbury and Angela Carter, 1979–1980), he remarks that 'when I wrote about Japan, something unlocked. One of the stories I showed the class was set in Nagasaki at the time the bomb dropped [...] I got a tremendous boost to my confidence from my fellow students' (Hunnewell and Ishiguro, 2008). The world's first wartime atomic detonation carries much resonance (even if Ishiguro refuses to attribute the bombing to US aggression, preferring the more passive, almost accidental 'dropped'), but the story told by a young author born in Nagasaki inevitably invests the narrative with a further degree of urgency. Spurred by his fellow students' approval, Ishiguro pursued his Japanese settings, resulting in the publication of his MA thesis in 1982 as *A Pale View of Hills* and of *An Artist of the Floating World* in 1986, his two 'Japanese' works.

Following the success of his first two novels, Ishiguro endeavoured to steer popular and critical attention away from such a direct link between his country of birth and his fictions. As he said to Dylan Krider: 'In the first two books, I very much wanted to appeal to the Japanese side of me. But by the time the second novel came out and I was starting to get known in Great Britain, I was very conscious that I was getting cast in this role as a kind of Japanese foreign correspondent in residence in London' (1998: 149). In an awkward 1986 interview with the British novelist Clive Sinclair, and in a subsequent 1987 Bookmark interview, an increasingly exasperated Ishiguro surmises that his reduction to a Japanese 'correspondent' resulted from 'projection on the part of a lot of reviewers, they see a Japanese name [and] attribute anything that is noticeable to Japaneseness' (Ishiguro, 1987). While Ishiguro's annoyance derives in part from reviewers associating him with a country he had left at the age of five, this critical tendency also exacerbated Ishiguro's related unease about the 'issue of people taking [my books] literally', that he became subject to 'a certain kind of misreader', expecting his fictions to 'reveal interesting information [about Japan] in the way that an anthropologist' might (Wood, 2017; Mason, 1989: 340; Wong, 2008: 182).[1] By choosing to set his third novel, *The Remains of the Day*, in the archetypal British country estate with a parodically traditional butler as lead character, and his fourth, most experimental novel *The Unconsoled* (1995) in an unspecified Eastern European city, Ishiguro hoped to counteract 'literal', 'realist' or 'Japanese' readings of his works.[2]

While his Japanese heritage influenced his cultural exposure, scholars have highlighted the ways in which the painterly style of gradual revelation characteristic of all Ishiguro's narratives borrows tonal, structural and visual techniques from Japanese film. Reflecting on the urban geographies of his first works, Motoyuki Shibata notes that Ishiguro's visions of Japan 'resemble not so much the Nagasaki of the late 1940s/early 1950s as the Japanese films by Ozu depicting those times' (2011: 46).³ The influence is more than pictorial; Rebecca Karni argues that the 'unique and subtle self-consciousness' which has come to typify Ishiguro's narrative voice derives from the 'post-World-War I Japanese film aesthetic' (2015: 328). Ishiguro has confirmed that he drew more from Japanese cinema than Japanese literature, admitting that 'the visual images of Japan have a great poignancy for me, particularly in domestic films like those of Ozu or Naruse' (Mason, 1989: 336). Interestingly, Ishiguro's current film project is an adaptation of Akira Kurosawa's *Ikiru* (1952), which stars Bill Nighy as a terminally ill bureaucrat hoping to make some contribution after a life of ineffectual servitude. Regardless of protestations, then, Ishiguro's relationship to and borrowings from his Japanese heritage are numerous, significant and ongoing; the connection continues to yield fruitful insights, reflected in this collection's chapters by Karni, Emily Horton and Anni Shen.

Yet, despite the clear importance of his Japanese parentage to Ishiguro's work, Barry Lewis reminds us that, after arriving in Britain he was 'brought up on the great canon, both English and European' and describes himself as being 'very much in the Western tradition' (2000: 12; Mason, 1989: 336). Although he refers to Jun'ichiro Tanizaki and Natsume Soseki, his most often cited influences are (perhaps predictably) Fyodor Dostoevsky, Anton Chekhov, Franz Kafka, Harold Pinter, Marcel Proust and Samuel Beckett.⁴ Moreover, in his official Nobel interview he confides that 'the novelist that has influenced me the most is Charlotte Brontë'; he told *The New York Times* that 'I owe my career, and a lot else besides, to "Jane Eyre" and "Villette"' (Ishiguro, 2017; Ishiguro, 2015). We can see from these names that Ishiguro's inheritance is from the realist and modernist European tradition. In terms of style, however, Ishiguro stands in an ambiguous relation to realism, modernism and postmodernism, the dominant modes of nineteenth- and twentieth-century fiction. His most characteristic technique is a quintessentially modernist unreliable narration, with a series of protagonists variously deceiving, deceived, uninformed or radically excluded from knowledge about their own situation. However, there are also elements of historiographic metafiction, pastiche, even magical realism, tropes commonly associated with postmodernist fiction.

This tendency to read Ishiguro through his national or ethnic background often neglects the complex global and cosmopolitan facets of his body of work, which uncover deeper, more existential questions of identity, memory, belonging, loss and responsibility. For Rebecca Walkowitz (2001), Ishiguro's works are reflective of the globalised condition of world literature in the contemporary moment, while Pico Iyer asserts that he is 'a paradigm of the polycultural order' (1993: 54) and it would be a mistake to contextualise his writings as stereotypical of a particular culture. Indeed Ishiguro came to view himself as a 'homeless' writer on account of his early exposure to diverse cultural settings: 'Nobody's history seemed to be my history' (Ōe and Ishiguro, 1991: 115). Nevertheless, attempts to read Ishiguro in relation to national forms of identification remain, although there has been a shift from Japan to Britain; Jed Etsy, for example, positions him alongside Ian McEwan as '[t]wo writers whose names now crop up as representatives of the English novel' (2012: 211). Though his own biography clearly imbued his writing with a different perspective on postwar society, it would, perhaps, be more accurate to describe Ishiguro as a humanist writer, invested in transcending the rooted specificities of time and place, of nationhood and language, to speak directly to the human condition.

Ishiguro, then, is difficult to situate in any discrete cultural, national or literary tradition, and seems to have created a category of writing which stands both within and between realism, modernism and postmodernism, while also gesturing towards a literature of sincere connection, which Sloane describes in his chapter as 'neo-humanism'. His deceptively experimental works conduct subtle but sustained interrogations of the form of the novel, yet at their core they demonstrate a commitment to the humanist tradition which has often been read as co-arising with the European novel (an idea explored by the curiously enlightened curriculum of *Never Let Me Go*'s Hailsham, which encourages students to read Victorian fiction). None the less, if humanism foregrounds or is predicated on the perfectibility of reason and the centrality of the transhistorical human subject, Ishiguro's hyperrational yet misguided and uninformed narrators also constitute a critique of traditional humanism, pointing towards the more complex ethical landscapes of the late twentieth and twenty-first centuries. Any desire to situate Ishiguro in some geospecific literary tradition is perhaps arbitrary; he is fundamentally a cosmopolitan writer, or what Kristian Shaw and Sara Upstone (2021) have elsewhere described as 'transglossic', not interested in parochial or narrowly national concerns but attuned to global and pan-human considerations. As Walkowitz argues, Ishiguro's fictions develop 'new models of the nation', in order to make 'national culture less homogenous' (2006: 25). That is to say, there is nothing peculiarly or uniquely British or Japanese about memory, or regret, or loneliness; recurring thematic concerns speak more broadly to what it means to be human, a question foregrounded in *Never Let Me Go* and *Klara and the Sun*, but which also textures the background of each of his fictions.

The emotive power of memory and memory's paradoxical fragility and permanence remains the most central recurring theme throughout his career (even in Klara, who cannot herself draw from a past, it is the memories of social and family tragedies lingering in the text's background which makes the novel's narrated present so affectively resonant). As Ishiguro writes, memory is 'the filter through which we read our past [...] [the] tool by which people tell themselves things about the lives they've led and about who they've become' (Ishiguro, 2000). While his early 'Japanese' novels look back to periods of collective mourning and the horrors of the Second World War, exposing the unreliability and delusions of national narratives (evident in Shaw's notion of what he terms the 'English sublime'), his later work unearths the wider implications of individual and collective memory, as characters seek to break cycles of retribution and make atonement for the past. As Robert Eaglestone argues here, it is precisely forgiveness which offers a means by which to escape the economies of retribution. *The Buried Giant* (2015), Ishiguro's foray into the quasi-fantasy genre, is a kind of parable which makes explicit his career-long preoccupation with the relationship between personal and national mourning; in *Klara and the Sun*, his second speculative fiction and clearly a response to, even a reading of, *Never Let Me Go*, he creates a character incapable of memory in the traditional sense, or even regret, because Klara is 'new', 'artificial', and, as Bruce Robbins argues below in 'Klara in the junkyard', immune to the loneliness which has become so characteristic of Ishiguro's works. In the background of each work is war and its aftermath, the scars left on landscape and memory, the traumas suffered by characters subjected to both national and personal wounds.

While much critical attention has been paid to the early decades of Ishiguro's literary career, *Kazuo Ishiguro: Twenty-First-Century Fictions* is the first collection to consider all of Ishiguro's novels from 1982 to the present, while also including a chapter on his screenplays and making reference to his short-story collection, *Nocturnes* (2009). Bringing together leading Ishiguro scholars and emerging critics of contemporary literature, the collection contributes to ongoing discussions prevalent in the contemporary novel, including national identity, Britishness, cosmopolitanism, memory, biotechnology, art practice, trauma, posthumanism, Brexit, immigration and populist politics.

Foregrounding Ishiguro's cultural profile and recent critical and commercial success, the collection also considers his personal contribution to current political debates and the ways in which his work speaks to emergent developments in contemporary British literature. Ishiguro is not simply a British author but a complex cultural figure crafting global fictions which are as broad in their geographical and thematic scope as in their stylistic diversity. Ishiguro is the most celebrated and successful British author writing today, and his work exemplifies attempts to move beyond modernist and postmodernist paradigms and has proved to be exceptionally prescient; while *The Remains of the Day* and *The Buried Giant* speak to the class divides, internal divisions and imperial nostalgia surrounding recent moments of political rupture, *Never Let Me Go* and *Klara and the Sun* respond to recent technological developments and tensions surrounding identity politics. The following chapters offer timely re-evaluations of Ishiguro's novels, short stories and screenplays to ensure that the collection is of relevance to those interested in his growing cultural profile as much as his celebrated literary fiction. Each chapter aims to extend and update existing criticism on Ishiguro via engagement with the most up-to-date critical frameworks, while at the same time staying true to each text's most prominent thematic concerns. Taken together, the chapters collected here offer fresh insights on Ishiguro's writing, charting his development as a writer, his commitment to the dynamic synergy of individual and collective experience, and the haunting qualities of grief, trauma and regret that pervade his work. Ishiguro's allegories are so open to interpretation that these singular moments of crisis transcend historical specificity and assume new resonance with each passing year, gesturing to the universal implications of his work.

In the volume's opening chapter, 'Diaspora, trauma, spectrality and world literary writing in *A Pale View of Hills*', Emily Horton explores Kazuo Ishiguro's first novel, considering his negotiation of the discourses of memory and trauma in order to investigate their relevance to postwar migrant experience. Focusing on *A Pale View of Hills*'s repeated engagement with Puccini's opera *Madama Butterfly*, Horton demonstrates how Ishiguro provides a world literary critique of Orientalist thinking and exposes the discriminatory discourses underpinning Western accounts of Japanese culture. The novel, in this sense, questions stereotypical accounts of 'Eastern fragility' and victimhood, and their role in nurturing 'false nationalist mythologies' that fail to align with complexities of migratory experience. In addition to this world literary rereading, the chapter investigates the lingering impact of memorial revision, guilt and disavowal in relation to the mother–daughter relationship of Etsuko and Niki, particularly in relation to their diasporic negotiation of the past. Providing a finely balanced critique of postwar Orientalism, as well as an acknowledgement of the historical ties to prewar Japanese imperialism, *A Pale View of Hills* negotiates what Horton terms 'a multi-directional approach to history and memory', disrupting any simplistic East versus West cultural binaries. Horton's concentration on Ishiguro's authorial fascination with the migratory nature of memory and the lingering effects of trauma develops a common thread that runs throughout the following chapters.

Cynthia F. Wong's 'Eloquence and empathy in *A Pale View of Hills* and *An Artist of the Floating World*' builds on Horton's analysis of Ishiguro's first novel, offering a comparative reading of his first, and most typical, narrators. Indeed, Ishiguro's early novels (his 'Japanese' works) share many geographical, thematic and stylistic similarities, perhaps foremost an exploitation of narrators rendered unreliable both because they suffer with imperfect memory and because they have, or appear to have, regrettable pasts. In her chapter Wong pays particular and careful attention to Etsuko and Ono, two characters who, as she argues counter to Ishiguro, are 'more distinct and contrasting characters [than] claimed by their author'. In the first part of her chapter, 'The duplicity of eloquence', Wong traces the often-conflicted critical responses to her chosen subjects, indicating an ongoing ambiguity about whether their accounts of their occluded pasts are wilfully duplicitous or simply inaccurate, partial. In 'Family resemblances and the domestic drama', Wong focuses on Ono's complex relationship with family understood both literally and figuratively, while also highlighting Ishiguro's recurring interest in family resemblance, and the manner in which this resemblance manifests as an organising principle in his body of work. Finally, in 'Empathy unrealised' Wong continues her exploration of familial relationships, this time thinking through the various characteristic failures of empathy and the fraught interpersonal relations negotiated in these two early novels.

Continuing the discussion of Ishiguro's formal sensibilities but focusing exclusively on *An Artist of the Floating World*, Rebecca Karni interrogates what she describes as 'Ishiguro's tempered presentational realism and practice'. Karni proposes that those aspects of Ishiguro's writing which appear to offer points of entry into a complex and ambiguous body of work – 'the deceptive surface transparency of the author's prose, in addition to his Japanese background' – often result in readings which are inherently reductive (essentialist or Orientalist). Karni explores Ishiguro's tactics of evasion, which, she argues, result in texts which sustain 'meaning in ways that go beyond signification'. Taking the idea of 'presentation' from Hans-Georg Gadamer – refining this with the usage of the same term in Japanese cinema studies – Karni thinks through the ways in which Ishiguro both borrows from the expectations of traditional realist texts and undercuts these through his characteristic narrative and narratological techniques. Ishiguro's first two novels, Karni suggests, are peculiarly apposite examples of his presentational realism. Her chapter interrogates the ways in which the novels provoke the reader's hermeneutic impulse, the desire to uncover, to move 'from signifier to the supposedly "hidden" signified', while simultaneously playing on the futility of such interpretative practices. In this way, Karni argues, Ishiguro's literary devices work to provoke more profound and wide-ranging questions about fiction, the novel as form, and the practice of reading more broadly.

Moving away from the Japanese setting of his early works, Sara Upstone's chapter, '"An inevitable course": political responsibility in *The Remains of the Day*' offers a re-evaluation of Ishiguro's most celebrated novel. In the first part of the chapter Upstone draws on Derrida to advance the notion of '*nonresponsibility*', suggesting that Stevens, as a butler, struggles to move beyond conditional hospitality and claim personal responsibility when confronted with socio-political events beyond his remit. Developing this line of thought, the second half of the chapter goes on to consider the fruitful consequences of rereading the novel in light of the 2016 British EU referendum, where questions of accountability are brought to the fore, forming parallels with Shaw's reading of *The Buried Giant* in the process. For Upstone, then, Stevens functions as 'a synecdoche for the British voting public and its emergent political consciousness', with the fateful Brexit vote not an aberration but rather 'an inevitable course that has its roots in twentieth-century attitudes towards political responsibility'. In this sense *The Remains of the Day* emerges as a prescient novel which taps into the early stirrings of an exclusive English nationalism and Britain's wider desire for a more accountable politics. However, Upstone provides a delicate balance by also acknowledging Ishiguro's claim that the novel is a work of fabulism, rather than direct political commentary, gesturing to the novel form's more general function 'as an abstract space for applicable meaning': a quality that assumes a fresh piquancy in Ishiguro's later works.

In his moving chapter 'Klara in the junkyard: on loneliness in *The Unconsoled*' Bruce Robbins unites Ishiguro's most recent and most narratologically complex works through their mutual interest in feelings of loneliness. Beginning with a short exemplary analysis of the final scenes of Ishiguro's Artificial Intelligence fiction, Robbins opens his chapter by pondering whether Klara herself is immune to the loneliness which she is ironically designed to remedy, and therefore in some sense immune from the fate of many of Ishiguro's most iconic characters, perhaps foremost *The Unconsoled*'s Mr Ryder. As he argues, Ishiguro's characters tend to find themselves personally isolated, most often because of their prioritising of their professional lives, before seeking some final yet ultimately unavailable consolation at the novels' end. Avoiding the critical tendency to simply condemn these characters, to hold them accountable for their own various neglects (of family, of morality, of society) and to see in their aloneness some poetic justice, Robbins instead argues that 'Ishiguro lays out elements of an ethical case in favour of the professional, impersonal, cosmopolitan commitments that are set against intimacy and that lead both figures into their final solitude'. Indeed, Robbins asks provocatively, do Ishiguro's fictions – in which familial, romantic and friendly relations often involve complex forms of ridicule and exclusion – promote the idea 'that belonging as such is inextricable from cruelty'? Robbins teases out the economies of belonging and loneliness which foster the interpersonal tensions so typical of Ishiguro's fictions and figured most powerfully in *The Unconsoled*.

Building on Karni's thoughtful interrogation of the ways in which Ishiguro's narrative techniques inspire questions about the novel as form, in his chapter, 'Novel dysfunction in *When We Were Orphans*', Andrew Bennett takes a similar approach, arguing that Ishiguro's deployment of the detective genre both exploits and confounds expectations that the novel is a 'meaning-producing artefact'. In his reading of Ishiguro's possibly least reliable narrator (and possibly the only cognitively impaired), Bennett deconstructs the flawed logic of the fantastic narrative, suggesting that various causal uncertainties which appear to be simply locally inexplicable in fact indicate the 'more fundamental failure of the novel to *work* in the way that its readers might reasonably expect'. Taking two recurring symbols, the idea of blindness and the prominence of severed body parts, Bennett playfully foregrounds the 'narratological, hermeneutic, and intertextual' failures of the novel, arguing ultimately that the novel's paradox is that its success as a literary artefact derives from these structural and signifying failures. In this way his chapter performs a critique of the novel form, the traditions of realism and the reader's desire to understand what is, ultimately, meaningless.

In a reading of Ishiguro's most affecting novel, *Never Let Me Go*, Peter Sloane situates the work in a longer context of clone and posthuman fictions, beginning with *Frankenstein*, *Brave New World* and *Where Late the Sweet Birds Sang*. Informed by and developing from Suzanne Keen's, Martha Nussbaum's and Anne Whitehead's important and influential insights into the complicated causal relationship between novel reading and the capacity for empathy, Sloane proposes that literary fiction has a peculiar power to provoke empathy, but that empathy is predicated on finding in its subject something which resembles the 'human', an uncovering of shared values, shared traits, shared hopes. However, he argues, *Never Let Me Go* very deliberately resists readings of the clones as human, and rather fosters an empathetic environment in which compassion is founded not on our shared humanity but on our shared posthumanity. The novel very pointedly highlights the various ways in which the clones, Kathy H. and her small, tragic band of friends, do not simply lack fundamental human attributes but are in fact defined by these apparent absences (futurity, fertility, self-actuation). Yet, as Sloane argues, in the posthuman age and in the contemporary novel, 'both text and reader need to be epistemologically and even ontologically resituated in relation to the refiguration of the humanities to the posthumanities'. Necessarily, these questions will recur in relation to Ishiguro's own response to *Never Let Me Go* and *Klara and the Sun*.

In his chapter on *Nocturnes*, Ishiguro's only collection of short fiction, Yugin Teo delicately unthreads the stories' engagement with the feeling of nostalgia which plays such a prominent role in Ishiguro's fictions. Teo thinks through this 'longing for a better world' as it manifests in three ways: home and the desire to return to innocence; the utopian spaces facilitated by shared reminiscence; and the form of the short story itself as a medium through which to convey the fleeting nature of nostalgic hope. Developing from insights in his own important monograph *Kazuo Ishiguro and Memory* (2014), Teo thinks through the complex relationships and tensions which nostalgia presupposes between longings for the past and hopes for the future; as he remarks, the 'collection of stories is ultimately about dreams and dreamers, and the difficulties of holding on to one's dreams and initial optimism for the future'. Questions also arise which have implications for Ishiguro's works more broadly, to do with regret, whether or not characters experience epiphanies (the traditional heart of the short story) from which they learn, somehow, to negotiate their pasts and alter their futures. However, as Teo points out, there remains a characteristic ambiguity in the stories, and one can never be sure whether nostalgia enables or hinders elusive happiness.

For some critics Ishiguro's 2015 novel *The Buried Giant* marked an unexpected turn to fantasy, serving as an urgent parable for a nation hung up on the former glories of its cultural past. In 'Disinterring the English sublime: haunted atmospherics in *The Buried Giant*', Kristian Shaw frames the novel in relation to the political climate of twenty-first-century Britain. Drawing on Ishiguro's own comments relating to nationalism, populism and the recent rise in xenophobic political rhetoric, Shaw suggests that Ishiguro's post-Arthurian landscape contains allusions to mythical constructions of Englishness which were also deployed during the 2016 British EU referendum campaign. Despite being published in the months leading to the referendum, the novel carries a clear anticipatory logic, gesturing to the nationalist violence and cultural amnesia which would come to define the subsequent post-Brexit period. The chapter goes on to demonstrate how Ishiguro utilises the fantasy genre to expose the fallacious nature of our foundational myths and warn of the dangers in assuming a backward-looking national perspective to attend to our troubled present. In developing these ties, Shaw argues that *The Buried Giant* attempts to disrupt what he terms the 'English sublime', forcing us to consider 'the internal ailments affecting the body politic' and pointing towards the need for England to radically overhaul its comforting cultural imaginary.

Ishiguro's most recent novel, *Klara and the Sun* (2021), seemingly marks a return to the posthuman speculative future of *Never Let Me Go*, but also offers a quiet meditation on what it means to be human. In 'Klara and the humans: agency, Hannah Arendt and forgiveness', Robert Eaglestone suggests that the novel utilises science fiction tropes to interrogate personal agency, the possibility of forgiveness and the complications of technological design. Though Klara, an Artificial Friend, is exceptionally intelligent, the chapter suggests that she can only follow her programming in matters of agency; however, her limitations come to reveal what is truly human in her fellow characters. Drawing on the philosophical works of Plato, Arendt and Heidegger, the chapter argues that *Klara and the Sun* responds to the foundational questions of Western thought, projecting an uncertain future to highlight the choices of the past. As Eaglestone goes on to demonstrate, the novel contains powerful echoes of – and forges a dialogue with – Ishiguro's earlier works, revealing the universality of his characters and authorial vision.

Moving beyond Ishiguro's literary output, in the collection's final chapter, Anni Shen explores 'Kazuo Ishiguro's film and television scriptwriting'. Making extensive use of the archive held at the Harry Ransom Center, Shen's uniquely informed chapter argues that Ishiguro 'expresses his ideas, in terms of themes, narrative voice and character relationships, through screenplays before finalising them in novels'.

While countering the notion that Ishiguro's screenwriting is something of an offshoot, a secondary form of his art, Shen demonstrates the centrality of *A Profile of Arthur J. Mason* (1984), *The Gourmet* (1986), *The Saddest Music in the World* (2003) and *The White Countess* (2005) to Ishiguro's development of themes and characters that would become typical of and most prevalent in his fictions. Supported by unprecedented use of Ishiguro's draft materials and his own thoughts about the relationships between screen and page, Shen traces the rich interconnectedness between his fictions and films. While uncovering these similarities, Shen also provides an insight into Ishiguro's own meditations on his developing oeuvre, while highlighting the fact that film 'remains at the centre of Ishiguro's art [because] he divides his energy, especially at the beginning of his career, almost equally between these two media'. Concluding with a nod towards *Living*, Ishiguro's English-language adaption of Akira Kurosawa's quintessentially Japanese *Ikiru*, Shen powerfully resituates his screenwriting with the fiction.

Speaking in a BBC interview in 2021, Ishiguro suggested that his novels are becoming 'increasing more hopeful' and, though it may be a 'pathetically futile hope, it speaks to some part of human nature, that courage that people will have until the bitter end'. His works speak to the potent capacity of literature to communicate our greatest fears, aspirations and dreams: a voice reaching out through the page to let us know that our thoughts and feelings are shared and universal. As Ishiguro (2017) so succinctly puts it, 'in the end, stories are about one person saying to another: This is the way it feels to me. Can you understand what I'm saying? Does it feel this way to you?'

Notes

1 Peter Sloane discusses Ishiguro's fear of being mistaken for a realist writer in *Kazuo Ishiguro's Gestural Poetics* (2021).
2 Although Ishiguro's first two novels were set in Japan, his first two screenplays were distinctively British, focusing on an ageing butler in *A Profile of Arthur J. Mason* which has obvious links to *The Remains of the Day* (1989) and a stereotypically British food fanatic in *The Gourmet* (1986) seeking a ghastly meal in London.

3 In the Bookmark interview, as the camera scans Ishiguro's bookshelf it reveals a copy of Donald Richie's *Ozu: His Life and Films* (1974).
4 Ishiguro was asked by James Ivory to adapt Tanizaki's *Diary of a Mad Old Man* (1952) for the screen, but Ishiguro instead wrote what would become the screenplay for *The White Countess* (2005).

References

Etsy, Jed (2012). *Unseasonable Youth: Modernism, Colonialism, and the Fiction of Development* (Oxford: Oxford University Press).
Hunnewell, Susannah and Kazuo Ishiguro (2008). 'Kazuo Ishiguro: The Art of Fiction No. 196', *The Paris Review*, 184. www.theparisreview.org/interviews/5829/the-art-of-fiction-no-196-kazuo-ishiguro (accessed May 2021).
Ishiguro, Kazuo (1987). 'Kazuo Ishiguro', *Bookmark*, BBC Archive.
—. (2000). 'Author Q & A: A Conversation with Kazuo Ishiguro about His New Novel *When We Were Orphans*', Knopf Publishing, www.penguinrandomhouse.com/books/85614/when-we-were-orphans-by-kazuo-ishiguro/9780375724404 (accessed May 2021).
—. (2015). 'Kazuo Ishiguro: By the Book', *The New York Times*, 5 March. www.nytimes.com/2015/03/08/books/review/kazuo-ishiguro-by-the-book.html (accessed May 2021).
—. (2017). 'My Twentieth Century Evening – and Other Small Breakthroughs', 7 December. *The Nobel Foundation.* www.nobelprize.org/uploads/2018/06/ishiguro-lecture_en-1.pdf (accessed June 2022).
Iyer, Pico (1993). 'The Empire Writes Back', *Time*, 8 February.
Karni, Rebecca (2015). 'Made in Translation: Language, "Japaneseness", "Englishness", and "Global Culture" in Ishiguro', *Comparative Literature*, 52:2, 318–348.
Krider, Dylan Otto (1998). 'Rooted in a Small Space: An Interview with Kazuo Ishiguro', *The Kenyon Review*, 20:2, 146–154.
Lewis, Barry (2000). *Kazuo Ishiguro: Contemporary World Writers* (Manchester: Manchester University Press).
Mason, Gregory (1989). 'An Interview with Kazuo Ishiguro', *Contemporary Literature*, 30:3, 335–347.
Oe, Kenzaburo and Kazuo Ishiguro (1991). 'The Novelist in Today's World: A Conversation', *boundary 2*, 18:3, 109–122.
Shaw, Kristian and Sara Upstone (2021). 'The Transglossic: Contemporary Fiction and the Limitations of the Modern', *English Studies*, 102:5, 573–600.

Shibata, Motoyuki (2011). 'Lost and Found: On the Japanese Translations of Kazuo Ishiguro', in Sebastian Groes and Barry Lewis (eds), *Kazuo Ishiguro: New Critical Visions of the Novels* (London: Palgrave Macmillan), 43–56.
Sloane, Peter (2021). *Kazuo Ishiguro's Gestural Poetics* (New York: Bloomsbury).
Walkowitz, Rebecca L. (2001). 'Ishiguro's Floating Worlds', *ELH*, 68:4, 1049–1076.
—. (2006). *Cosmopolitan Style: Modernism Beyond the Nation* (New York: Columbia University Press).
Wong, Cynthia F. (2008). 'Like Idealism is to the Intellect: An Interview with Kazuo Ishiguro', in Brian W. Shaffer and Cynthia F. Wong (eds), *Conversations with Kazuo Ishiguro* (Jackson: University Press of Mississippi), 174–188.
Wood, Gaby (2017). 'There Is a Slightly Chilly Aspect to Writing Fiction', *The Telegraph*, 5 October. www.telegraph.co.uk/books/authors/kazuo-ishiguro-countries-have-got-big-things-buried/ (accessed May 2021).

1

Diaspora, trauma, spectrality and world literary writing in *A Pale View of Hills*

Emily Horton

Central to diaspora studies is an appreciation of the experience of cross-cultural liminality or in-betweenness – an attempt to balance diverse and sometimes conflicting loyalties to home and host country. As James Clifford puts this, 'Diaspora cultures [...] mediate, in a lived tension, the experiences of separation and entanglement, of living here and remembering/desiring another place' (1994: 311). Moreover, 'at the core of the concept of diaspora lies the image of a remembered home', a space of origin which may be both nostalgic and traumatic (Stock, 2010: 24). From this perspective the immigrant retains a sense of ongoing connection to the homeland, sustained through processes of memory and retrospection, which complicate the experience of identity and belonging within the host country. Such an understanding situates diasporic identity as temporally and spatially split: always to some extent in the past and at a distance from the location of current residence.

Trauma memory, potentially both as a cause and as a consequence of migration, complicates this split self even further. To borrow Jill Bennett's phrasing, the traumatic subject 'is not so much *speaking of* but *speaking out of* a particular memory or experience' (Bennett, 2003: 33) and, as such, their relationship to truth as historical fact is inevitably complicated. The memory of home becomes shaped by an experience (or experiences) of trauma which often carry repercussions into the present day, defining the meaning and value attached to migration. As John Sundholm explains, 'in this framework [of trauma], the relation between event (origin) and its meaning (trauma) is foremost considered to be a question of social value rather than of epistemology' (2011: 121). In other words, central to understanding migratory trauma is an appreciation of how the present (host) context impacts upon the remembrance of past events, including those within the home country: the present 'triggers' the memory and in this way factors into its meaning (Sundholm, 2011: 122). Memory itself might in this way be read as inherently migratory, to the extent that its shape and significance depend upon the changing circumstances in which it is constructed (Creet, 2011: 9).

In Ishiguro's first novel, *A Pale View of Hills* (1982), this migratory understanding of memory underpins the narrative structure, where a focus on retrospection and revision complicates the representation of diasporic selfhood in ways that reinforce this split or 'in-between' reality, underlining the conflicting affects attached to home and host countries, and the migratory quality of memory itself. The fragmented first-person narrative recounts a Japanese woman, Etsuko's, recollections of postwar Japan from the perspective of her present residence in early 1980s Britain, as she reassesses the complex series of events, desires, fears and fantasies surrounding her decision to migrate. The recent suicide of her first daughter, Keiko, with whom she migrated from Japan, invests this narrative with trauma, as it shifts between past and present, home and abroad, and nostalgia and regret in ways that might be read as rehearsing iconic tensions aligned to diasporic consciousness, or what Homi Bhabha famously refers to as a 'third space' of enunciation (1994: 36). As Bhabha writes, this third space 'makes the structure of meaning and reference an ambivalent process [and] destroys this mirror of representation in which cultural knowledge is customarily revealed as an integrated, open, expanding code' (1994: 37). Indeed, in Etsuko's often disturbed and unintegrated reflections, what Bhabha refers to as the 'uncanny literary and social effects of enforced social accommodation, or historical migration' become overtly apparent as a filter on her subjectivity, drawing attention to her estranged experience of life in Britain, as well as to the contradictory quality of memory that her position of in-betweenness obliges (1992: 141). The novel's title itself, with its reference to a 'pale view' (*PVH*: 103), can be read to underline this in-between perspective, emphasising the ambivalence and equivocation with which Etsuko approaches her remembered Japan, as well as that with which she negotiates her migrant experience in Britain.

Such a reading reinforces the textual centrality of diaspora within the novel, specifically as this introduces a perspective of distance and critique with respect to both Japanese and English cultural norms. As Rebecca Walkowitz writes, the 'sly humour and dramatic irony' of Ishiguro's early novels 'depend on the reader's sense of distance both from the interwar confidence of the early 1930s and from the Cold War hypocrisy of the 1950s'; the texts juxtapose historical and cultural settings such that 'no country looks like a perpetrator or a victim only, or like a major power or a minor supplicant all the time' (2006: 110). More specifically, in the novel's attention to the implicit ties between Etsuko's current experiences of racism in early 1980s England, and her past engagements with Japanese militarism and American neo-imperialism, Ishiguro brings into play a critical world literary perspective that moves between East and West, and past and present, making evident the transcultural and transhistoric dimensions of this oppressive encounter. This multi-perspectival outlook, combined with a textual irony regarding the narrator's claims to have confronted her past and moved on from it, gives shape to the novel's diasporic reading of late twentieth-century geopolitical relations, in particular as these impact upon Etsuko's own understandings of motherhood and migration.

In this chapter I seek to explore this diasporic representation in more detail, underlining in particular its challenge to reactionary nationalist and imperialist cultural ideas. The novel is especially attentive to how these right-wing ideologies inform the narrator's diasporic experience and how they structure her reading of the past in complex ways. Even so, noting a prominent postcolonial critique of diasporic thinking, which questions this outlook's emphasis on 'in-betweenness' as a necessarily *enlightened* mode of perception, 'blessed with a specific awareness of the relativity of cultural rules and forms', I want to suggest a note of caution here (Smith, 2004: 246). Thus, while diaspora has been celebrated critically as 'a kind of superior cultural intelligence owing to the advantage of in-betweenness, the straddling of two cultures and the consequent ability to negotiate difference', on the whole, I would argue, this is *not* the perspective aligned to Etsuko in the novel (Hoogvelt, 1997: 158). To the contrary, throughout the text, precisely in accordance with her identification as a migrant, Etsuko battles with a sense of regret and culpability around her past, which mars her narrative authority. Put differently, this celebratory reading of diaspora overlooks the many ways in which Etsuko's 'split' subjectivity emerges here *not* from a self-conscious 'third space' of enunciation so much as from a deeply repressed and traumatic self-association with her patriarchal and imperial oppressor(s). The trauma produced by this *ethical* 'in-betweenness' obstructs her capacity to successfully inhabit an empowering third space, instead tying her narrative to discourses of complicity and disavowal.

In order to recognise this repressed and conflicted outlook explicitly, and to further appreciate how it inheres within the novel's world literary thinking, I suggest three key textual strategies by which diaspora is approached in the narrative. These include, firstly, Etsuko's narrative unreliability, in connection with her experience of guilt and trauma regarding her migration; secondly, the text's engagement with dreams and nightmares, as a means to exploring Etsuko's ongoing narrative insecurity; and, lastly, intertextuality, which through repeated engagements with Puccini's *Madama Butterfly*, brings to light the novel's central organising concern with guilt and abandonment, while at the same time invoking a world literary critique of Orientalist thinking.[1] Each of these techniques functions to shape the text's diasporic depiction of Etsuko's story, but also to complicate the 'third space' narrative she seeks to offer, again foregrounding her and her father-in-law's attachment to repressed nationalist and imperialist agendas. Before going on to examine these ideas, however, I want to take a moment to survey more closely Ishiguro's own comments on diaspora in interviews, considering how his own experience as a migrant writer might come into this representation.

Having arrived in the UK at the age of five and lived here ever since, Ishiguro has notably stronger ties with the country than his migrant protagonist. He does not speak fluent Japanese and, after arriving in England, returned to visit Japan only at the age of thirty in 1989 (Oe and Ishiguro, 1991: 109). As such, he is often at pains to underline the Western cultural and literary influences on his work and has invoked 'impatience' regarding the burden of authority placed on him as a spokesperson for Japanese culture (Mason, 1989: 336). Regarding his early reputation, in an interview with Suzie Mackenzie, he recalls, 'People seemed to think that I was some sort of Japanese foreign correspondent. I remember Channel 4 once asking me to appear to talk about the trade war between America and Japan' (Mackenzie, 2000). Perhaps as a result of such expectations, which Peter Morey aptly describes as part of a long-standing tendency within Western literary scholarship 'to view non-Western literatures as essentially anthropological in nature' (2018: 6), Ishiguro's early interviews often stress his 'caution' regarding the topic of Japan and its importance to his work: as he relates as late as 2000, Japan remains 'a place I have only been to once' (Mackenzie, 2000).

Indeed, an emphasis on the invented quality of his 'Japanese' geographies often underpins Ishiguro's reflections on his Japanese settings, reaffirming their fictional contours in opposition to a historical realist reading. 'When I wrote, say, *The [sic] Artist of the Floating World*', he explains, 'I wasn't terribly interested in researching history books. I very much wanted to put down onto paper this particular idea of Japan that I had in my own mind, and in a way I didn't really care if my fictional world didn't correspond to a historical reality' (Oe and Ishiguro, 1991: 110–111). By contrast, what Ishiguro claims to want to highlight throughout his writing are 'themes with an emotional dimension' including especially 'how one uses memory for one's own purposes, one's own ends' (Mason, 1989: 346; 347). In this way Salman Rushdie's concept of an 'imaginary homeland', coined in the same year as *A Pale View of Hills*, becomes notably *psychologically* invested; aligned not simply to diasporic nostalgia or cultural in-betweenness but equally, to memorial revision, guilt and disavowal.

In fact numerous critics have commented on Ishiguro's narrative investment in memorial psychology, linking this particularly to his novels' repeated engagement with unreliable narration, often through the lens of Freudian psychoanalysis and trauma theory. Writing on *A Pale View of Hills*, Brian Shaffer references Etsuko's numerous strategies to confront her past indirectly, including projection, rationalisation and suppression of memory (1998: 16; 17; 24–25). Noting how 'such defence mechanisms allow [Etsuko] to transfer feelings of personal guilt onto the external world', he sees her constructing an 'elaborate subterfuge' (1998: 24) to avoid responsibility. More forgivingly, Ljubica Matek writes that 'Etsuko's unreliable narration reflects the complexity and elusiveness of the process of migration which, for her, never seems to be complete, leaving her torn between who she was and who she is now' (2018: 130). Such readings, despite their differences, aptly capture the layeredness of Etsuko's narrative, as she endeavours to navigate the past, while at the same time finding mechanisms through which to evade her sense of guilt and regret.

Unreliable narration thus features centrally within this novel's engagement with diaspora, structuring its complex and multi-layered representation of Etsuko's emotional ambivalence regarding her migration. It also arguably explains what is so often regarded as lying at the heart of Ishiguro's popularity, namely his self-declared interest in universal human feelings and relationships. As Ishiguro states in his 2017 Nobel Prize speech, 'I wanted, like [Salman Rushdie and V.S. Naipaul], to write "international" fiction, that could easily cross cultural and linguistic boundaries', further emphasising that, for him, 'the essential thing is that [his stories] communicate feelings. That they appeal to what we share as human beings across our borders and divides' (Ishiguro, 2017: 18). His emphasis on motherhood and trauma in *A Pale View of Hills* might tentatively be read to speak to this ambition, in so far as the former encompasses a ubiquitous, if widely varying, experience, and the latter a common, if again culturally and historically varying, psychological condition. Borrowing Stef Craps's phrasing, Ishiguro could in this way be read as seeking to 'redeem [trauma's] promise of cross-cultural ethical engagement', precisely by linking it to 'the sufferings of those belonging to non-Western or minority cultures' (2014: 46), including not only wartime Japan but also a larger postwar Asian diaspora. In emphasising particularly Etsuko's traumatic 'structure of reception' (Caruth, 1995: 4) in confronting her past, defined by certain memorial gaps and lacunae around which her narrative circles, *A Pale View of Hills* would in this way seem to echo Cathy Caruth's classic reading of trauma psychology, invoking a common experience of traumatic belatedness, relevant across various cultures and histories, and invested in the project of 'reveal[ing] how and why traumas become interlaced with each other, both within the individual psyche and in the social world' (Rothberg, 2003: 149).

Even so, as Justine Baillie and Sean Matthews assert, despite the 'universal questions' invoked throughout Ishiguro's work through his engagement with memory and psychology, '[his] narrators are nonetheless situated at precise points of imperial crisis and collapse [...] and it is significant [...] the ways in which the stories they tell involve the construction of historically specific identities' (2009: 46). Moreover, as Craps writes, it is necessary to be cautious regarding the application of such 'single, uniform, timeless, and universal' Western readings of trauma, which often result as 'culturally insensitive and exclusionary', incurring 'charges of cultural imperialism' and 'uncritical cross-cultural application' (2014: 3). In this case the very specific trauma of the Nagasaki bomb, here framed within the context of postwar American occupation and a neo-imperialist narrative of Oriental fragility and Western delivery, helps to explain Etsuko's hesitancy regarding the appositeness of such narratives as applied to her story, as these arguably fail to capture the historical uniqueness and complexity of her situation. By engaging with this larger context of postwar transition and reassessment, then, seen retrospectively through the lens of diasporic loss, the text thus addresses and deconstructs Western readings of Etsuko's 'Nagasaki narrative', bringing to attention the discriminatory Orientalist discourses within which these accounts position her and Keiko.

As several critics have noted, one of the most obvious historical markers in Etsuko's narrative, the event of the nuclear bomb, emerges most clearly here not as a presence but rather an absence, marking Etsuko's expression precisely through its weighted omission (Eckert, 2012: 79; Lewis, 2000: 39). While Etsuko does speak to Ogata-san, Mrs Fujiwara and Sachiko at various points about the bomb and its impact, learning from Ogata-san that she 'was like a mad person' in the weeks following its occurrence (*PVH*: 58), her trauma itself, encompassing the loss of a lover and possibly her family (*PVH*: 71; 13), surfaces most clearly *not* in its telling but rather precisely in her failure to directly confront and process this event, in this way echoing a classic trauma theory diagnosis of memorial non-assimilation: 'the event is not assimilated or experienced fully at the time, but only belatedly, in its repeated *possession* of the one who experiences it' (Caruth, 1995: 4). That Etsuko is indeed possessed by this event is visible in her stepfather's memories of her violin-playing 'in the dead of night' (*PVH*: 57), as well as in her general sense of numbness and disconnection throughout her narrative – she recounts 'gazing emptily at the view from her apartment window' during her pregnancy with Keiko (*PVH*: 99), and, indeed, repeatedly she returns to images of unseeing eyes and vacant staring (*PVH*: 40; 74).

To recall Jill Bennett's phrasing, Etsuko is speaking 'out of' rather than 'of' her memories of the bomb, and, in this way, often fails to comprehend its psychic significance for her, instead approaching it obliquely through the medium of dreams, fantasies, and images. She navigates the layered symbolism of multiple traumas, including Keiko's death and the bomb, in ways that testify to her continued confusion and displacement following these events. To quote James Berger, her language suggests a darkly poetic 'combining [of] conscious and unconscious motives and powers – that arise out of horror and confusion' (2003: 52). Her recourse to repeated spectral and morbid images speaks strongly to this impression, capturing her overwhelming distress following these stratified catastrophes. Even so, despite her attention to the bomb's impact, the date which most directly absorbs Etsuko's focus is *not* that of 9 August 1945, but rather several years later, during the final months of the American occupation. As she reflects, 'The worst days were over by then. American soldiers were as numerous as ever – for there was fighting in Korea – but in Nagasaki, after what had gone before, those were days of calm and relief. The world had a feeling of change about it' (*PVH*: 11). It is on this period of transition and change, also the time of Etsuko's pregnancy with Keiko, that the narrative concentrates, reconsidering the contextual and ideational details surrounding her decision to emigrate.

What is notable about this period from the start is the overt negativity with which Etsuko invests it, even while the banner of change itself is ostensibly optimistic. The city is in the process of rebuilding itself, yet her building, as she describes it, is situated on a 'wasteground', laden with 'craters filled with stagnant water' and swarming insects (*PVH*: 11), while a series of local child murders dominate the news with images of batterings and hangings (*PVH*: 100). Likewise, while the Occupation is publicly presented as inaugurating a new more progressive administration, as well as new fashions and appliances meant to improve women's domestic lives (*PVH*: 152), Etsuko and her community remain visibly cynical about this new government, aware of continued political in-fighting and the perseverance in power of earlier militarist leaders (*PVH*: 31; 99–100). Reflective of the instability of the transition period politically, these passages also suggest Etsuko's personal inability to find hope in the promise of marriage and family, where the prospect of a child seems merely to increase her burden, rather than lightening it. As she recalls, she was haunted during this time by 'misgivings about motherhood' (*PVH*: 17; 99), which have a visible effect on her appearance and demeanour. Mrs Fujiwara comments on how 'unhappy' – indeed 'miserable' – she looks, despite the event of her pregnancy, and both she and Ogata-san urge her not to dwell so much on the past (*PVH*: 24, 77). There seems little reason, indeed, for Etsuko to be happy within her marriage, as despite the good intentions she retrospectively ascribes to Jiro as a husband and father (*PVH*: 90), he emerges as here pointedly domineering and uncommunicative, eager to establish his authority within the household, while otherwise inattentive to Etsuko and his elderly father's needs. In this respect, Etsuko's depression is seemingly further compounded by the tensions within her marriage, where she finds no real space for working through her pain with any support or consideration.

This is also the period in which Etsuko befriends Sachiko and Mariko, the mother–daughter duo in relation to whom her narrative unreliability emerges most clearly. The imprecise contours of Etsuko's relationship with Sachiko and Mariko become evident from early on in the text, when she responds to overheard gossip about Sachiko's unfriendliness by reclaiming *her own* (rather than Sachiko's) innocence: 'It was never *my* intention to appear unfriendly', she maintains (*PVH*: 13 – emphasis added), in this way suggesting a narrative focus on her own story *by means of* Sachiko's. This conflation of identities then re-emerges at two key moments in the text: firstly, when Etsuko takes it upon herself to convince Mariko that she will enjoy *their* move to America (*PVH*: 173); and, secondly, when, in explaining her photo of Inasa, she suggests that it portrays a 'happy memory' of Keiko, rather than Mariko (*PVH*: 182). These three slippages represent the most obvious reminders of Etsuko's unreliability as a narrator, suggesting an unconscious projection of personal guilt on to this real or imaginary duo (see also Eckert, 2012: 77, and Lewis, 2000: 36). Whatever the reality or fictiveness of Sachiko and Mariko, then, their equivocal status within the narrative reinforces the gaps within Etsuko's story, situating them as strategic vehicles for her (conscious or unconscious) negotiation of a haunting past.

What is compelling about this postwar narrative with respect to Etsuko's diasporic trauma is how its recourse to Sachiko's story suggests a very different form of traumatic reaction to that displayed in the immediate aftermath of the bomb, one which sees Etsuko regretting her past and reconstructing this gradually to account for perceived transgression. Rather than failing, as in the case of the bomb, to assimilate the overwhelming catastrophe of this event's occurrence, in accordance with a classic trauma theory diagnosis, what appears to happen is that Etsuko identifies with a particular set of troubling attachments, which she then strategically disavows, as a means to denying responsibility and preserving her integrity as a notionally 'good mother'. To quote Susannah Radstone, these events 'prove traumatic [...] not because of [their] inherently shocking nature but due to the unbearable or forbidden fantasies that [they] prompt' (2003: 20), in this case, of conscious maternal violence in the event of her early treatment of Keiko, and, later, her migration. Despite her eagerness to forget the past, then, these memories haunt Etsuko with guilt regarding her motherhood and her relocation, as she sees herself symbolically in the role of persecutor and failed mother.

Her fascination throughout this text with images of ropes and drowning reinforces this symbolic association directly, seeing her trauma as a distraught response to a personal identification as her daughter's murderer. The rope upon which Keiko hangs herself thus finds its way inadvertently into Etsuko's memories, as Mariko comments on its threatening presence in her possession: 'Why have you got the rope? [...] signs of fear [...] appear[ed] on her face' (*PVH*: 84). This happens in the moment in which Etsuko first refuses to take one of Mariko's kittens, and later when she promises that *they* (she and Mariko) will 'come straight back' if Mariko does not like America (*PVH*: 84, 173). In this way these fantasies of abandonment and deception underline the self-castigating impulse in Etsuko's narrative; this is further underscored by parallel stories of Sachiko drowning the kittens and another mother drowning her infant child (*PVH*: 74). Etsuko's decision ultimately to bring Keiko to England becomes here symbolically tied to maternal infanticide, as she psychically punishes herself for her dreams of escape from her domestic reality.

Jenny Edkins's notion of 'trauma time' is useful in capturing the jointly personal and political dimensions of this encounter, encompassing not only Etsuko's regret and self-castigation but also the transitional political order which surrounds and feeds into this narrative. For Jenny Edkins, trauma time 'is a time where events that we call traumatic or unspeakable both expose the lack that underpins a sovereign political symbolic order and reveal the radical relationality of life' (2014: 127). Keiko's suicide places Etsuko in trauma time in so far as it reveals the simultaneous violence and contingency of her motherhood, trapping her in a still-unprocessed past in which her daughter was yet living. As she puts it, 'I feel only regret now for those attitudes I displayed toward Keiko. [...] I never imagined she could so quickly vanish beyond my reach' (*PVH*: 88). Nevertheless, this time also functions politically in that it reveals the lie of Japan's postwar optimism, making clear the underlying insecurity of this era of confidence. In effect, Etsuko's trauma here exposes the error of refusing to interrogate the past in the way that Ogata-san and Mrs Fujiwara advise, as they urge her to 'keep thinking about the future' and to '[start] looking ahead' to motherhood (*PVH*: 25). As Edkins puts it, 'In trauma time [...] we have a disruption of this linearity. Something happens that doesn't fit [.... This] demands that we invent a new account, one that will produce a place for what has happened and make it meaningful' (2003: xiv). Trauma time is thus significant to the narrative in that it enjoins a reassessment of Japan's postwar politics from the perspective of diasporic trauma, demonstrating the necessity of confronting a militant past and its postwar continuation.

Indeed Etsuko's earlier experience of trauma following the bomb also participates in this political reckoning, as her depression sees her hesitantly questioning the patriarchal and imperialist status quo which continues to shape her marriage and pregnancy. For example, her 'misgivings about motherhood' might be read as a politically attuned response to Jiro's authoritarianism, as well as to the shallowness of her society's invocations that she remain positive. Sachiko is the most overt spokesperson for this political critique, as she directly refuses society's consolations, dismissing the hypocrisy of those who claim to befriend her, whilst whispering behind her back, as well as the expectation that she should embrace motherhood as a form of consolation. Denouncing the boredom of her uncle's household, where 'it [was] surprising how slowly the time [went] by', as well as the tyranny of her former husband's dictates, which forbade her to learn English (*PVH*: 102, 110), she instead opts to leave Japan for America to claim her independence and begin anew, affirming the many 'opportunities' (*PVH*: 46) that America promises both for her and her daughter. Significantly, this promise of Western delivery turns out itself to be deceptive, as Sachiko is left behind by her American lover in a plot twist which directly invokes *Madama Butterfly*. Nevertheless, the transgressiveness of her outlook in these passages illuminates the hidden frustration and rebellion fuelling Etsuko's own migration, exposing the incredulity towards tradition and domesticity that marks her experience of postwar trauma.

That this decision has resulted in Keiko's suicide is thus traumatic on multiple levels, where what was intended as a gesture of self-assertion is now revealed as selfish, a dismissal of Keiko's perspective and well-being. As Gregory Mason puts it, within this context Etsuko 'lashes herself with grief and guilt at the suicide of her daughter' (1989: 338), reproaching herself as the ultimate cause of her daughter's unhappiness. What is noticeable about this second trauma, however, is how it brings into question the discourse of Western emancipation in which Etsuko has thus far maintained an obstinate faith, what Shunya Yoshimi refers to as the discourse of 'America as desire' within Cold War Asia (2003: 433). Thus, while Etsuko has moved to England rather than America, from the very start of her narrative we see her compelled by the lure of Western delivery narratives, eager to investigate just 'what things are possible out there' (*PVH*: 46) as opposed to in Japan. Indeed, at the very close of her narrative, she spells this out directly, in relation to a fantasy of pastoral England to which she continues to cling. As she comments to Niki, 'When your father first brought me down here, [...] I remember thinking how truly like England everything looks. [...] It was just the way I always imagined England would be and I was so pleased' (*PVH*: 182). Here the discourse of cultural authenticity, encased in a form of pastoral aesthetics ('all these fields', 'the orchard behind us' (*PVH*: 182)), functions to explain Etsuko's self-deception regarding her expectations as a migrant, where this 'truly English' landscape is far from the utopia she paints it to be.

By contrast, following Keiko's suicide, we see Etsuko beginning to question this cultural narrative, willing now (at least tentatively) to see how this discourse has impacted upon her and her daughter. As she puts it, 'The English are fond of their idea that our race has an instinct for suicide [...] for that was all they reported, that she was Japanese and that she hung herself in her room' (*PVH*: 10). In short this self-conscious framing at the start of the narrative denounces the Orientalist tendencies that underpin traditional Western accounts of Japanese culture, both in *Madama Butterfly* itself, and in the postwar and late century. Indeed, as John Lie explains, this account became especially prominent during the postwar period through the publication and promotion of Ruth Benedict's *The Chrysanthemum and the Sword* (1946), a US-government-commissioned inquiry into Japanese culture intended precisely to defend US neo-imperialism in the region, and which radically 'ignores the considerable diversity [of postwar Japanese culture] and the impact of rapid change experienced by modern, industrial, and complex society' (2001: 253–254). In rejecting this essentialist Orientalist narrative, then, which sees Japan as 'the most alien enemy the United States had ever fought in an all-out struggle' (Benedict, 1946: 1), Etsuko begins to reconceive her past home's meaning, and likewise to rethink the Western romance of Occupation-era delivery. In connection with the *Madama Butterfly* intertext, then, Etsuko's narrative becomes an implicit critique of this text's very foundations, questioning its underlying defence of migration to the West as a supposed means to freedom. Likewise, Keiko's suicide stands in here *not* for Asian frailty, as in Puccini's opera, but rather precisely for the implicit violence that Orientalist discourse has enacted upon Etsuko and her daughter, alongside a wider diasporic Asian community in the context of late century Reaganite and Thatcherite geopolitics. Etsuko's experience of loss following Keiko's death enlivens her to the lie of this conservative political and ideological programme, allowing her to begin to question her mistaken faith in Western redemption.

In accordance with this idea of post-traumatic revision, there are two other dimensions to this narrative project that I want to briefly address: firstly, Etsuko's faith in her marriage to Sheringham, which comes under the same scrutiny that Etsuko grants to the English media, and, secondly, her understanding of Nagasaki's trauma itself in her conversations with Niki. With respect to the first of these, Etsuko's English husband is seen here to be, if not as a tyrant, nevertheless deeply mistaken in his claims to understand Japanese culture, and likewise himself largely responsible for Keiko's unhappiness due to his own cultural prejudice. As Etsuko explains, 'it became his view that Keiko was a difficult person by nature and there was little we could do for her. In fact, although he never claimed it outright, he would imply that Keiko had inherited her personality from her father' (*PVH*: 94). This discourse of paternal blame, and the stereotyping of Japanese masculinity that it negotiates, fall in line with what Nadia Y. Kim identifies as a prominent discourse of postwar global relations, wherein 'the dominance of white masculinity depends on a subordinate nonwhite masculinity (e.g., as "patriarchal," less desirable)' (2006: 520). In this case this binary reading of Eastern and Western masculinities is suggested as one possible foundation for Etsuko's decision to migrate, now under revision as she comes to question her English husband's claims to authority regarding Japanese culture. Noting how 'despite all the impressive articles he wrote about Japan, my husband never understood the ways of our culture, even less a man like Jiro' (*PVH*: 90), she here reaffirms the deception thus forth tentatively maintained in her narrative regarding Western Orientalist readings of Japan. If Jiro is responsible in part for *Etsuko's* own past unhappiness, she implies, he is not so for Keiko's – to the contrary, her daughter felt a strong affection for her father (*PVH*: 90), and here it is Sheringham who plays the part of the oppressive (and culturally insensitive) patriarch.

Niki's response to Etsuko's suffering also emerges in conjunction with this Orientalist discourse, as she depends upon her father's writing to understand her mother's past and respond to her current suffering (*PVH*: 91). Thus, while Niki is depicted as in many ways attentive to her mother's predicament and eager to reassure her regarding past decisions, her strategy for doing so is distinctly informed by her sense of closeness to her father and distance from her sister, the latter implicitly a figure for a wider Japanese 'otherness'. 'Sisters are supposed to be people you're close to, aren't they', she reflects, '[...] I don't even remember what she looked like now. [...] I just remember her as someone who used to make me miserable' (*PVH*: 10). Moreover, Niki's eagerness to defend Etsuko's migration to England in Western terms – as at once a result of her trauma and a valiant refusal to 'get stuck with kids and [a] lousy [husband]' (*PVH*: 89–90) – itself falls back upon stereotypical understandings of Eastern fragility and oppression, themselves promoted by her father, which shamefacedly ignore the particularity and complexity of Etsuko's experience. As Etsuko reflects, 'One supposes she has built up some sort of picture from what her father has told her.

Such a picture, inevitably, would have its inaccuracies' (*PVH*: 94). In effect, such discourses rely on an Orientalist perspective which essentialises and exoticises Etsuko's past, seeing this as a product of cultural otherness and a locus of pity.

It is not merely Etsuko's supposed bravery in leaving her Japanese husband which defines Niki's version of her narrative here but, more centrally, the aesthetic dimensions of her suffering as a vision of female Oriental trauma personified. Requesting an artefact from her mother's past ('a photo or something' (*PVH:* 177)) to illustrate the nature of her suffering to her friends, Niki at once reduces postwar Nagasaki to a poignant poem or postcard image, and simultaneously exoticises Etsuko's pain to inspire her companions' curiosity. As she affirms, 'You know that friend I was telling you about, the one writing the poem about you. [...] She's been through a lot, you see. That's why I told her about you' (*PVH*: 177). Here the suggestion that her young friend's poetry, itself based on a mere photo of postwar Nagasaki, might make accessible her mother's trauma for a Western audience, involves a problematic exhibition of Asian pain, combined with a supposition of Oriental psychologically transparency, which again reinforces a narrative of cultural 'truth' framed by melodramatic tragedy. In effect Niki reads her mother's story through the Orientalist lens of the *Madama Butterfly* narrative, and Etsuko very rightly resists this as a discriminatory product of the Western imperial imagination.

I return to this relationship in the section that follows, as I consider more closely the novel's rewriting of *Madama Butterfly* and its ideological implications. Nevertheless, noting Niki's considerable anxiety regarding Keiko's death, even despite her apparent disconnection from her Japanese sister, I want to take a moment to examine the role of dreams and nightmares in the novel, in particular as these comment on unconscious fantasies shaping both mother and daughter's diasporic negotiation of the past. Recognising in particular the spectral and uncanny quality of these dream sequences, which bear witness to a form of the return of the repressed, I read these scenes as commenting on the unconscious personal and collective psychologies underpinning right-wing cultural dogma and shaping the idea of truth that such discourses put forward.

One particularly Gothic 'dream' narrative that emerges near the start of the novel involves the figure of an unnamed woman who

Mariko claims has been visiting her, whom she describes as pale and thin, and living in the woods on the other side of the river. While never explicitly naming this tradition, the woman conjures the figure of the *onryo*, a classic Japanese avenging spirit, with long black hair, a white kimono robe and staring eyes, often associated with male domestic violence, but also demonic motherhood. As Ada Lovelace writes, 'onryo is most often represented in literature and theatre as a wronged woman who has been murdered, or subjected to a traumatising event during life that has instigated her demise. The powerful and overwhelming emotions that have originated in such an instance function as the catalyst for administering vengeance upon the living' (2008: 31). In this case, the *onryo* is explained by Sachiko as a fantasy figure resulting from Mariko's trauma in seeing a woman drown her infant child during the war: 'She saw other things in Tokyo, some terrible things, but she's always remembered that woman' (*PVH*: 73). The traumatising 'event' being revenged is in this way doubly explained: firstly, as connected to the war itself, which, in its violence, has brought this unknown woman to murder her child, but also, in so far as Mariko is concerned, as linking to the experience itself of *witnessing* maternal violence, which produces fantastic associations likewise capable of wreaking incredible damage.

These conjoint understandings of the *onryo*'s haunting violence – on the one hand, memorial, and on the other, fantastic – help to elucidate the novel's layered portrait of postwar trauma, as reflecting unprocessed horror, but also lost innocence. Etsuko's account of her own dreamlife overtly reasserts this depiction, as she notes how, having dreamt of a little girl that she and Niki saw swinging in the park, 'I had doubts even then as to its innocence [...] the dream had to do not so much with the little girl we had watched, but with my having remembered Sachiko two days previously' (*PVH*: 55). In this passage Etsuko's dreams of ropes and swinging children become connected not only to the horrific event of Keiko's suicide but also, and more centrally, to her sense of complicity in the postwar maternal violence which she here associates with Sachiko and Mariko's story. As she later puts it, stutteringly, 'it isn't that little girl at all [...] It was just a little girl I knew once [...] A long time ago [...] the little girl isn't on a swing at all [...] it's not a swing she on' (*PVH*: 95). By making explicit these symbolic associations, linking them to her relationship with Keiko during the postwar period, the novel thus uncovers Etsuko's underlying regret over her past behaviour, explaining this as a result not simply of trauma but also of profound guilt over how she has treated Keiko.

Indeed there is a strong sense in which this haunting spirit stands in both for Etsuko herself and Keiko, in so far as both women are imagined as enacting ghostly vengeance over their households. The novel makes this first connection (to Etsuko) explicit when, following Mariko's first mention of the woman, at the start of the novel, Etsuko responds, 'But that was me, Mariko-san. Don't you remember?' (*PVH*: 18). That Etsuko should see herself in this role affirms again her guilt for bringing Keiko to England, but also, implicitly, a suggestion that her rejection of motherhood during the postwar period acts as a form of revenge on an oppressive patriarchy, what Stephanie Lai identifies as 'the monstrous female ghosts [...] [and their] ability to punish their aggressors and the patriarchal society that has left them to rot' (2014: 18). By aligning violence to a balancing of debts in this way, within the context of continued postwar traditionalism, Etsuko thus implicitly rationalises her actions, even while chastising herself with respect to her daughter's unhappiness.

Meanwhile Keiko becomes associated with the *onryo* through Etsuko and Niki's anxieties regarding their English home, where night-time noises, coming from Keiko's former bedroom, evoke fears about a ghostly presence: 'A strange spell seemed to linger [in her room] even now, six years after she had left it – a spell that had grown all the stronger now that Keiko was dead' (*PVH*: 53). By spectrally inhabiting the family's domestic space in this way, both in life and, now, death, Keiko invokes the responsibility that her mother and sister share over her suicide, which again manifests as an unease regarding an invisible avenging spirit. 'I haven't slept very well lately', Niki confesses, 'I think I'm getting bad dreams, but I can never remember them properly once I wake up' (*PVH*: 55). Etsuko, as noted above, likewise struggles with disturbing nightmares, which increasingly become associated not only with Keiko's death but equally with her treatment of her daughter back in Nagasaki. As mentioned, her dream about 'the little girl' shifts in its meaning across the novel, first taking into consideration the links between this girl and Mariko, and, later, Mariko and Keiko. That Etsuko here inadvertently identifies with Sachiko, as a kind of uncanny doppelgänger, whose story again intersects with her own at several key points (see also Sim, 2006: 55–57), thus reaffirms her sense that Keiko is wreaking ghostly vengeance upon her, reminding her of a past she attempts to forget, but which keeps returning. Commenting on this understanding of the spectral as explained from a specifically Derridean point of view, Stephen Frosh writes, 'If the truth is spectral, then there is something true about what has been repressed, lost, maybe murdered too. These lost truths keep coming back to haunt us, and demand recompense. They are unwanted apparitions, truths troubling us; we often wish they would let us alone' (2012: 247). In this context this reading encompasses not only Etsuko's guilt and regret regarding her decision to migrate but also the mythologised understanding of English cultural authenticity she espouses in an effort to justify her migration. Her view of Keiko's room as 'the most pleasant in the house, with a splendid view across the orchard' (*PVH*: 53) emerges here as especially telling, reinforcing the repression implicit in her pastoral view of England, which radically contrasts the depressing truth of Keiko's suicide. That Keiko's ghost haunts the room and effectively bars Etsuko's access to this view reminds the reader of spectral truth behind her passing, which involves the need for critical reassessment in the face of nationalist cultural mythologies.

The novel's intertextual engagement with Puccini's *Madama Butterfly* further affirms this critical challenge to reactionary ideals, both in the case of prewar Japanese militarism, postwar American neo-liberalism and Thatcherite traditionalism. Indeed, considering both texts' interest in negotiating key moments of global historical change following American neo-imperial involvement in Asia – in *Madama Butterfly*'s case, following the Spanish-American and Philippine–American wars (Yoshihara, 2004: 975), and in *A Pale View of Hills*, following the Second World War and later the Cold War – both can be read to underline the shifting and overlapping nature of imperial power, as a triumphalist and militarised East confronts an equally aggressive and expansionary West. Moreover, the opera's salient interest not simply in negotiating this key moment of geopolitical transition but more centrally in 'creating its own Orientalism at a time when the geopolitics of East–West relations underwent a rapid change' (Yoshihara, 2004: 975), explains its central intertextual importance to the novel's diasporic critique, as the novel identifies and *inverts* this imperialist American Orientalism within postwar and late-century contexts, in this way disrupting the discriminatory representation of Japanese cultural otherness that it upholds. The stereotypes enacted within Puccini's *fin-de-siècle* opera might thus be seen as lying at the heart of *A Pale View of Hills*'s world literary project, as the novel investigates how such othering narratives become political instruments for systemic oppression.

To explain this I have commented above on the implicit connections drawn between the figure of Sachiko and Puccini's Cio-Cio-San, both of whom experience abandonment in the event of intended (but unsuccessful) migration. In the novel this connection is complicated by Sachiko's position as a counterpoint to Etsuko's narrative, wherein the latter is not abandoned by her lover but rather sees herself in the role of abandoner. Thus, while Sachiko is left behind by her Western lover, in a mimetic rehearsal of Puccini's melodrama, by contrast Etsuko's 'successful' migration story sees her racked with guilt over the death of her daughter, as she debates her complicity alongside her Western neo-imperialist oppressor. In this case the violent implications of Western 'delivery' are made ironically explicit, as Etsuko reviews their devastating impact upon the life of her daughter.

Likewise the ties drawn between Cio-Cio-San and Keiko in the event of the latter's suicide are here also complicated through textual attention to the discourse of Orientalism, wherein rather than supposedly explaining this tragic occurrence in terms of an inherent Eastern tendency, and in this way contributing to an exotifying melodrama of Eastern fragility (as in Puccini's opera), in this case this discourse *itself* is seen as responsible for Keiko's passing, its disregard for this young woman's personhood, a cause for her radical unhappiness in the West. In this way, in the mould of David Cronenberg's filmic remake of David Henry Hwang's Broadway play *M. Butterfly* (1993), Ishiguro 'reframes the narrative in the ironic mode of postmodernist aesthetics, articulating it to the cultural issues of gender, race, and sexuality in a postcolonial West' (de Lauretis, 2007: 127). What I would emphasise about this rereading is the revisionary nature of Ishiguro's project, as, rather than reinvesting in traditional Orientalist dichotomies between East and West, or in authorising the opera's gendered narrative of Eastern fragility and Western delivery, what *A Pale View of Hills* does is precisely to revoke such traditionalist ideologies in favour of critique, seeing Orientalism itself as the (often disguised and/or aestheticised) culprit of imperialist violence. In this way the novel illustrates this discourse's role not only in fuelling discrimination but also in nurturing false nationalist mythologies, which obscure difference and diversity.

Conclusion

Ishiguro's debut novel brings into play a diasporic critique of both postwar and 1980s Orientalism, while at the same time recognising links to a prewar Japanese imperialism with its own traditionalist tendencies. Indeed, noting the novel's central interest in highlighting such cross-cultural and cross-historical comparisons, and in drawing links between supposedly disconnected and contrasting settings, the text might be said to negotiate a multi-directional approach to history and memory, reinforcing what Michael Rothberg sees as 'the dynamic transfers that take place between diverse places and times during the act of remembrance', and which, he insists, '[help] to explain the spiralling interactions that characterize the politics of memory' (2009: 11). As Etsuko looks back over her past and reflects on such linkages, her narrative makes clear the critical significance of this multi-directional perspective, which recognises overlaps and reciprocities between imperialist projects, in this way disrupting any simplistic East versus West cultural binary. Through this act of memorial revision she begins a process of critical reassessment which gradually and tentatively allows her to confront her past mistakes and to begin to move on. While this project is not finished in this novel, it nevertheless brings to bear a new form of critical thinking, with an emphasis on commonalities, in acts of both violence and reassessment.

Note

1 Barry Lewis (2000) and Wai-chew Sim (2006) also see *Madama Butterfly* as a central intertext for the novel, and their ideas on this inform my reading here. Indeed, while Sim rejects the central importance of diaspora to the novel, in this way contrasting my own interpretation,

nevertheless his focus on a critique of Orientalism in *A Pale View of Hills* via engagement with this intertext very much inspires my analysis, and for this I am grateful to him.

References

Baillie, Justine and Sean Matthews (2009). 'History, Memory and the Construction of Gender in Kazuo Ishiguro's *A Pale View of Hills*', in Sean Matthews and Sebastian Groes (eds), *Kazuo Ishiguro: Contemporary Critical Perspectives* (London: Continuum), 45–53.
Benedict, Ruth (1946). *The Chrysanthemum and the Sword* (Boston, MA: Houghton Mifflin).
Bennett, Jill (2003). 'The Aesthetics of Sense-memory: Theorizing Trauma through the Visual Arts', in Susannah Radstone and Katharine Hodgkin (eds), *Memory Cultures: Memory, Subjectivity and Recognition* (Piscataway: Transaction Publishers), 27–39.
Berger J. and J. Greenberg (2003) 'There's No Backhand to This', in Judith Greenberg (ed.), *Trauma at Home: After 9/11* (Lincoln: Bison Books), 52–59.
Bhabha, Homi (1992). 'The World and the Home', *Social Text*, 31/32, 141–153.
—. (1994). *The Location of Culture* (New York: Routledge).
Caruth, Cathy (ed.) (1995). *Trauma: Explorations in Memory* (Baltimore: Johns Hopkins University Press).
Clifford, James (1994). 'Diasporas', *Cultural Anthropology*, 9:3, 302–338.
Craps, Stef (2014). *Postcolonial Witnessing: Trauma out of Bounds* (London: Palgrave Macmillan).
Creet, Julia (2011). 'Introduction: The Migration of Memory and Memories of Migration' in Julia Creet and Andreas Kitzmann (eds), *Memory and Migration: Multidisciplinary Approaches to Memory Studies* (Toronto: University of Toronto Press), 3–26.
Eckert, Ken (2012). 'Evasion and the Unsaid in Kazuo Ishiguro's *A Pale View of Hills*', *Partial Answers: Journal of Literature and the History of Ideas*, 10:1, 77–92.
Edkins, Jenny (2003). *Trauma and the Memory of Politics* (Cambridge: Cambridge University Press).
—. (2014). 'Time, Personhood, Politics', in Gert Buelens, Sam Durrant and Robert Eaglestone (eds), *The Future of Trauma Theory: Contemporary Literary and Cultural Criticism* (London: Routledge), 127–139.
Frosh, Stephen (2012). 'Hauntings: Psychoanalysis and Ghostly Transmission', *American Imago*, 69:2, 241–264.

Hoogvelt, Ankie (1997). *Globalization and the Postcolonial World* (Baltimore: Johns Hopkins University Press).
Ishiguro, Kazuo (1982). *A Pale View of Hills* (London: Faber and Faber).
—. (2017). 'My Twentieth Century Evening – and Other Small Breakthroughs', 7 December. *The Nobel Foundation*. www.nobelprize.org/uploads/2018/06/ishiguro-lecture_en-1.pdf (accessed June 2022).
Kim, Nadia Y. (2006). '"Patriarchy Is So Third World": Korean Immigrant Women and "Migrating" White Western Masculinity', *Social Problems*, 53:4, 519–536.
Lai, Stephanie (2014). 'Sympathy for Lady Vengeance: Feminist Ghosts and Monstrous Women of Asia', *The Lifted Brow*, 23, 18–22.
Lauretis, Teresa de (2007). 'Private and Public Fantasies in M. Butterfly', in P. White (ed.), *Figures of Resistance: Essays in Feminist Theory* (Champaign: University of Illinois Press), 118–148.
Lewis, Barry (2000). *Kazuo Ishiguro: Contemporary World Writers* (Manchester: Manchester University Press).
Lie, John (2001). 'Ruth Benedict's Legacy of Shame: Orientalism and Occidentalism in the Study of Japan', *Asian Journal of Social Science*, 29:2, 249–261.
Lovelace, Ada (2008). 'Ghostly and Monstrous Manifestations of Women: Edo to Contemporary', *The Irish Journal of Gothic and Horror Studies*, 5, 30–45.
Mackenzie, Suzie (2000). 'Between Two Worlds', *The Guardian*, 25 March, www.theguardian.com/books/2000/mar/25/fiction.bookerprize2000.
Mason, Gregory (1989). 'An Interview with Kazuo Ishiguro', *Contemporary Literature*, 30:3, 335–347.
Matek, Ljubica (2018). 'Narrating Migration and Trauma in Kazuo Ishiguro's *A Pale View of Hills*', *American, British and Canadian Studies*, 31:1, 129–146.
Morey, Peter (2018). *Islamophobia and the Novel* (New York: Columbia University Press).
Oe, Kenzaburo and Kazuo Ishiguro (1991). 'The Novelist in Today's World: A Conversation', *boundary 2*, 18:3, 109–122.
Radstone, Susannah (2003). 'The War of the Fathers: Trauma, Fantasy, and Sept 11', in Judith Greenberg (ed.), *Trauma at Home: After 9/11* (Lincoln: Bison Books), 117–123.
Rothberg, Michael (2003). '"There Is no Poetry in This": Writing, Trauma, and Home', in Judith Greenberg (ed.), *Trauma at Home: After 9/11* (Lincoln: Bison Books), 147–157.
—. (2009). *Multidirectional Memory* (Redwood City: Stanford University Press).
Shaffer, Brian W. (1998). *Understanding Kazuo Ishiguro* (Columbia: University of South Carolina Press).

Sim, Wai-chew (2006). *Globalization and Dislocation in the Novels of Kazuo Ishiguro* (Lewiston: Edwin Mellen Press).

Smith, Andrew (2004). 'Migrancy, Hybridity, and Postcolonial Literary Studies', in Neil Lazarus (ed.), *The Cambridge Companion to Postcolonial Literary Studies* (Cambridge: Cambridge University Press), 241–261.

Stock, F. (2010). 'Home and Memory', in Kim Knott and Sean McLoughlin (eds), *Diasporas: Concepts, Intersections, Identities* (New York: Zed Books), 24–28.

Sundholm, John (2011). 'The Cultural Trauma Process, or the Ethics and Mobility of Memory', in Julia Creet and Andreas Kitzmann (eds), *Memory and Migration: Multidisciplinary Approaches to Memory Studies* (Toronto: University of Toronto Press), 120–134.

Walkowitz, Rebecca (2006). *Cosmopolitan Style: Modernism Beyond the Nation* (New York: Columbia University Press).

Yoshihara, Mari (2004). 'The Flight of the Japanese Butterfly: Orientalism, Nationalism, and Performances of Japanese Womanhood', *American Quarterly*, 56:4, 975–1001.

Yoshimi, Shunya (2003). '"America" as Desire and Violence: Americanization in Postwar Japan and Asia during the Cold War', *Inter-Asia Cultural Studies*, 4.3: 433–450.

2

Eloquence and empathy in *A Pale View of Hills* and *An Artist of the Floating World*

Cynthia F. Wong

Are the narrators of Kazuo Ishiguro's first two novels set in Japan innocents recovering from a tormented life or murderous villains covertly shielding their deceits? Etsuko from *A Pale View of Hills* and Ono from *An Artist of the Floating World* have sparked both empathy and antipathy in unequal measure when reflected in psychological, cinematic or feminist readings of their characterisation. Interpretations vary on charges of unreliable narration stemming from emotional instability, on Ishiguro's reworking of Japanese cultural stereotypes and nationalist themes, and on consequences of personal trauma leading to some potential catharsis. Other contextual and extra-textual approaches to these novels take on fascinating cultural and historical interpretations, particularly the entwined postwar complexities pertaining to Japan, Great Britain and America during the middle of the twentieth century. As well, the political implications of Ishiguro's depictions of Japanese nationals tormented by their individual choices amidst broad public histories have produced lively debates about these intriguing narrators. The personal remembrances of Etsuko and Ono set during the postwar period among Ishiguro's imaginary contexts are scintillating, because of the author's nuanced craft in tone, diction and character complexity – indeed, precisely from the novels' literariness.[1]

The equivocating narratives by Etsuko and Ono in the respective novels originate from the author's perceptive portrayals of his characters set in a decimated but recovering Nagasaki in the late 1940s to 1950s: Japan's rebuilding period after the American bombing in 1945. *A Pale View of Hills* is set around 1955, almost ten years beyond, while events in *An Artist of the Floating World* are recounted by Ono from October 1948 to June 1950. Ishiguro explained: 'I wrote about these people [Etsuko and Ono] not actually to pass judgment on them because I am interested in people who do have a certain amount of talent. Not just talent, but how they have a certain passion, a certain real urge, to do a little bit more than the average person. They've got this urge to contribute to something larger' (Vorda and Herzinger, 2008: 86). These remarks came early on in Ishiguro's career, and the ensuing critical analyses of these characters actually challenge the author's sense of his literary characters. The narrators struggle for clarity amidst their emotional uneasiness, certainly, but they also may deceive in order to endure. Are their anecdotal fragments nevertheless continuous and coherent, culminating into a satisfying self-reflection or confession? Or are the pieces of stories and events each a distinct element reflecting their fractured disorientation, producing a profound sense of discontinuity with their place in time, or setting forth outright deception and emotional manipulation? These types of queries have guided these novels' reception and criticism. I will highlight the literary acumen with which Ishiguro wrote indeterminate yet perhaps vulnerable characters that have encouraged as well as upheld contradictory interpretations. As Ishiguro's first and only Japanese narrators, Etsuko and Ono turn out to be much more distinct and contrasting characters in their own right than as claimed by their author.

The duplicity of eloquence

Readers are more divided about the veracity of Ono's narrative than they are about the motives behind Etsuko's account. The spectrum of his personality is also much wider, ranging from psychological assessments of him as a weak and stunned old man to being a deliberately murderous tyrant. Brian W. Shaffer sees 'surface calm and tempestuous depths' (1998: 39) in both novels, with 'Sachiko's symbolic murder of [daughter] Mariko' standing in for Etsuko driving the death of her daughter, Keiko, and, in the second novel, of Ono as 'indirectly accountable for the deaths of his son, Kenji, and wife, Michiko' (1998: 39; 40). Peter Wain takes on Ono's culpability for disaster to highlight his vanity and need for celebrity status (1992: 187). Peter Sloane, on the other hand, deepens the characterisation of Ono's nefariousness in his charge that Ishiguro's novel is propaganda, and Ono exaggerates and revels in his artistic career with extreme reprehensibility (2018: 156). Barry Lewis's engrossing examination of Ono with reference to Japanese political history and cultural movements concurs with Wain's that Ono is 'a vain, self-serving man' but notes how at that juncture of vanity Ono turned out to have been 'just a minor functionary who is now burdened with an inappropriate sense of guilt' (2000: 54). In navigating a postwar world that seems to have forgotten about men like him, it is only Ono who seems to inflate how others revered or sympathised with him.[2] Timothy Wright also examines the variety of indictments against Ono and proceeds to extend the degree of 'self-deception and concealment at the level of nation' (2014: 63). The degree of villainy associated with Ono's character far exceeds those few (but still serious) recriminations directed at Etsuko. The trajectory of these compelling discussions over three decades of criticism ranges from analyses of Ishiguro's textual elements such as narrative tone, sophistication of figurative language, the novel's structure and themes of self-deception and cultural survival, as well as extra-textual elements such as Ishiguro's references to politics, history and artistic movements. These types of issues have a variety of possible answers for narrative motives in the first two novels, and readers continue to be beguiled by Ishiguro's characterisations.

Readers tend to be more sympathetic towards Etsuko's plight that is set in the context of her grief and guilt. In remembering herself nearly thirty years prior during the reconstruction period around 1955 when she was pregnant with Keiko, she admits that 'the Nakagawa district still provoked in me mixed emotions of sadness and pleasure [...] [and] a deep sense of loss' (*PVH*: 23). Many readers, including myself in the 1995 article, assumed Etsuko's story is set somewhere in the immediate aftermath of the bombing in 1945 and prior to the end of the American occupation in 1952. However, the Peace Park visit indicates that it must be 1955 or after. This kind of discrepancy – or miscalculation of dates and events to reflect Etsuko's imprecise memory – is what makes the novel so intriguing and irreducible. Rebecca Walkowitz identifies Etsuko's complex construction of her postwar experiences as her 'recounting and juxtaposing, in a palimpsest of memories, several stories at once' (2001: 1069), which would produce the temporal

Eloquence and empathy   43

and referential confusions. Michael Molino would concur with this claim on the relationship of Etsuko's narrative aligning but also remaining ineffable with her psychological state in his study of her trauma. As such, the confusions, gaps and omissions of the narrative reflect the deeply embedded stress that she experienced in the postwar period. Molino highlights that 'Etsuko's narrative, in other words, occupies a space of hermeneutical uncertainty in which she can recall and retell portions of her story – in all its ambiguity, displacements, anxieties, and dispossessions – without relaying it to a listener who will interpret and respond to it' (2012: 326). Walkowitz and Molino each use different theoretical methods to arrive at a similar point about an ambiguity of Etsuko's recounts creating several trajectories to pursue: is the memory of Sachiko a deliberate act of self-consolation for her grief over Keiko, or is Molino's 'hermeneutical uncertainty' a sign of her waning mental and emotional faculties caused by both guilt and shame? Are these two sensibilities about Etsuko's eloquence warring with some other kind of narrative uncertainty? Ljubica Matek addresses some of these compelling yet open-ended questions to reflect the sophistication of Ishiguro's suspenseful plotting and thematic unfolding:

> Ishiguro purposely chooses to leave certain issues unresolved so that the novel (and Etsuko's story) remains open to various interpretations and the ambiguity is such that the reader continues to wonder about the exact nature of Etsuko's trauma well after the story has ended. The traumatized protagonist-narrator either underreports or misreports traumatic events in order to protect herself from them. (2018: 144)

Ken Eckert (2012) also addresses the narrative's essential ambiguity and echoes Matek's and Molino's sense that Etsuko is working through these postwar events privately and not invoking a direct listener, adding to critical insight that determines psychological repercussions not only for Etsuko's particular postwar situation but as valuable ways for addressing physical and psychic trauma broadly.

Some readers have presumed incorrectly, but understandably, that Etsuko's private ruminations are actually conversations that she is having with her visiting daughter, given a particular fluency, vividness or relevance with particular accounts. But Molino explains that 'Etsuko is organizing knowledge not bonding socially with Niki or anyone else' (2012: 326) and therefore emphasises both the privacy and the silence of Etsuko's narrative processing. Readers might hope that she presents to herself a coherent rationalisation of her postwar remembrances in order to hone an acceptable fiction that would lessen her guilty feelings, but the effort is less on coherence and consistency than retracing key remembered episodes as signs for an attempt at contextualising and understanding her circumstances. In fact Etsuko's eloquence masks these type of disruptions to coherence, a mode that would come to characterise many of Ishiguro's future narrators as they work their stories. Even Ishiguro critiqued his characterisation of Etsuko by noting that 'the flashbacks are too clear, in a way [...] [and don't quite] have the same murkiness of someone trying to wade through their memories, trying to manipulate memories' (Mason, 1989: 5). Etsuko chides herself at times for imprecise accounts due to a failing memory, which can be read as both a reflective and a deflective gesture that captures truth-telling in all its uncertainties and possibly reroutes the painful story of maternal culpability towards a more ameliorating version. Yugin Teo writes that, at such turns in the remembrances, she in fact experiences 'self-recognition [that] occurs when the line between Etsuko's seemingly innocent recollections and her inner self-examinations is blurred in a flashback sequence' (2014: 64).

When examining some of the conversations between Etsuko and her daughter Niki – as I do later – readers would be persuaded with assessments by Molino and Eckert about the complexity of Etsuko's expressive styles, as well as Teo's remarks about Etsuko's recognition of her past deeds and remarks. Etsuko indeed works through her anecdotes in order to untangle her memories from a variety of time periods (prewar; postwar; contemporary present) throughout her narrative, and this dynamic process is conducted privately within her own diegesis. Whether she takes such care to reconstruct her failings as a mother to depressed and suicidal Keiko after their migration to England, or to escape and perhaps shield her inner torment about her decisions from the postwar period and beyond, is one fine point of contention among readers, who either judge negatively her shortcomings or sympathise with her difficulties in presenting a more traditional or logical account of her past.

Eckert analyses the repressions and evasions in Etsuko's account to assess her as neither 'a duplicitous [n]or insane narrator' (2012: 87). Sensitivity for Etsuko's situation evolves in further criticism such as the analysis by Ljubica Matek that adds another dimension to trauma by factoring in migration. Matek analyses 'how the novel's narrative strategies mimic the actual coping mechanisms of displaced people who, in the process of migration, experience a traumatic event' (2018: 130). Adding to the psychological and cultural ramifications of Etsuko's characterisation, Rebecca Karni focuses on Etsuko's 'conscious–unconscious feelings of guilt' to underscore how the novel's literary elements, including 'mood and themes of transience, flux, and changing values' (2015: 331) reflect and support such diverse interpretations. When contrasted with the array and degree of differences from critical assessments of Ono's character, those of Etsuko's nearly form a consensus with the caveat I noted above about few readers judging her negatively. Ishiguro's first two narrators, both elderly Japanese characters, are in fact much more distinct and unusual than the author himself and early critics assessed, and which evolving criticism continues to elucidate.

Family resemblances and the domestic drama

In the third of his four diary-like entries (November 1949), Ono reflects pleasantly on family resemblances when he takes his visiting grandson on an outing and notices how Ichiro's 'mannerisms and little facial habits' resembled his mother Setsuko's. Ono notices that his son-in-law's traits were evident as well and that, moreover, Ichiro 'was coming to resemble his father' (*AFW*: 136). This amiable observation leads Ono to remark on family resemblances and inheritances that offer a natural bridge of his observations about family with the reflections of his involvement as a propagandist painter:

> I was struck yet again by the similarity Ichiro bore to how my own son, Kenji [now dead], had been at that age. I confess I take a strange comfort from observing children inherit these resemblances from other members of the family […] Of course, it is not only when we are children that we are open to these small inheritances; a teacher or mentor whom one admires greatly in early adulthood will leave his mark. (*AFW*: 136)

In addition to spinning a web about resemblances and inheritances in these otherwise innocuous remarks, Ono applies the observation to an explanatory function of his employers, Takeda and Mori-san, regarding the justification of his art career. Family members or close working colleagues might provide 'strange comfort' to one another, might enmesh one another with their blood or employment ties of duty and loyalty, or might involuntarily provoke and help retrieve an image or memory associated with shared ties, such as when Ono sees Ichiro's resemblance to Ono's own son, Ichiro's uncle. Ono sets forth that family and work relationships are continuous and flow naturally in some order of things, and this is a concept that some could be persuaded into believing from his amiable tone. Omitted from Ono's rationalisation, though, is the way that he extricated himself vehemently from his father in order to move into the world of art with his mentors and employers (AFW: 41–47). Does Ono not see his father's ruthless ambition, acquisition of wealth and fame or vindictive nature in himself? It is within these failures of self-recognition, omissions in the storytelling and his breaks with primary ties that Ono double-exposes himself as someone simultaneously ashamed, proud and pompous, particularly when examining his self-defences against estrangement from his father and his teachers over his artistic production and employment.

Early in his narrative Ono presents broad positive strokes about family unity and legacy to which he seems to adhere in the time spent with his daughters and grandson, but his own history points to irrevocable rifts and vindictiveness with his own father, his employer-mentors, and even his students. With respect to his former student, Kuroda, Ono causes him and his mother physical harm and arrest (AFW: 181–182). On the surface these rifts appear to originate from irreconcilable ideological differences about money or artistic purpose, but beneath may be a loose foundation of the morality and work ethic that Ono often propounds. Ono's illusion of continuity shrouds the ruptures and breaks, but it is a duplicity that he cannot maintain for long. Chu-Chueh Cheng aptly describes Ono as 'an old man haunted by his earlier misdeeds' in her examination of 'the disquieting estrangement individuals sustain' (2010: 227) in their relationships to important others. Such a division of self-knowledge and one's subsequent presentation in narrative form is important to both of the first novels, but, in Ono's case, readers can gauge his being a decent, well-meaning but short-sighted man or an arrogant, degenerate and disgraced careerist on the basis of their sense of Ishiguro's complex portrayal. Ishiguro's construction of Ono's interior self has garnered a wide character spectrum as evidenced from the array of criticism about his personal and national character. Unlike Etsuko, whose irregularities of temporal representations might be explicable through examining her grief and guilt, Ono's misdirection seems more calculated and devious, according to these well-illustrated and diverse readings. Ishiguro sets the foundation for these duplicitous characterisations when he places Ono in physical settings in which he is above or beyond others, such as in the novel's opening lines of climbing 'the steep path leading up from the little wooden bridge still referred to around here as "the Bridge of Hesitation"' (*AFW*: 7), and at the novel's end, when Ono, among people but still on the outskirts, is watching young office workers and saying he feels both nostalgia and hope for Japan and its people while perhaps shrouding emotions about self-regret and disappointment.

Ono's considerations about inheritances from family members, formal teachers and other mentors serve as an organising principle for Ishiguro's own artistic rendering of his characters in these 'Japanese novels'. Among Ishiguro's novels are many family resemblances, particularly in his first three, that he said were essentially revisions of one after the other:

> In the first three novels, I was rewriting the same thing. I was on the same piece of territory, and each time I was refining what I wanted to say. So, you consider the move between my second and my third novels: my second novel was an expansion of the sub-plot of my first novel, but it's about how somebody wasted his life in terms of his career. It's about well-meaning but misguided efforts to lead a good life, but it seems to happen only in the realm of one's career. It seemed to me at the end of writing that book, that if you're talking about wasted lives, you can't just talk about career, you have to talk about the personal arena as well. (Wong and Crummett, 2008: 208)

Of the three novels, the elderly narrators' reflection of their personal lives helps reveal both their own personality as well as the way they were affected by the historical conditions of their times. A theme of career ambitions conflicting with one's emotional needs is present in *An Artist of the Floating World* and his third novel *The Remains of the Day*, providing some of the most satisfying Ishiguro literary criticism. My focus here on the first two novels from the 1980s ascertains how the relatively tranquil narrative surface provided by Etsuko and Ono shields much darker and more complicated situations and emotions. This duplicity of his eloquent representations to signify desperate and painful human experiences would come to mark Ishiguro's evolving literary work and affirm the Swedish Academy's anointing 'his novels of great emotional force [that] have uncovered the abyss beneath our illusory connection with the world' (Ishiguro, 2017).

In both of the first two novels Ishiguro's remarks about rewriting and expanding his topics are valid and indicate that he was doing a version of 'family resemblances' among his own evolving literary writing.[3] As an example, Cheng notes, 'A sub-plot concerning the generation gap in *A Pale View of Hills* expands into a major plot in *An Artist of the Floating World*, in which the narrator Masuji Ono articulates what Ogata-San might have expressed if he were more fully developed' (231). But Ishiguro may have been overly modest about certain recurrences found across novels. The first two novels focus on one family but bring in relationships with other families to affirm or contest values of the primary one; deaths of family members are at the centre of unspoken crises but often not explicitly referenced or discussed; and recurrent dramas enacted by members provide insight into the pattern and tenor of relationships.

Etsuko does not have a career per se, one for which she is remunerated for employment as Ono would have been. Justine Baillie and Sean Matthews note that her roles as wife and mother, though, very much occupy her as these demanding duties were 'socially defined within a conservative and patriarchal environment' (2009: 50). We wonder whether Jiro, Keiko's father, would assume a similar emotional or psychological responsibility for contributing to his daughter's death, if we were to get his first-person account of his familial authority. Much of Etsuko's anguish stems from her tormented evasions about the quality of her mothering and the guilt and shame associated with her unspecified failures but which one might deduce from her memories about Sachiko and Mariko. Both Ono and Etsuko return to factual and emotional traces of their lives, but, in so doing, they reveal the strains, changes and even ruptures that paradoxically propelled their lives forward in time. Their self-accounts grow more strange, perhaps even emotionally regressive, rather than more familiar or clearer to readers, who must untangle their myriad attributes only still to find the characters elusive (Walkowitz, 2001: 1072). Ishiguro focused on the richness of family dynamics in his novels to create unique 'couples' with interesting similarities and differences from one another, in order to organise the ruptures in narrator accounts. Each of Ono's teachers and students might form a new coupling, for instance, with Ono and Matsuda paired to show their extreme nationalism in the prewar period. Etsuko and Sachiko are mother pairs, while their daughters Keiko and Mariko form daughter pairs; Mrs Fujiwara, the optimistic mother figure for Etsuko, is paired with the funereal elderly cousin of Sachiko's to represent hope and despair, respectively.

It is now a well-known fact that Ishiguro drew from his own childhood memories before age five when he lived in Japan with his extended family, as well as borrowing from Japanese films of the mid-twentieth century as part of his creative reconstruction of his birthplace (Dasgupta, 2015: 14). In particular the *shomin-geki*, or domestic drama, from Japanese cinema has provided Ishiguro with a great deal of inspiration for character situations in the novels. Karni notes that in the first two novels, 'besides an aesthetics and poetics of change, nostalgia, and the pathos of things as described above, an aesthetics of suggestion and indirection goes hand in hand with the formulation of an enigma on the levels of both *story* and *discourse*' (2015: 331 – emphasis in original). Through the visual imagery of these films Ishiguro added details from his child's memory of Nagasaki before his family immigrated to and eventually remained in England.[4] Ishiguro's socialisation into England and his respect for the Japanese representations in films such as Yasujiro Ozu's *Tokyo Story* (1953) help him explore, for example, the estranging nature of relations between parents and children in the postwar period. In that film the likeable elderly couple, Shukishi and Tomi – perhaps prefiguring the sojourn that Axl and Beatrice would make in Ishiguro's 2015 novel *The Buried Giant* – undertake a long return train journey from their small village to the big city of Tokyo where their grown and married children, along with their war widow daughter-in-law, now reside. One of the main themes that Ishiguro seemed to have borrowed from Ozu is the prevalence of family disunity and estrangement rather than the conventional ideal theme of unity and strong bonds during the postwar period.

Grown children move away from parents to follow employment in the big city, as they also crave much-needed physical and emotional distance from their parents in order to root and flourish. The son and the daughter, Koichi and Shige, seem indifferent to the visit and act burdened by the time they must withdraw from their usual daily life to tend to the parents' visit. At one point the doctor son Koichi cancels the entire Sunday family outing because he claims he must treat an ill patient and emphasises in the process the community's great need for his medical services. The daughter-in-law, Noriko, is the most attentive and empathetic to the elderly couple's abandonment by their own children (who at one point send them to an ill-suited youth-populated spa in Atami). None of the biological children's irritations about their parents impinging on their current lives are explicit but their actions and attitudes suggest that they feel annoyingly strained by the visit. En route home, the elderly mother sickens and shortly dies at home. Only then, in the immediate aftermath of her dying and death do the children switch course and express deeper emotions about their mother. Though passionate, the expressions of grief are brief, which anger the youngest daughter still living at home, Kyoko, who shares her frustration with Noriko, only to learn from her sister-in-law that life inevitably and invariably will be disappointing. The family members gather dutifully for the funeral, pay their respects to their widowed father, share a post-funeral meal that is peppered with some joyous remembrances of Tomi and immediately make plans to return to their own lives. Arguably, their stoicism – or pragmatism – affirms a societal need to return to a productive life for economic productivity and stability, and even a period of familial mourning has its due course.

When drunk one night, though, the father, Shukishi, in Ozu's *Tokyo Story* laments mutually with his old friends that their children are huge disappointments. The drunken confessional outburst is at once astonishing and edifying. The drunkenness of that night seems to signify many such nights while his children were young, a point frustratingly recalled by the daughter when father shows up late at night, inebriated and accompanied by the police. Family solidarity and sympathy are further tested when the grown children start showing signs that life growing up was far less rosy than the gentleness and patience we see reflected in the elderly couple at present. The father's inebriation in Tokyo is a stunning repetition to Shige of his past frequent drunkenness, to which Ishiguro might have alluded for Ono's own drinking past and his misguided insistence that his son Kenji and grandson Ichiro get early tastes of sake, much to the rightful disdain of Ono's daughters. Director Ozu's way of disorienting audience expectations of children dutifully respecting their elderly parents while also suggesting darker events in the family past – such as cruel behaviours from parents when their children were young that may account for their adult resentments – is subtle yet powerful and must have resonated with Ishiguro. The implication of disrupted family cohesion would not be lost on Ishiguro, who used similar overlaps of past and present to wrench the many textures wrought by time upon human lives and their family relationships.

In Ishiguro's first two novels, family strife is never far beneath the surface of seeming cordiality, if we might read the novels through thematic and dynamic lens provided by Ozu's film, *Tokyo Story*: the strained family visit, the difficulties of maintaining calm and order among varied members and in-laws, the need to focus on present matters and not return to oppressive past events or forecast anxious future ones that create constant challenges to civility, and the veiled desire to depart to somewhere else far from the family abode – all of these moments figure into the literary constructions of time and space in the two novels, where Ishiguro is 'stressing the interaction between literary utterances, on the one hand, and the social and mental activities of writers and readers, on the other' to produce these thematic connections (Keunen, 2000: 2). Gingerly we might accept the Academy's point about a yawning 'abyss' beneath the illusions that people devise for connecting their relationships as found in Ishiguro's novels to discover how his works can be simultaneously uplifting and depressing. Ironically, these illusions provide the impetus to follow a prevailing sense of the importance of one's family, for good and ill, while forging one's self and stories.

Empathy unrealised

In *A Pale View of Hills* the family visit is set in reverse from Ozu's film. Etsuko's remembrances are stimulated by her second daughter Niki's April 1982 visit from London to her childhood home.[5] Etsuko's lugubrious retirement contrasts with her daughter's probably more boisterous London life, but Niki does not take the bait when her mother complains that she does not 'seem sensitive to the feel of the countryside despite having grown up here' (*PVH*: 47). Niki in turn charges that her mother's home and village are 'not the real countryside, just a residential version to cater for the wealthy people who lived here' (*PVH*: 47). This disagreement about authenticity portends the many others that pepper the different perspectives and miscommunications characterising their relationship. Their activities are quite mundane and Etsuko senses Niki's boredom or restlessness during this return to the childhood home and village. Over five days the two women walk around the village, have stilted and relatively unproductive conversations, fuss around plants and discuss the impact of Keiko's former room intruding upon restful sleep. Niki takes time away from her mother to go through her father's journalism. Their missteps but also their seemingly genuine endeavour to be present for one another find one obstacle after another towards a warmer, more stable bond.

We sense immediately the friction of the mother–daughter relationship, and the emotional weight each carries in trying to maintain cordial demeanours; we sense, as well, the burdens of the past and the attempts from both women to tread carefully. Mainly we sense their feeling of being haunted by their blended family past and the deaths of half their family. The occasion for recalling the friendship with Sachiko in 1955 is stirred by the recent event of Keiko's suicide and when Etsuko and Niki see a young girl in the village. For most of the novel Etsuko tries to maintain this sense or guise of temporal distinction in her accounts but the result is a much more complicated and traumatic working of her thoughts about both becoming and being a mother, as many critics have noted. Jane Hu observes not only that Etsuko's first-person narration creates 'a formal entanglement between Etsuko's and Sachiko's plots' but that a 'stark antinomy between Sachiko's American progressivism and Etsuko's Japanese subordination becomes increasingly blurred' (2021: 129) as the novel progresses.

Similarly Ono's remembrances are invigorated by the failure of his second daughter Noriko's prior marriage negotiations and the recent, more propitious possibility of a second attempt at an engagement. The novel is also punctuated with family visits from the elder daughter Setsuko with her son Ichiro on two separate occasions which mark the division of apprehension and relief on Ono's part as he works through his memories. Both daughters seem to try and veil their concerns that Ono is wrong for thinking so highly of his artistic past and might contemplate or commit suicide to placate the family's assumed diminishing reputation. At one point Ono expresses, 'I now find myself becoming increasingly irritated by certain things [Setsuko] said to me' (*AFW*: 132) and gets no satisfaction from his daughter when he believes she has been proved wrong. Whether Ono remembers correctly or not a luminous career in the prewar nationalist period, his family members seem united in an unspoken consensus about his perhaps unmerited self-importance as a public figure, as Ichiro inadvertently lets on that he has been privy to their probably frequent discussions of his grandfather. Ichiro asks Ono in one of their more sombre moments together, 'Was Mr Naguchi [who killed himself out of supposed honour] like Oji [who was a famous painter]?' (*AFW*: 154) and opens a Pandora box for the much deeper problems provoked by Ono's self-misrepresentations.

Ono's passionate work in pro-Nationalist painting and his own drunken forays in the floating world probably caused a great deal of strife for his wife and children, but these are not scenes given in the novel. Ono makes no mention of how his indulgences in work and after-work pleasure might have negatively affected them, but Noriko's mistrust of and irritations with her father – which he blames on her stress about the upcoming *miai* (the formal meeting between his daughter and future son-in-law and their respective families) – indicate a more disoriented parent–child relationship than the one he tries to conjure for his audience (*AFW*: 105–108). As in Ozu's film, the daughter Shige still nurses psychological wounds caused by her parents while growing up; Noriko's aloofness also signals her general negative attitude towards her father during this time. Ono's ideal audience would be a sympathetic and compassionate person – like his conservative friend Matsuda – who cannot fault someone for not being able to read into the future the fatal consequences of his artistic endeavours or the sacrifices he made for work at the expense of his family relationships.

From their very beginning, Ishiguro's first two novels contain mysteries that pull the disparate narrative threads forward, and readers might hope for disclosure, unearthing of secrets, or, at the very least, the narrators locating root causes to provide both explanatory and consolatory closure. At the start of *A Pale View of Hills* Etsuko observes that a palpable tension shrouded the visit, particularly 'the subject of Keiko's death' which 'we never dwelt long on [...] [but] it was never far away, hovering over us whenever we talked' (*PVH*: 10). In one seemingly ordinary domestic conversation, Ishiguro writes tellingly of Etsuko's perceptiveness about her hampered communications with her daughter and their failure to hear the other:

> 'If you're cold at night, Niki, you can simply turn up the heating'.
> 'I suppose so', She gave a sigh. 'I haven't slept very well lately, I think I'm getting bad dreams, but I can never remember them properly once I wake up'.
> 'I had a dream last night', I said.
> 'I think it might be to do with the quiet. I'm not used to it being so quiet at night'.
> 'I dreamt about that little girl. The one we were watching yesterday. The little girl in the park'.
> 'I can sleep right through traffic, but I've forgotten what it's like, sleeping in the quiet'. Niki shrugged and dropped some cutlery in to the drawer. 'Perhaps I'll sleep better in the spare room'. (*PVH*: 54–55)

Niki seems to have missed entirely her mother's reference to the dream about a girl in the park, an image that is linked with Keiko's suicide by hanging. She talks over her mother's two utterances about that dream. Or she ignores or avoids them, as she does with maternal advice about turning up the heat to address the cold. Niki continues her one-sided reflections about the quiet affecting her sleep while Etsuko fails to interest her daughter in her own disturbing dream that was provoked by their afternoon walk into the village. Niki's frustration with not remembering her bad dreams is also symbolic of the women's ability to ignore, deflect or honestly attempt to evade difficult subjects in order to maintain domestic peace.

Furthermore Niki plans to entrust her friend, who has 'been through a lot', to write a poem about her mother's life (*PVH*: 177). This impressive feat, if accomplished however, would be less a tribute to Etsuko's life than a simplification or, worse, a reduction or diminishing of her wartime losses as well as indicting her for failures at marriage and child-rearing. Perhaps this is what Niki desires: to make her mother's experiences reducible, compact, manageable. As rendered by a complete outsider of her mother's life, the friend's poem would be filtered through her personal difficulties and would be an attempt at an empathetic retelling of Etsuko's life. The friend's intended ekphrasis of Etsuko's experiences would be influenced by the last remaining photo of Inasa from an old calendar (*PVH*: 179).[6] Etsuko, also trying to maintain a warm regard for her daughter, says actually with tinged sarcasm or veiled dread, 'I'm sure your friend will write a marvelous poem' (*PVH*: 89), just as she notes when Niki reports that her friends admire Etsuko's courage for fleeing a distressful life in Japan, 'I'm very flattered. Please thank your marvelous friends' (*PVH*: 90). While Niki insists that her mother is not to blame for Keiko's death, she is understandably uneasy broaching the subject any further. Etsuko herself makes subtle references to Niki's hesitancy to bring up Keiko and seems to prefer the silence over any confrontation. The presence of the dead daughter/sister haunts Etsuko and Niki and strains their ability to converse in what a reader might hope is a more heartfelt and open manner.

Like Noriko's responses to her father Ono in the second novel, Niki's emotions of frustration and fear about her mother are veiled in defensive language. Noriko hopes to become engaged; Niki refuses to subject herself to the prison house of marriage and having children. Noriko critiques her father's gardening, his 'meddling' of it and signifies her dread that his past will mar her chances for marital union (*AFW*: 106–107). Etsuko counters Niki's surprise about her pretending that Keiko is still alive by anticipating it before Niki confronts her, to which Etsuko snaps back, 'I don't enjoy deceiving people' (*PVH*: 52). Niki's advance manoeuvre may be the kind of protective devising of her past actions against Keiko that contributed to her death.

Keiko's migration to England was an unhappy uprooting, if we are to infer her isolation from the story of Mariko that is remembered in Etsuko's narration. As a Japanese child with a Japanese mother and British stepfather, Keiko might have been accepted by the community or shunned for her foreignness. Her half-sister Niki could have come to represent for Keiko the preferred child of possibly loving and well-matched parents while Keiko's estrangement from her Japanese father would have left a large gap in her sense of connectedness and belongingness. Near the novel's end, in a kind of denouement, Etsuko finally brings herself to tell Niki, 'I knew all along she wouldn't be happy over here. But I decided to bring her just the same' (*PVH*: 176), confirming a reader's dread that Keiko inherited the intergenerational harms of many of her mother's own traumas about loss, dispossession and failed belongingness. Matek observes the heart-breaking dilemma in which Keiko 'suspects that she is a burden to her mother and feels both neglected and invisible as well as forcefully uprooted from her Japanese heritage and homeland' (2018: 138). Etsuko's own blanks in the narrative about this highly critical period in her daughter's removal from home and country provoke these and other kinds of speculations regarding Etsuko's narrative motives. Etsuko's socialised deference to her first husband Jiro and her genuine, loyal affection for her father-in-law during her first pregnancy belie the eventual dissolution of her marriage to Keiko's father. In England she may have come to regret their migration to follow her second husband Sheringham. Her choices irreparably hurt and harmed Keiko; her silence about those choices could come to produce estrangement with Niki as well. Caroline Bennett assesses that, in studying relations between parents and their children in the two novels, '[t]rauma lies at the heart' of Ishiguro's explorations (2011: 91). As Matek declares, the story stays with the reader long after the novel is completed and is a testament to Ishiguro's subtle and significant portrayals of guarded family lives. Instead of reconciliation and unity, though, *A Pale View of Hills* emphasises a person's inability to manifest an empathetic connection, as well as underscoring the predominance of fragmentation and disunity possible among family members. All of Etsuko's households – with her biological family that is never named or elaborated, with the Ogatas' in Japan and with Sheringham's in the UK – have been irreparably broken, and the spring visit serves rather as a eulogy to failed families and their ideals. The death of a child signifies the inversion of the order of life; the death of a parent forecasts the absence of authority and guidance in the family hierarchy – Etsuko experienced both these kinds of losses. In the first two novels these profound losses within the family unit are real and symbolic, simultaneously.

Conclusion

Ishiguro's focus on domestic drama and universal themes about parents and their children offers poignant storytelling through a variety of literary elements. His tonal modulations in both novels provide a unique signature regarding the complexity of human emotions, causing readers to pause and reconfigure their literary expectations. While the characters have difficulty forging empathy with one another, Ishiguro capably opens the emotional arena for readers to find substance and complexity in his characters' lives. The elegiac tone, particularly in the first novel, becomes more a mood or attitude of defiance and defence of misbehaviours in the second, reflecting Ishiguro's early and successful ability to create affective worlds for his reader's engagement. Readers' sympathy for Etsuko is contrasted with a mix of repulsion and pity for Ono, as borne out by nearly thirty years of criticism for these novels. Indeed, while both are set in Ishiguro's imagined Japan, these tonal differences account for the much greater diversity of Ishiguro's literary imagination than one might expect initially, but to which his subsequent six novels attest.

Speaking in 1904, Franz Kafka said, 'But we need books that affect us like a disaster, that grieve us deeply, like the death of someone we loved more than ourselves, like being banished into forests far from anyone, like a suicide. A book must be an axe for the frozen sea within us.' Ishiguro's debut novels borrowed from his memory and imagination of a childhood Japan that was built by his immersion in Japanese films (Shen, 2021: 2). Through the rich complexity of his characterisations and the emotional heft of his narrative constructions, through his eloquent style and empathetic narrator portrayals, he compels us to witness human failings as well as support endeavours to reflect and to never stop searching for plausible ways of persisting.

Notes

1 The concept of literariness is first introduced in 1919 by Roman Jakobson and developed by Russian Formalists: 'the object of literary science is not literature but literariness, that is, what makes a given work a literary work'. See Marko Juvan (2000) for a more thorough assessment of literariness and defamiliarisation, which will provide structure for my discussion. Since Ishiguro's first two novels have been assessed through a variety of theoretical lens and through their realism, as well as modern and postmodern tendencies, returning to elements of what constitutes the texts' 'literariness' will support the tremendous appeal of his works across a span of fascinating critical readings.

2 In conversation with Ishiguro in 2006, he told me that after he read the first edition of my monograph (2000): 'I thought that you were quite harsh in your assessment about Ono's character and less so with Stevens [in *RD*]' (2012: 6). Along the spectrum of criticism to date, my 2000 assessment of Ono would now be identified as relatively sympathetic.

3 More recently, a concept of Ishiguro's 'intertexts', or echoes and overlaps, has occupied critics who find all kinds of family and thematic resemblances across all of the novels. As mentioned earlier, Ono is an echo of the character Ogata-san from the first novel; Lewis identifies Ishiguro's early short story, 'The Summer After the War' as an early source for *An Artist of the Floating World* (2000: 48); and even characters as diverse as Ryder from *The Unconsoled* bear some resemblance to the Artificial Intelligence friend in *Klara and the Sun*.

4 See Ria Taketomi's (2020) informative analysis of Japanese sites familiar to Ishiguro and his literary reconstruction of, for instance, the symbolic river in the first novel.

5 In keeping with the timeline that Etsuko's account of Sachiko takes place in 1955 (or after) when she is pregnant with Keiko that spring, the migration to the UK would have occurred in 1962 when Keiko is about seven years old. Niki is twenty when she visits her mother in the novel's present tense, the same age that Keiko left the family for good to live and die in Manchester. Keiko's death at the age of twenty-six also would have occurred in 1982, not many years prior as a few critics and reviewers have mistakenly noted. The year that Niki's father Sheringham died is not noted, but the proximity and propinquity of Keiko's suicide certainly would account for the taut tension between Niki and Etsuko, who quibble about attendance at the family members' funerals (*PVH*: 52).

6 The calendar photo is cued to a memory of Keiko that Etsuko mentions to Niki but for which she does not provide details. Instead, Inasa is one of the places that she went to with Sachiko and Mariko, and Etsuko conflates the two Inasa outings. Other symbolisms that have been addressed by critics over the years include the rope around Etsuko's ankle when she talks to 'the child' who could be either Mariko or Keiko; the 'ruined' tomato plants that Niki tries to straighten; and Sachiko's drowning of Mariko's kittens (*PVH*: 173; 91; 92; 168).

References

Baillie, Justine and Sean Matthews (2009). 'History, Memory and the Construction of Gender in Kazuo Ishiguro's *A Pale View of Hills*', in

Sean Matthews and Sebastian Groes (eds), *Kazuo Ishiguro: Contemporary Critical Perspectives* (London: Continuum), 45–53.

Bennett, Caroline (2011). '"Cemeteries are no places for young people": Children and Trauma in the Early Novels of Kazuo Ishiguro', in Sebastian Groes and Barry Lewis (eds), *Kazuo Ishiguro: New Critical Visions of the Novels* (London: Palgrave Macmillan), 82–92.

Cheng, Chu-Chueh (2010). 'Cosmopolitan Alterity: America as a Mutual Alien of Britain and Japan in Kazuo Ishiguro's Novels', *Journal of Commonwealth Literature*, 45:2, 227–244.

Dasgupta, Romit (2015). 'Kazuo Ishiguro and "Imagining Japan"', in Cynthia F. Wong and Hülya Yıldız (eds), *Kazuo Ishiguro in a Global Context* (London: Ashgate/Routledge), 11–22.

Eckert, Ken (2012). 'Evasion and the Unsaid in Kazuo Ishiguro's *A Pale View of Hills*', *Partial Answers: Journal of Literature and the History of Ideas*, 10:1, 77–92.

Hu, Jane (2021). 'Typical Japanese: Kazuo Ishiguro and the Asian Anglophone Historical Novel', *Modern Fiction Studies*, 67:1, 123–148.

Ishiguro, Kazuo (1982). *A Pale View of Hills* (London: Faber and Faber).

—. (1986). *An Artist of the Floating World* (London: Faber and Faber).

—. (2017) 'My Twentieth Century Evening – and Other Small Breakthroughs', 7 December. *The Nobel Foundation*. www.nobelprize.org/uploads/2018/06/ishiguro-lecture_en-1.pdf (accessed June 2022).

Juvan, Marko (2000). 'In Literariness: From Post-Structuralism to Systems Theory', *CLCWeb: Comparative Literature and Culture*, 2:2, 1–12.

Karni, Rebecca (2015). 'Made in Translation: Language, "Japaneseness", "Englishness", and "Global Culture" in Ishiguro', *Comparative Literature*, 52:2, 318–348.

Keunen, Bart (2000). 'Bakhtin, Genre Formation, and the Cognitive Turn: Chronotopes as Memory Schemata', *Comparative Literature and Culture*, 2:2, http://docs.lib.purdue.edu/clcweb/vol2/iss2/2 (accessed June 2021).

Lewis, Barry (2000). *Kazuo Ishiguro: Contemporary World Writers* (Manchester: Manchester University Press).

Mason, Gregory (1989). 'An Interview with Kazuo Ishiguro', *Contemporary Literature*, 30: 3, 335–347.

Matek, Ljubica (2018). 'Narrating Migration and Trauma in Kazuo Ishiguro's *A Pale View of Hills*', *American, British and Canadian Studies*, 31:1, 129–146.

Molino, Michael (2012). 'Traumatic Memory and Narrative Isolation in Ishiguro's *A Pale View of Hills*'. *Critique*, 53:4, 322–336.

Ozu, Yasujiro (1953). *Tokyo Story*, Criterion, DVD.

Shaffer, Brian W. (1998). *Understanding Kazuo Ishiguro* (Columbia: University of South Carolina Press).

Shen, Anni (2021). 'Adapting Mizoguchi's Ugestsu in Kazuo Ishiguro's *The Buried Giant*', *Adaptations*, 10:1, 1–21.

Sloane, Peter (2018). 'Literatures of Resistance Under U.S. "Cultural Siege": Kazuo Ishiguro's Narratives of Occupation', *Studies in Contemporary Fiction*, 59:2, 154–167.

Taketomi, Ria (2020). 'The Image of the River in Ishiguro's *A Pale View of Hills*', *East-West Cultural Passage*, 74–93.

Teo, Yugin (2014). *Kazuo Ishiguro and Memory* (Basingstoke: Palgrave Macmillan).

Vorda, Allan and Kim Herzinger (2008). 'An Interview with Kazuo Ishiguro', in Brian W. Shaffer and Cynthia Wong (eds), *Conversations with Kazuo Ishiguro* (Jackson: University Press of Mississippi), 66–88.

Wain, Peter (1992). 'The Historical-Political Aspect of the Novels of Kazuo Ishiguro', *Language and Culture*, 23:1, 177–205.

Walkowitz, Rebecca L. (2001). 'Ishiguro's Floating Worlds', *English Literary History*, 68:4, 1049–1076.

Wong, Cynthia F. and Grace Crummett (2008). 'A Conversation about Life and Art with Kazuo Ishiguro', in Brian W. Shaffer and Cynthia F. Wong (eds), *Conversations with Kazuo Ishiguro* (Jackson: University Press of Mississippi), 204–220.

Wright, Timothy (2014). 'No Homelike Place: The Lesson of History in Kazuo Ishiguro's *An Artist of the Floating World*', *Contemporary Literature*, 55:1, 58–88.

3

Ishiguro's tempered presentational realism and practice

Rebecca Karni

Making sense of worlds of ambiguous, ambivalent, treacherous and often contradictory signs as well as of silences and pauses emerges as a central concern for both narrator-protagonists and readers of Kazuo Ishiguro's novels. These slippery signs and the deceptive surface transparency of the author's prose, in addition to his Japanese background, have compelled many readers to attribute to the narratives' blanks and ambiguities the kinds of meanings on the levels of character, culture, aesthetics and ethics that Ishiguro's texts so intriguingly defy, resulting, for example, in essentialist or Orientalist interpretations of his work. My focus here is precisely on the ways in which Ishiguro's texts resist, even as they invoke, expectations on the levels of form, content and genre, entangling us in the affective and ethical intricacies of the characters' experiences and their reading, while simultaneously directing our attention to these expectations and sense-making processes themselves. More specifically, while signs and represented (fictional) reality are concerns for both characters in and readers of Ishiguro's fiction, these signs themselves, as I argue in this chapter, subtly train us in alternative ways of reading them, the author's texts, and of reading as such. In acquiring meaning in ways that go beyond signification, the narratives foreground and confront us with their own limits and liminality, thus prompting reflection on and modelling an awareness of novel ways of meaning-making and its implications for interpretation as such.

Based on a close reading of Ishiguro's second novel, *An Artist of the Floating World* (1986), this chapter examines the foundations of the gestural, and more specifically presentational, techniques by means of which Ishiguro interrupts and redirects signification or the narrative flow of his novels. More particularly, the chapter highlights the presentational characteristics of these techniques and Ishiguro's writing, which I view as central to a tempered presentational realism at the heart of the author's fiction and to the ways in which his first-person narratives entangle us in the affective and ethical conundrums of the narrator-protagonists' experiences as well as in the complexities of their narration and reading.[1]

The notion of 'presentational' as I use it here involves both aspects associated with the term in narrative contexts, aesthetics, philosophy – particularly Hans-Georg Gadamer's conception of it – and in Japanese film studies. Gadamer's notion of 'presentation' (*Darstellung*) refers to the meaning of a work of art or thing existing in the work or thing itself and not independently of it. Meaning, to him, is therefore presented rather than represented.[2] But 'presentational' in this essay is ultimately meant to designate a combination of qualities unique to Ishiguro's fiction adapted from characteristics that have been related to the term. They include interrupted signification processes so that meaning is conveyed gesturally, and more specifically presentationally, rather than through signification;[3] thwarted and recast reader expectations both about the stories and the narratives' own procedures; and a gestural and subtly deictic textual self-consciousness, directing our attention to, and involving us in, the narratives' meaning-making processes.

Elements discussed as 'presentational' in Japanese film studies, I argue, are an important factor in the formation of Ishiguro's tempered presentational realism.[4] This link between Ishiguro's prose and Japanese film is based on his self-stated attraction to a particular Japanese film aesthetic, especially evident in the films of Yasujiro Ozu, Kenji Mizoguchi and Mikio Naruse, as well as considerations of specific narrative and significatory characteristics and their functions in his work (rather than an essentialist connection established between the two simply based on the author's Japanese background).[5] Examples of presentational practices particularly relevant in this context are subtle techniques, especially notable in Ozu's films, that continuously undercut the films' underlying realism, linear representation and the transparency of the sign. In similar ways as do Ozu's films, I argue, Ishiguro's fictions balance realism with a delicate focus on form and a peculiar consciousness of its own construction that includes a gestural and subtly deictic quality and embroils the reader in novel ways. Moreover, a set of presentational techniques serves to gently recast the reader's assumptions and expectations both about the stories and about the narratives' own procedures.

Gregory Mason argues that certain strategies adapted from Japanese film aesthetics influenced Ishiguro's character depictions.[6] My chapter foregrounds how and argues that, even more fundamentally, these and other techniques inspired and helped shape the author's style and a particular type of presentational realism central to his fiction.[7] My argument thus entails, in part, a re-examination of the author's self-stated attraction to Japanese cinema and its influence on his prose. Ishiguro's early novels *Pale View* and *Artist* are especially relevant in this respect because, in part owing to their visual images of a partly remembered, partly imagined 'Japan' as well as their relationship to the narratives' progression, these works speak to the ways that a visual dimension contributed to the formation of Ishiguro's narrative style and presentational realism. This is one of the reasons why the gestural and more specifically presentational elements at issue here are, literally, more visible in these two early novels than in his later texts. *Artist* is especially interesting in this context because narrative unreliability contributes to the novel's subtle presentational realism for the first time similarly as in Ishiguro's subsequent texts and because of the manner in which variations of a particular motif prefigure similar moments in Ishiguro's subsequent novels.

Ultimately, this chapter considers the ways in which Ishiguro's fiction, in its tempered presentational realism and practices, embroils us in its significatory limits on the levels of narration, character and reading, thus training us in navigating the liminality of both the characters' affective and ethical quandaries as well as those pertaining to their reading and interpretation, while simultaneously commenting implicitly on its implications for reading and interpreting fiction in our current moment. The chapter considers *Artist* from a presentational perspective first compositionally, then by looking at individual textual moments. Its last part focuses on liminal meaning-making and presentational strategies in Ishiguro's fiction beyond *Artist*.

Compositional presentationalism

Artist further develops the diegetic strategies of his short story 'A Family Supper' and first novel, *Pale View*, central to his fiction and particularly conspicuous in his early work, that simultaneously invite, redirect, reflect on and subtly expose readers' assumptions and expectations. While the discourse in *Pale View* is already marked as that of an unreliable first-person narrator, narrative unreliability is more saliently involved in formulating a mystery apparently at the heart of the story in *Artist*. And, through the ways in which the narrator-protagonist's perceptions and interpretations of his experience are linked to the text's construction of something that is seemingly withheld from the reader, narrative unreliability in *Artist* contributes to the novel's subtle presentational realism for the first time similarly as in Ishiguro's subsequent texts.

Artist is narrated by Masuji Ono, a retired painter whose mind tracks back through an unsettling mist of memories related to his career as an artist, which emerges as in complex ways entangled with Japan's imperialist propaganda leading up to its involvement in the Second World War.[8] As in *Pale View* and Ishiguro's subsequent novels, particularly *The Remains of the Day*, Ono's wistful, remorseful and at times self-defensive narrative – typically read as a subdued confession of shame and guilt – draws attention to its own peculiar formality and indirectness, raising questions as to its purpose and reliability. The narrative present is set in 1949 and 1950, in an unnamed Japanese city whose fictional geography suggests Tokyo. Just as *Pale View* and *Remains* open or are concerned with a visit, so does/is *Artist*. After reflecting proudly on the honourable way in which he was once elected buyer of his stately, yet presently war-damaged, house, Ono recalls the recent visit of his married daughter, Setsuko, who had come with her grandson Ichiro to discuss marriage plans for her sister Noriko. Ono is evidently a man of substance who can look back on a successful career as an artist. Despite the bomb damage, his house is still comfortable and distinguished. His wife and only son were killed during the war, but he has two caring daughters and a grandson he loves. Yet the reader soon realises that all is not as well as it seems. Ono's paintings, of which he appears to be rather proud, so he tells his grandson, are '"tidied away for the moment"'; his former pupils are either embarrassed by or do not wish to see him; and, most conspicuously, his daughters worry about the forthcoming marriage negotiations for Noriko. One set of negotiations has already mysteriously collapsed, and Setsuko now repeatedly urges her father to take '"certain precautionary steps"' against the investigations to be pursued, as a matter of course, by his prospective son-in-law's family. In order to prevent '"unnecessary misunderstandings"', furthermore, she advises him, both implicitly and explicitly, '"to speak to certain acquaintances from his past"' (*AFW*: 18, 32, 49, 50, 51, 52, 79, 85, 102–104, 113).[9]

Thus *Artist* activates what Roland Barthes has referred to as the 'hermeneutic code',[10] or suggests the presence of an enigma, which, for the narrative context, could be defined as 'a signifier whose signified is disturbingly suppressed by the narration' (Cohan and Shires, 1988: 123).[11] The reader soon cannot help but wonder what is being withheld, not least because, whatever the novel's mystery may be, it seems as if it cannot be openly stated before Ono himself. Instead, his daughters allude to 'the past' with a peculiar formality, leave sentences unfinished ('"I didn't mean to imply ..."' (*AFW*: 18)), exchange glances (*AFW*: 8, 83, 157) and break off their discussions as soon as Ono enters the room (*AFW*: 51). Not only his daughters but also his former colleagues and friends seem to make allusions to Ono's past: the director of a company involved in 'certain undertakings' during the war is reported to have gassed himself after a futile attempt – betrayed by 'minor scratches around his stomach' – to perform *seppuku*, or ritual suicide (*AFW*: 55); and a famous composer of patriotic songs, Ono is told, has committed suicide (*AFW*: 154). The reports of these suicides as a form of public apology following Japan's Second World War defeat vaguely suggest that a similar apology may be expected of Ono, too. Ono himself appears in fact to have alluded to parallels between the dead composer Naguchi's and his own past, although, according to Ono, it was only '"a sort of joke"' (*AFW*: 154–155).

On one level the text thus emphasises the presence of an enigma and hence appears to invite a binary process of decoding, of moving from signifier to the supposedly 'hidden' signified. From this perspective Ono's own and other characters' allusions to his past could be read as disclosing just that signified. Thus it slowly emerges that the ageing painter began his career as a pupil in a school of bohemian artists, happy to paint only the delights of the 'floating world', of the night life in the pleasure districts; that he then apparently betrayed his master, moving with the times from 'escapist' romantic art to social realism and, in the 1930s, to imperialist propaganda for the regime that eventually led Japan into the calamitous war against America; and that, when his most talented pupil, Kuroda, began to develop a style no longer commensurate with the principles of Ono's own propagandist endeavours, as 'official adviser to the Committee of Unpatriotic Activities', he – albeit not realising what consequences for his mentee this would entail – reported Kuroda to the police (*AFW*: 182).

Despite this apparent disclosure, however, the text's supposed mystery is far from solved. For one thing, besides the formulation of a riddle and its gradual revelation, a third dimension can be discerned in Ono's discourse: the hint that the story he is telling may be largely, or to some degree, imagined. At the *miai*, the formal meeting between his daughter and future son-in-law and their respective families, where, as usual, Ono has the impression that the whole table is gazing at him in 'hostility and accusation', he admits for the first time that '[i]t is quite possible, of course, that I imagined this' (*AFW*: 119). When he finally rouses himself to admit openly that he made political mistakes in the past, everyone looks up 'with a puzzled expression' (*AFW*: 122, 123) and stares at him 'in astonishment' (*AFW*: 124). Later on, Setsuko tells Ono about a letter she has received from her younger sister, Noriko, repeating how '"surprised"' and '"extremely puzzled"' everyone was at her father's behaviour. Even Suichi, Setsuko's husband, who has earlier been reported to display 'signs of bitterness' towards Ono's generation, now appears to have expressed 'his bewilderment' at the contents of Noriko's letter (*AFW*: 50, 191). Towards the end of the novel, further, Setsuko remarks that '"it is some mystery to me why Father's career should have been of any particular relevance to the [marriage] negotiations"', expresses her concern about her father's comparing his own past to that of the composer who committed suicide, and even denies ever having advised her father to take any '"precautionary steps"' in view of Noriko's upcoming marriage negotiations (*AFW*: 191, 193).

Thus the disoriented reader, whose awareness has already been sharpened by the text's apparently withholding something, is likely to attribute new or double meanings to statements like 'it was one of those instances last month when I got a distinct impression they [Ono's daughters] had at some point been discussing certain things about me' (*AFW*: 83). Comments like these are not frequent in the first half of the novel, and readers may not immediately, and perhaps only on second reading of the novel, see them as suggesting not only Ono's past artistic and political involvement as described above but also the possibility that the web of shame and guilt he is seemingly constructing may be largely, or to a certain degree, imagined. Then again, since none of the discourses that appear to compete for supremacy here is entirely cancelled by another, it is in their multifaceted relationships to each other that they gesture towards core aspects of Ono's feelings and experience. Moreover, in so doing, they subtly perform and point to the limitations of the kind of reading *Artist* on one level invites.

The novel's ending contributes further to the text's tempered compositional presentationalism. It concludes anticlimactically the text's enigma-plot by questioning (even though not proving entirely unfounded), and thus directing our attention to, readers' assumptions and expectations as to a dramatic guilt-plot involving suicide. Thus Setsuko tells Ono that '"Father was simply a painter"', that he '"must stop believing he has done some great wrong"' and that '"no one has ever considered Father's past something to view with recrimination"'. And Ono, for his part, states explicitly that while he is '"not too proud to see that [he] too was a man of some influence, who used that influence towards a disastrous end"', he '"wouldn't for a moment consider the sort of action Naguchi took"' (*AFW*: 192, 193). Moreover, the novel ends on a cautiously optimistic and modest note with Ono wishing the younger generation well and his acknowledgement that he and his last mentor, Matsuda, were simply '[o]rdinary men with no special gifts of insight', so of his limited perspective (*AFW*: 200).

While *Artist* thus on one level invites decoding and moving from signifier to signified, it acquires meaning principally by way of continuous presentational decentring techniques thwarting signification and creating distance between signifier and supposed signified. The novel's subtle compositional presentationalism in this way gives expression to affective and ethical aporias and ever-changing realities beyond simply suppression, shame or guilt and opens up the text to a far richer reading experience than its slippery signs on one level suggest.

Another aspect that functions presentationally in Ishiguro's first two novels and is an important element in their presentational realism is the manner in which both novels gesture vaguely towards connections between their compositionally constructed and invoked mysteries and meanings related to Japanese culture. In effect the texts' silences, hesitations, circuitousness and restraint work together with readers' preconceptions and expectations associated with Japan and the Japanese to create these meanings. Western readers may therefore wonder, for example, whether, or to what extent, the fact that aspects of Ono's past cannot be openly expressed or stated before him may be a reflection of a cultural code of politeness and deference to elders. This sense is reinforced by the fact that many of these textual gaps occur during conversations given in direct, supposedly Japanese, speech so that the text's silences and ambivalences coincide with readers' notions of polite Japanese speech behaviour. This is also in the sense that these pauses frequently consist in descriptions of non-linguistic signs, or gestures, such as respectful bows, nods and smiles taking the place of speech. Narrative disorientation and estrangement are seemingly tied to otherness, further, through repeated references and allusions to suicide, which clearly does have its place within Japanese literature and culture and is a serious problem in contemporary Japan, but is also a prominent stereotype often associated with essentialist notions of 'Japaneseness'. The text's mystery, suggested compositionally, thematically and generically, is in this way tied inextricably to, and complicated by, readers' assumptions and expectations related to a presumed Japanese otherness.

At the same time, the enigma plot's 'unnarrating' itself by means of the presentational techniques described here, including the anticlimactic ending, functions to reveal the limits of, and as inadequate, the meanings apparently tied to Japanese culture that the text simultaneously invokes. Genre, too, becomes a signifier detached from its apparent signified, in the ways in which it resists fulfilling its generic promise. Ishiguro's inherently mediated and stylised use of genre – for which, in his first two novels set in Japan, the *shomingeki*, or family drama, associated notably with Yasujiro Ozu's mature films, provided the author with a generic model to subvert reductive notions of Japanese culture centring on samurais and suicide – ultimately defies readers' generic expectations.[12] (Particularly in *Remains* and *Orphans* a supposedly central enigma is in similarly presentational ways linked to 'Englishness'.)

In these subtly experimental ways, then, the novel compositionally and presentationally resists, and embroils us in its sense-making procedures tied to its affective and ethical aporias in ways that go beyond, the decoding and signification processes that it – on another level – invites. It thus gestures towards core aspects of Ono's experience that defy direct expression while holding up a mirror to, indirectly commenting on and prompting critique of and reflection on, our interpretative practices and presumptions.

Presentational moments and motifs

In both *Pale View* and *Artist* descriptions of specific and repeated images and motifs that reverberate across the narratives' past and present, resulting in intriguing moments of failed signification, are crucial elements of Ishiguro's tempered presentational realism and techniques. In balancing realism with subtly presentational qualities these moments present both narrators and readers with affective and ethical territories far less tangible than the novel's signs on one level seem to imply, thus entangling us in a novel sense-making experience attuned to the text's ambivalent signs, silences and hesitations that goes well beyond what the novel's superficial invitation to decipher suggests. The interrupted and recast signification processes as well as liminal meaning-making central to these moments are, in *Artist*, tied to repetitions of a particular motif.[13]

More specifically, details linked to variations of the teacher–pupil motif gesture synecdochically and synaesthetically towards what emerge as key aspects of Ono's past as well as relationships between particular memories and scenes, whether represented in the text or not. The earliest version of this motif is given in Ono's recollection of his authoritatarian father who, in an attempt to convince his young son to pursue a more honourable and lucrative profession than that of an artist, apparently burns his first paintings (*AFW*: 43–47). True to Ishiguro's presentational principles of indirectness, allusion and metonymic effect for cause, Ono did not see his father burn the paintings but recalls only the 'smell of burning in the air' and 'around the house' following the conversation with his father (*AFW*: 44, 47). Seemingly further supporting, but never conclusively substantiating, Ono's suspicion is his impression at the time – which he admits could have been 'simply [his] imagination' – that an 'earthenware ashpot' and a candle had been moved closer together since he left the room where he spoke with his father a little while earlier (*AFW*: 44). This is also a synaesthetic experience for Ono because he recalls alternately the meeting room's candlelight as well as, three times during the scene and tied to the earthenware pot, 'the smell of burning' (*AFW*: 44–47). The synaesthetic connection between the candle and the ash pot suggests, but never confirms, Ono's suspicion mentioned above, as well as contributing to the scene's ominous atmosphere. 'The smell of burning' comes to eventually link, albeit only gesturally, and more specifically presentationally, all key scenes in the narrative and moments in Ono's past related to this motif, thus foregrounding its significance.

Before focusing on the intriguing ways in which the novel hints at inexpressible meanings through the presentational links between these key moments in the narrative and Ono's experience, it is interesting to note the manner in which the text subtly points to the importance of these scenes also through Ono's conscious-unconscious deferral of them. While his visiting certain 'acquaintances from the past' in view of the upcoming marriage negotiations for his younger daughter, Noriko, is mentioned and apparently suggested by his older daughter, Setsuko, early in the novel, he does not act upon it until the end of the book's first part, when he visits Matsuda, his mentor during the last stage of his career. It emerges that this iteration of the teacher–pupil motif is the least problematic for Ono and contributes to the effect of a continuous suspension of sense-making in the novel and a gradual, hesitant peeling back of layer after layer of emotions before he finally, and primarily by metonymy, gets to the more painful memories of his other mentor–mentee relationships.

These relationships include Ono's first important mentor, Mori, and himself, which mirrors Ono's later association with his most talented student, Kuroda. Ono is Mori's 'most accomplished pupil' (*AFW*: 177, 180), just as Kuroda later becomes 'the most gifted of [Ono's] pupils' (*AFW*: 175). And just as first one of Ono's fellow-artists, Sasaki, is called a 'traitor' when he develops a style at odds with Mori's, so is eventually Ono himself, for moving from Mori's artistic ideals of the floating world towards those of imperialist propaganda and a new mentor, Matsuda, referred to as a 'traitor' by his colleagues (*AFW*: 143, 165). This in turn foreshadows and hints at how Ono will treat his own protégé, Kuroda, once the latter starts to paint in ways no longer commensurate with Ono's nationalist style. Indeed, since, as Ono recalls, his last conversation with Mori took place in 'that same pavilion' as the final one, many years later with Kuroda, and Ono admits that a certain phrase used by Mori, '"exploring curious avenues"', could have been his own words to Kuroda, it is possible to read the scene involving his mentor as mirroring, or in part mirroring, the later meeting between himself and his student omitted from the narrative (*AFW*: 175, 177).

The 'smell of burning' is attached not only to Ono's memory of his meeting with his father but also to his last conversation with Mori. Mori has at this point confiscated those of Ono's paintings with which, as the mentor puts it euphemistically, Ono seems to be '"exploring curious avenues"' (*AFW*: 177). As did Ono's father before him, Mori understands that his mentee has stored the paintings he is most fond of in a separate place and orders Ono to hand over these pieces to him as well. When, unlike in the earlier scene with his father, Ono refuses, Mori gives him a sharp reply essentially expressing the end of his mentorship. If, as suggested above, this scene reflects, or reflects in part, the later one between Ono and Kuroda, then Ono's subsequent remarks on the 'arrogance' and 'possessiveness' of his former teacher may be read as applying equally to himself (*AFW*: 181). His point that 'such arrogance and possessiveness on the part of a teacher [...] is to be regretted', too, can be read as gesturing towards his own regret (*AFW*: 181). At the same time, however, it is important to highlight the text's liminal quality in this respect, the ways in which these meanings are merely suggested to us. Upon closer reading, furthermore, the above-mentioned burning smell can be read as applying not just to the final meeting with Mori but also to two other scenes, one of which is only alluded to and omitted from the narrative, involving Kuroda.

The phrase 'the smell of burning' is part of a short passage of which only the last sentence marks it as a transition to another scene and of which several phrases turn out to be referentially ambiguous, so that these phrases come to perform, and in this way foreground, their inherent referential uncertainty as well as the text's transitional and liminal process of creating meaning:

> For all that, it is clear that such *arrogance and possessiveness* on the part of a teacher – however renowned he may be – *is to be regretted*. From time to time, I still turn over in my mind *that cold winter's morning* and *the smell of burning* growing ever stronger in my nostrils. It was the winter before the outbreak of war and I was standing anxiously at the door of Kuroda's house – a shabby little affair he used to rent in the Nakamachi area. (*AFW*: 181; emphases added)

Following as it does Ono's comment on Mori's 'arrogance' and 'possessiveness', 'the smell of burning', too, appears at first to relate to the immediately preceding exchange between Mori and Ono, which in turn mirrors and prefigures a very similar one between Ono and Kuroda – until the next sentence marks the passage as a transition, making it clear that we have moved ahead in time to yet another episode involving Kuroda, a visit to his house, where Ono is astonished to find that his report of Kuroda's autonomous style has resulted in his former mentee being considered an unpatriotic artist, his paintings being burned and his house searched by police agents. Thus the burning smell can be read as connected to either or both the conversation with Mori or/and the visit to Kuroda's house, the former of which prefigures a very similar exchange between Ono and Kuroda and the latter of which also evokes indirectly Ono's report of Kuroda to the police – another of the novel's many meaningful narrative gaps. Reinforcing this pregnant ambiguity is the phrase 'that cold winter's morning', whose deictic seems to be associating it with the previously mentioned 'that same pavilion' (*AFW*: 175, 177), but which too can be linked to either or both the Mori meeting or/and the Kuroda house visit episodes evoked in the quotation above. In this way 'the smell of burning', while it appears initially related to the one, or essentially two, immediately preceding scene(s), comes to link, albeit only gesturally, and more specifically presentationally, all moments in the novel directly involving Ono in which someone, principally Ono, is either treated or seemingly behaves like a 'traitor' (three of them evoked in the preceding quotation, one of which implies metonymically Ono's report of Kuroda, and one being the earlier meeting between Ono and his father).

Later in his narrative Ono associates 'the smell of burning' also with 'bombings and fire' and so indirectly with the death of his wife and son Kenji during the war (*AFW*: 200). The novel thus alludes to Ono's possible 'treacherous' behaviour as well as to his own feelings of betrayal and remorse on the personal and artistic as well as political levels. Yet once again nothing is either directly shown or told. Where Mori's actions and words end and Ono's begin is ultimately impossible for both Ono's older, narrating self and the reader to tell. Instead, meaning is suggested synecdochically and liminally through the multi-faceted ways the invoked scenes echo and relate to each other as well as gesture towards Ono's predicament, interrupting and continually recasting signification, thus making visible for both Ono and the reader – if only for a fleeting instant – and directing our attention to the ethical and affective complexities of Ono's experience and the intricacies involved in its reading.

A remarkable descriptive diegetic pause and yet another iteration of the teacher–pupil motif in the novel emblematises the delicately presentational procedures of the passage above and of a number of others throughout Ishiguro's oeuvre: Ono remembers seeing from a distance, on a rainy morning shortly after Japan's surrender, a 'figure' he believes was watching him. He recognised the person as Kuroda, his former protégé, whose artistic style Ono had eventually considered unpatriotic and, even though evidently not realising what consequences for his mentee this would entail, had reported to the police. The 'figure' 'moved his head very slightly', and Ono is in the narrative present, and was at the time, 'not sure if it was the beginning of a bow, or if he was just adjusting his head to get out of the splash of rainwater from his broken umbrella' (*AFW*: 77, 78). Kuroda's gesture illustrates wonderfully the ambiguities and complexities of Ono's past actions and his present feelings about them. If, given that his former pupil recognised him as well, which the text does not unambiguously state, Kuroda's movement encompassed a hint, or even just the possibility, of a bow, and hence an expression of politeness and respect on the part of his former protégé towards him – which, based on the text's presentation of both Ono's values and his cultural context, is clearly of great importance to him – then his past behaviour may not have been so problematic after all. As is typical of Ishiguro's fleeting, presentational signs, to what extent the bow is indeed a possible interpretation of Kuroda's gesture, and to what degree it is Ono's wishful thinking, or perhaps the result of his distant observation in another of the author's misty landscapes, is in the end impossible for Ono and both the implied and real reader to discern.

Instead we witness and are involved in a moment of hesitation, liminality and provisional meanings, encompassing both what could have been and might still be, possibility and potential, its various thresholds literally made visible and held in balance here through the non-verbal gesture of the bow. Kuroda's bow is in fact a presentational moment par excellence: it presents, holds within itself, suggests and performs the momentary reality of Ono's situation that defies direct expression, thus subtly gesturing towards unspeakable core aspects of his experience as well as its own expressive procedures. Another moment in the text where meaning does not follow as expected, it requires both Ono and us to pause and, in bringing into sudden (literal) perspective intricately entangled details of his reality, constitutes and enacts an instant of increased awareness and reflection for both Ono's younger and older narrating selves as well as the reader.

Overall, the type of meaning-making at the heart of the tempered presentational realism focused on here produces meanings gesturally and palimpsestically through the ways in which they relate to each other and the story, both compositionally and in individual moments, by means of balancing realism with a subtle focus on form – in this case the incongruities of the first-person narration and reverberating repetitions of the teacher–protégé motif. It sets itself apart from postmodern relativity through the novel's interruption and redirection of signification as well as its simultaneous insistence on, and resistance to, the deciphering of signs, going hand in hand with a delicately deictic and gestural self-consciousness that immerses readers in the text's presentational procedures on the levels of both content and form. It also distinguishes itself from both a modernist emphasis on form over content and postmodernist experimentalism through its essentially realist mode, including subtly experimental elements that are fully integrated into, and do not detract from, the story. In its tempered presentational realism and practices the novel ultimately demands attention and reflection – directed towards the narrative's affective and ethical conundrums, their reading and beyond – thus embroiling us in the intricacies of Ono's experience and narration, while simultaneously commenting implicitly on the implications for interpretation itself.

Liminal meaning-making and presentational strategies beyond *An Artist of the Floating World*

While the compositional presentational realism and underlying individual moments described here are more visualised and therefore, literally, more visible in the early novels *Pale View* and *Artist* than in Ishiguro's subsequent ones, they are foundational to his prose. I offer in what follows a few examples of moments of interrupted, provisional and liminal meaning-making beyond signification, central to the author's presentational realism and tied to the texts' ethical and affective concerns, in Ishiguro's subsequent work. Consider in particular the ways in which diegetic friction between a surface–depth aesthetics and ethics, with characters and readers on a quest to distinguish between and move from the presumed superficial and/ to the expected essence, on the one hand and a conception of signs that thwarts such signifying processes, where signs are not expressive *of* anything but expressive *in themselves*, on the other, significant to the ethical and affective quandaries both narrator-protagonists and readers are asked to navigate, manifests itself in *Remains* and *Never*. A notable example in *Remains* is Miss Kenton's accusing Stevens of 'pretending' upon learning that, despite not having shared this with her at the time, he was just as dismayed as she was at their employer Lord Darlington's request that they dismiss two Jewish maids (*RD*: 154).[14] Her reproach reflects the reasoning that remaining silent while disagreeing with the dismissals is necessarily a sign of something else – of cowardice, insincerity or indifference. This, or in terms of a sign of Stevens's inability to distinguish between his private and professional selves or of his position as an unwitting cog in a corporate system, is also how readers of the novel have often interpreted this episode. To Stevens, however, his silence means just that. And as he explains: '"Naturally, one disapproved of the dismissals. One would have thought that quite self-evident"' (*RD*: 154). The butler's silence suggests a certain degree of awareness of the inadequacy of anything he could have said to her at the time and, on the level of narrative, of the same kinds of liminal sense-making strategies beyond signification that are at the heart of Ishiguro's presentational realism and style. Moreover, resisting the urge to read this and the novel's many silences as necessarily pointing to something more specific rather than something that defies expression is in this case, I suggest, to acknowledge Stevens's subjectivity and to attribute more awareness to him than he has typically been granted. Ishiguro's subtly presentational strategies and style train readers to do just that. And as with all the main and generally fleeting moments of interrupted signification described here, in this case, too, the episode reflects a sudden glimmer of insight as to his past experience as well as, more broadly, the limitations of meaning-making, language and his situation in the world on the part of the narrator-protagonist. He recognises it as one of the 'turning points' that thwarted the possibility of a closer relationship between him and Miss Kenton and led to her eventually getting married and leaving Darlington Hall (*RD*: 164, 175, 176).

We find echoes of this scene in *Never*, in an episode that the first-person narrator Kathy recalls as a transitory but significant moment – a 'turning point' for her as well – causing her and her childhood friend and later love interest Tommy to drift apart before finally reuniting belatedly in their truncated lives as clones. Witnessing their friend Ruth tell Tommy a lie, that Kathy finds animal drawings that are dear to him silly, Kathy hesitates while – as her older self has come to realise after revisiting the moment 'over and over' – quietly rehearsing different possible ways to respond, ultimately dismissing each of them as inadequate and futile and remaining silent (*NLMG*: 195).[15] Bruce Robbins has referred to such scenes in terms of moments of 'intimate cruelty', when 'a character behaves with sudden, inexplicable, astonishing cruelty – not to a stranger, but to an intimate' (2007: 289).[16] Though in different ways, my reading, like Robbins's, complicates the apparent 'cruelty' of these moments. Given that Kathy is a more introspective narrator than Stevens, it is apt that she is better able to articulate and illustrate the emotional complexities associated with her silence than Stevens. Here, too, the text performs Kathy's silence in terms of a thwarted signification process, a meaning expected but withheld, in this case by detailing Kathy's deliberations and possible responses and reactions prior to her dismissal of them. As in Stevens's case, the episode reflects, here more explicitly, the narrator-protagonist's cognisance of the constraints of language and communication and, more broadly, a similar sensitivity to the limits and limitations of signification that is at the core of Ishiguro's presentational strategies and prose. And here, too, reading Kathy's silence in this way is to attribute to her more awareness of her situation, including its constraints, than she is typically ascribed. Moreover, as seen above, in its significatory and affective omission, causing momentary perplexity, the text performs its silence and moment of heightened awareness, thus redirecting readers' assumptions as well as prompting reflection on the characters' affective and ethical conundrums, their reading and interpretation, and beyond.

Tempered presentational realism and practice 77

Contrasting with these episodes of interrupted and recast signification involving puzzling emotional blanks and misunderstanding are scenes depicting moments of unexpected respite or even elation set against the characters' bleak predicaments. Noteworthy in this respect is a scene in *Never* in which Kathy and Tommy unexpectedly have the chance to spend an hour alone together during a trip to Norfolk. The scene is particularly interesting in this context in part because of its self-consciousness, both compositionally and on the level of character, in respect to the aspects focused on in this chapter. It is part of a key episode in the novel that involves the three friends Kathy, Tommy and Ruth and two new acquaintances spending a day in Norfolk, where they have traced a woman who could be Ruth's 'possible', the human she may have been cloned after. Finding her is linked to their vague hope of alternative futures – what they call 'dream futures' including, for example, a job at an office like that of the potential 'possible' – to their pre-scripted and truncated lives as 'carers' of fellow clones donating their organs and eventually as 'donors' themselves (*NLMMG*: 142). In the clones' quest for the ultimate original or essence underlying their existence, the novel's apparent insistence on a hidden or core meaning, which, as the characters come to realise that the woman cannot be Ruth's 'possible', ultimately eludes them, the text in this case dramatises a thwarted signification process par excellence. Moreover, in enacting this significatory resistance, denying the clones and us the presumed signified, the novel values the clones *in themselves*, not simply as lesser humans, thus asserting their subjectivity and at the same time gesturing towards the role and agency of its presentational strategies in doing so.

I would like to draw our attention more particularly to a scene following the friends' disappointment pertaining to Ruth's 'possible', the trip's low point, when Kathy and Tommy unexpectedly find themselves alone and decide to look for a cassette tape that was one of Kathy's most treasured possessions at their boarding school Hailsham. Since going missing one day, the tape functions as a nostalgic object for Kathy, and both Ruth and, as she learns in this scene, Tommy have tried to find it for her, Tommy even imagining what doing so 'would be like' (*NLMG*: 173). The text's foregrounding of different versions and the copied nature of the tape is reflected, for example, in Ruth's gift to Kathy of another, in fact very different, tape to make up for the lost one as well as Kathy's comment in the second-hand store she and Tommy enter to look for it that '"there might be thousands of these knocking about"' (*NLMG*: 172). Rebecca Walkowitz has helpfully likened the different replica of the tape to other copied objects and the clones in the novel, arguing that they all accrue meaning through 'networks of production and consumption' based on their 'potential for comparison and likeness' (2015: 112). And indeed, on one level the novel does seem to privilege an aesthetics and ethics of cloned humans and objects. Thus, for example, while Ruth's gift of a tape to replace the original one 'has nothing to do with anything' and its music does not appeal to Kathy, it is, in the narrative present, one of Kathy's most treasured belongings, as is the cassette – of which she doesn't know whether it is a copy or possibly the original – she and Tommy find during their trip to Norfolk (*NLMG*: 76).

At the same time this particular scene also complicates such an aesthetics and ethics of copies and clones in that, here, it is the *tension* between the potentially original tape that disappeared many years ago and one or more possible replicas at the stores in Norfolk that serves as catalyst for the unexpected moments of shared anticipatory feeling and, later in the scene, what Kathy can only refer to as 'something more complicated' between her and Tommy, as well as of heightened affective awareness for Kathy's narrating self and the reader. From the beginning of the scene when they discuss looking for the cassette tape together and Kathy 'fe[els] [her] rotten mood evaporating', it is the possibility of finding the same, original tape that was Kathy's at Hailsham – made more probable because they half-seriously, half-playfully tie it to the myth popular at the boarding school that Norfolk is the 'lost corner of England', where all the country's lost property ends up – that contributes to their sudden childlike joy at the beginning of their search (*NLMG*: 169, 172). Immediately after finding the cassette, too, Tommy wonders whether it '"could be the same one [...] the *actual* one"' that Kathy lost (*NLMG*: 172; emphasis in original), to which she, having examined the tape, replies, '"For all I know, it might be"', but also that, at the same time, '"there might be thousands of these knocking about"' (*NLMG*: 172).

Ultimately, though, while in this case the cassette tape is found, it is nevertheless part of an interrupted signification process in which the signified remains elusive or without meaning. In fact, the scene functions like a *mise en abyme* – a performance of a thwarted signification process within a larger enactment of the same – in relation to the entire episode of the Norfolk trip (chapters thirteen to fifteen). The tape takes on the role of a catalyst and of subtly pointing to and redirecting both the narrator's and our attention to something more meaningful, namely, the unexpected moments of mostly unspoken connection between Kathy and Tommy.

Following their decision to look for the tape '[e]verything suddenly fe[els] perfect' for Kathy, and she experiences a rare instance of unfettered joy: 'I had to really hold myself back from giggling stupidly, or jumping up and down on the pavement like a little kid' (*NLMG*: 171). The moment is particularly meaningful for Kathy in the narrative present as she has since learnt that Tommy 'felt exactly the same' at the time (*NLMG*: 171). We note, too, that their shared feeling is anticipatory, articulated in relation to the *prospect* of finding the tape. As Kathy puts it: '*That moment when we decided to go searching for my lost tape*, it was like suddenly every cloud had blown away, and we had nothing but fun and laughter *before us*' (*NLMG*: 171; emphases added). The text foregrounds the role of another moment of delayed and interrupted meaning-making through Kathy's own awareness of it, reflected in her expression of her *desire*, once she suddenly finds the tape, to prolong this state: 'The tape had been the perfect excuse for all this fun, and now it had turned up, we'd have to stop' (*NLMG*: 172). She momentarily even considers not telling Tommy that she found it, and, when she does call him over, the lighthearted mood gives way to both a sudden 'huge pleasure' and what she can only refer to as 'something else, something more complicated' (*NLMG*: 172), signalling Kathy's conscious-unconscious realisation that her complex and conflicting range of emotions, involving joy but likely also an awareness of the belatedness, constraints and uncertainties of their newfound connection, defies words. Thus we witness, and are entangled in, another episode of interrupted, transitional and liminal meaning-making on the levels of form, composition, character and reading in which the (first potential, then found) cassette tape functions as a catalyst for the characters' transitory feelings of unbridled joy while also gesturing towards the constraints of these shared moments and their lives. And it is in and through the narrative's and the narrator's subtly self-conscious and self-reflexive awareness and performance of these instants *in* their limits and limitations, temporal and otherwise – hence these moments' inherently conflicting nature – that the latter demand attention and increased affective awareness on the part of not only the narrator-protagonist but also the reader.

Ishiguro has said about *Never* that '[a]lthough it's a story about mortality, I wanted it to be a quite positive story. By having this rather negative, bleak scenario, I thought it might highlight what is actually quite positive and valuable about being alive' (Wong and Crummett, 2008: 220).[17] More specifically, he has asked, 'What are the things you hold on to ...? What do you regret? What are the consolations?' (Freeman, 2008: 197).[18] His fiction's presentational realism and strategies, including interrupted, gestural and liminal meaning-making, register the inherently conflicting aspects, for both narrators and readers, of such transient moments that they and we 'hold on to', 'regret' or that console. Moreover, in these strategies' enactment of the transitory but profound instants in the characters' lives and novel described above – resulting in a productively complex, often dissonant, relationship between the expectations raised by both narrative form and content on the one hand and the fictional reality of the situation in these instances on the other – they assert the clones' subjectivity and draw attention to their own role and agency in articulating the text's ethical perspectives.

Ultimately, in their tempered presentational realism and practices, Ishiguro's fictional worlds embroil us in the characters' affective and ethical quandaries and their reading, while at the same time examining and commenting implicitly on our readerly and interpretative assumptions as well as the implications of the narratives' own procedures for interpretation as such. In so doing, the novels' silences and ambiguities, interrupted signification and liminal meaning-making perform textual and critical perspectives that involve a continuous unfolding and recasting of meaning that remains incomplete; entail a certain modesty in their acknowledgement of their own limits and limitations; entangle us in the latter by demonstrating on the levels of character, reading and interpretation the hazards of the type of meaning-making they on one level invoke; and that, based as they are on ongoing sense-making processes that are not object-centred, are open to novel and unexpected ways of making meaning. In this, Ishiguro's fiction models, and asks us to adopt, a readerly and critical disposition, too, one to which the kind of (affectively attuned) textual awareness, attention and reflection highlighted in the preceding discussion that the author's texts, in their tempered presentational realism and procedures, help us hone and demand are vital.

Notes

1 *The Buried Giant* is the only Ishiguro novel to date that is not a first-person narrative.
2 See in particular Gadamer (2004).
3 See also R. Karni (2010), particularly chapter 1 and p. 42 as well as Karni (2011), especially p. 21, where I argued that in combining representational and presentational elements Ishiguro's fiction conveys meaning primarily through gesture and allusion rather than signification.
4 In Japanese film studies primarily Western scholars have sometimes directly or indirectly linked the notion of the 'presentational' to essentialist conceptions of 'Japaneseness' and/or, in accounts of Japanese film history, viewed elements of a 'Japanese presentational aesthetics' as complementing Western film form, thus implicitly positing the latter as dominant. Due to the term's possible Orientalist connotations in the Japanese context it is important to note that I use it to refer to a set of narrative and significatory techniques associated with the notion of the 'presentational' in various contexts, including Japanese film studies, and, ultimately, to designate Ishiguro's unique version and blend of these strategies.
5 As Ishiguro has stated: 'Cinema is the one area of Japanese "culture" which I believe has had a direct effect on my writing' (Jongh (1982: 11). He comments, 'The visual images of Japan have a great poignancy for me, particularly in domestic films like those of Ozu and Naruse, set in the post-war era, the Japan I actually remember' (Mason (1989a: 336).
6 See Mason (1989).
7 In a forthcoming essay I consider another aspect of this realism, its 'translational' quality and the ways in which it contributes to an inherently translated dimension of Ishiguro's prose and fictional worlds (R. Karni, 'Ishiguro and Translation', in A. Bennett (ed.), *The Cambridge Companion to Kazuo Ishiguro* (Cambridge: Cambridge University Press, forthcoming)).
8 The following discussion of *Artist* from a presentational perspective partly revisits earlier close readings of the novel. See R. Karni (2010 and 2011).

9 Ishiguro, 1986.
10 See R. Barthes, *S/Z*, trans. Richard Miller (Oxford: Blackwell, 2002).
11 S. Cohan and L. M. Shires, 1988.
12 Elsewhere I have discussed in more detail the various ways in which genre and other narrative strategies in Ishiguro's fiction work to subtly expose and comment on the texts' own cultural constructions precisely *as* such (Karni, 2015).
13 For another example of a motif's designed failure to function according to novelistic conventions in Ishiguro's fiction see Andrew Bennett's perceptive reading of *When We Were Orphans* in Chapter 6 below.
14 Ishiguro, 1989.
15 Ishiguro, 2005.
16 Robbins, 2007.
17 Wong and Crummett, 2008.
18 Freeman, 2008.

References

Cohan, Steven and Linda M. Shires (1988). *Telling Stories: A Theoretical Analysis of Narrative Fiction* (London: Routledge).
Freeman, John (2008). 'Never Let Me Go: A Profile of Kazuo Ishiguro', in Brian W. Shaffer and Cynthia F. Wong (eds), *Conversations with Kazuo Ishiguro* (Jackson: University Press of Mississippi), 194–198.
Gadamer, Hans-Georg (2004). *Truth and Method*, translated by Donald G. Marshall (London: Continuum, 2nd edn).
Ishiguro, Kazuo (1986). *An Artist of the Floating World* (London: Faber and Faber).
—. (1989). *The Remains of the Day* (London: Faber and Faber).
—. (2005). *Never Let Me Go* (London: Faber and Faber).
Jongh, Nicholas de (1982). 'Life after the Bomb', *The Guardian*, 22 February.
Karni, Rebecca (2010). 'Kazuo Ishiguro and the Ethics of Reading World Literature' (PhD dissertation, University of California, Los Angeles).
—. (2011). 'Reflective Signs', *Studies in the Humanities*, 38:1–2, 112–137.
—. (2015). 'Made in Translation: Language, "Japaneseness", "Englishness", and "Global Culture" in Ishiguro', *Comparative Literature*, 52:2, 318–348.
Mason, Gregory (1989a). 'An Interview with Kazuo Ishiguro', *Contemporary Literature*, 30:3, 335–347.
—. (1989b). 'Inspiring Images: The Influence of the Japanese Cinema on the Writings of Kazuo Ishiguro', *East-West Film Journal*, 3:2, 39–52.
Robbins, Bruce (2007). 'Cruelty Is Bad: Banality and Proximity in *Never Let Me Go*', *NOVEL: A Forum on Fiction*, 40:3, 289–303.

Walkowitz, Rebecca L. (2015) *Born-Translated: The Contemporary Novel in an Age of World Literature* (New York: Columbia University Press).
Wong, Cynthia F. and Grace Crummett (2008). 'A Conversation about Life and Art with Kazuo Ishiguro', in Brian W. Shaffer and Cynthia F. Wong (eds), *Conversations with Kazuo Ishiguro* (Jackson: University Press of Mississippi), 204–220.

4

'An inevitable course': political responsibility in *The Remains of the Day*

Sara Upstone

A 2021 BBC documentary on the career of Kazuo Ishiguro begins with the unlikely image of an iconic scene from Buster Keaton's *Steamboat Bill Jr* (1928). A house collapses on the comic actor, only for him to emerge unscathed in the doorway space of the house's wooden frame. Explaining his fascination with the scene from the 1928 film, Ishiguro describes it as representative of his view of his own generation. As the author's commentary continues, the filmmakers replace Keaton in a still image with a small Japanese boy – a child Ishiguro. 'I've had this extraordinary escape' (Yentob, 2021), says Ishiguro, before cutting to newsreel footage of the mushroom cloud over Nagasaki, the author's place of birth and early childhood home.

The image of Keaton, caught within a catastrophe he is seemingly unaware of, emerging physically unscathed and yet perhaps more affected than he is aware, is also a theme of Ishiguro's fictions, in which characters frequently find themselves in the midst of huge events – not outside those events, yet untouched within them. *The Remains of the Day* (1989) recounts the first-person narrative of Stevens, a butler at the country house Darlington Hall, now owned by a wealthy American. Stevens is embarking on a road trip to visit his former housekeeper, Miss Kenton. During the journey he recounts through a series of incidents and reflections his past relationship to Miss Kenton, and his involvement in the political events of the house in the run up to the Second World War, during which time his employer, Lord Darlington, is involved in attempts to forge a relationship between Nazi Germany and the British government. Reflecting from the position of 1956, the year of the Suez Crisis, Stevens's remembrances raise questions about the nature of individual relation to the political – about what emerges when the house has fallen around you, and what it means to be still standing in the wake of the destruction. Reading the novel in such terms concurs with Kelly M. Rich's (2016) definition of the novel as a text engaged with the 'juxtapolitical', concerned with how intimate and domestic scenes sit alongside large-scale events. In particular it asks the reader to consider what it means in such circumstances to be unaware of those on whom the house might in fact fall; to ask what it means to be responsible for these others and to consider 'an individual's responsibility or complicity in the "widespread systemic attacks" that constitute crimes against humanity' (Rich, 2016: 501).

In interview Ishiguro has repeatedly cautioned the reader against taking *The Remains of the Day* as a comment on the specific contexts of its setting, declaring his 'trouble' with readers who thought the book to be about Suez or British appeasement (Vorda and Herzinger, 2008: 84). Rather than a realist novel, Ishiguro describes the novel as containing 'metaphorical intentions' (Vorda and Herzinger, 2008: 84), 'talking through the myth created around the figure of the English butler' to 'say various things that concern me as a person living in the 1990s, or the 1980s, when I wrote that book' (Swaim, 1990: 100). While critics have acknowledged this rejection of realism in the novel and the relevance of this to considering the text instead as a work of postmodern fiction (see for example MacPhee, 2011: 178), these acknowledgements tend to focus on Ishiguro's reference to pastiche, metaphor and fabulism. Yet another word that emerges in Ishiguro's discussion of the novel is 'parable' (Vorda and Herzinger, 2008: 75). This implies a level of abstraction which draws the reader towards larger metanarrative concerns rather than historical specifics, a word more usually associated with the realm of fairy-tale in which non-specific locations open up a space for transferable meanings. As a 'parable', Ishiguro suggests that it is more relevant to apply the messages of the novel to other historical events than to those that it explicitly evokes – this, then, is a dictate to the reader to engage in what Chris Holmes and Kelly Mee Rich have described as the particular quality of Ishiguro's fiction for processes of *rereading*: 'Ishiguro's relation to the very nature of the contemporary [...] Whatever force his works carry, it insists on being felt anew, striking each reader in the moment of transmission' (2021: 5). This parable is interwoven into the novel's carefully constructed narrative voice and form. As David James (2010) has noted, Ishiguro's employment of modesty throughout the narrative serves to direct the reader's point of view and highlight moments of emotional intensity whilst also self-referentially drawing attention to formal construction, yet the novel's lack of reveal can also be seen as a central formal device for the construction of a narrative designed to elide specifics in the service of what J.R.R. Tolkien (1947) calls applicability. As Ishiguro himself points to the novel as a work of fabulism, so it is that motifs of fantasy world-building are relevant to its construction; Ishiguro's England is a marvellous invention that employs the modesty of revelation not only to emphasise Stevens's emotional self-denial but also to serve simultaneously the novel's function as an abstract space for applicable meaning in ways which draw it much closer to later works such as *Never Let Me Go* (2005) and *The Buried Giant* (2015) than might be initially apparent.

In the discussion that follows I consider Ishiguro's representation of responsibility as the feature of a 'parable' via a Derridean reading which aims to expose how *The Remains of the Day* resonates with contemporary political debate. For Derrida responsibility is a matter of decision, knowledge and consciousness, a process intimately entwined with a relation to the other that, in its demand for infinite hospitality, is in conflict with the discrimination demanded by politics. In the first part of the chapter I argue that such thinking on responsibility provides the opportunity to rethink readings of Stevens as irresponsible, in favour of a notion of *non-responsibility* that holds relevance for wider questions of individual relation to the political. In the second part of the chapter I consider the consequences of this reading for the novel's relevance to a specific contemporary political event in which questions of accountability are brought to the fore, namely the 2016 UK European referendum, and its outcome in which the UK voted to leave the European Union. In this sense I argue that the 'parable' of the novel can also be read as what Michael Naas defines as the 'logic of the example' in Jacques Derrida's writing (1992: xvi): not merely a representation of current political circumstance but also a provocation towards an alternative. As Naas points out, the example is discussed explicitly in Derrida's *Edmund Husserl's 'Origin of Geometry': An Introduction* as that which is simultaneously 'an undistinguished *sample* and a teleological model' (1978: 115). Yet it also emerges as a recurring trope in Derrida's thought, standing for a mode of operation in which a particular circumstance is not that which illustrates a politics but that which creates the grounds for its invention. So, in *The Gift of Death* (2008), as illustration, Derrida recounts the Biblical story of Abraham's sacrifice of his son Isaac, examining the philosophical import of the narrative not to tell what the event meant, but to identify within it the foundations for what meaning could be. This understanding is not developed in abstraction but is directed towards a particular interest; in this case Abraham's actions are an *example* for the contemporary European moment – offering not 'a politics of which we would then give examples, but with *examples* out of which we might *invent* a politics' (Naas, 1992: xxii). Yet Europe itself also serves as an *example* for wider concepts of democratic thought, both in *Edmund Husserl's 'Origin of Geometry': An Introduction* and also in *The Other Heading* (1992), the text with which Naas is concerned. At the core of Derrida's use of Europe as an *example*, equally, lies an interest in responsibility. In *The Gift of Death* these associations are established via Derrida's discussion of the tension between Christian politics and Platonic influence; only with a 'new responsibility', he writes, 'will Europe have a future, and will there be a future in general' (2008: 30). That *the example* is directed specifically towards Europe, towards responsibility and also towards the parable offers a powerful connective thread between Ishiguro's novel and its relevance to considering the EU referendum of 2016.

As an *example* of responsibility, Stevens's professional role and his 'domestic' engagement are one where the role of 'butler' serves as synecdoche for the British voting public and its emerging political consciousness, so that the 2016 referendum is not an aberration but rather represents the concluding point of an inevitable course that has its roots in twentieth-century attitudes. Such representation not only questions the dominant media discourse surrounding Brexit, it also serves as stimulus to consider the promise of different modes of political responsibility with the potential to reshape how we consider both the outcome of the vote and its origins. Situated in a career which has been concerned for the ethico-political purchase of fiction, the novel thus illuminates Ishiguro's employment of literature as a form with the capacity not only to speak to political circumstance but also to pose a radical intervention that brings philosophical discussion into dialogue with real-world events.

Beyond politics: *The Remains of the Day* as responsibility

In interview Ishiguro has repeatedly pointed towards an association between progressive politics and the concept of the responsible. Describing Stevens's career, Ishiguro exclaims that it is deeply shaped by a lack of self-awareness that amounts to an 'abnegation of moral and political responsibility' (Yentob, 2021), resonating through the metaphor with contemporary concerns: 'Here I am', he says when speaking of the motivations behind the novel, 'somebody who was supposed to be educated, somebody with a certain sense of *responsibility*, living in a democratic country [...] I have this *responsibility* as a member of a democracy' (Swaim, 1990: 101 – emphasis added).

In keeping with Ishiguro's tendency for a gradual unfolding of meaning, it is at the end of the novel that this theme is made explicit. Departing from the main focus on Stevens's remembrance of the 1930s, the final section brings readers to the time of the narrative, 1956, and Stevens's trip to visit Miss Kenton after her departure from Darlington Hall and subsequent marriage. During this journey Stevens finds himself making an unexpected penultimate stop in the town of Moscombe in Devon. Mistaken for being a member of the landed gentry, Stevens becomes embroiled in a discussion regarding political action. Reflecting on their wartime experiences, the most vocal of the men, Harry Smith, argues that it is specifically a 'responsibility' of the men to get their strong opinions heard, the burden of those in a small village, and 'getting smaller', to get their opinions recognised in 'high places' (*RD*: 189). Discussing the notion of dignity, Stevens finds that what for him is a term associated with decorum is for the men of the town a specific response to the outcome of the war, a notion defined by the fact that 'it's one of the privileges of being born English that no matter who you are, no matter if you're rich or poor, you're born free and you're born so that you can express your opinion freely, and vote in your member of parliament or vote him out' (*RD*: 186). Assuming Stevens to be a gentleman,

Harry goes on, 'For the likes of yourself, it's always been easy to exert your influence [...] It gets easy for us here to forget *our responsibility* as citizens. Whether people agree or disagree [...] at least I'll get them thinking' (*RD*: 189 – emphasis added). This encounter marks Stevens's literal and figurative movement into a new world. The novel's earlier diegesis, all of Stevens's remembrance, can be seen as a necessary precursor, a series of proleptic ironies, to the rich significance of this encounter. For prior to this moment, as Ishiguro himself intimates, Stevens's actions have been wholly without responsibility.

Such a statement may seem at odds with the life of a man who is bound by obligation; a man who follows the rules and takes his occupation with great seriousness. Yet the narrative emphasises how Stevens's commitment to these rules does not translate into either speaking or acting in the name of a political cause as do the men he meets in Devon. Ishiguro places Stevens's remembrances in July 1956, the first month of the Suez Crisis in which Britain saw the last vestiges of its imperial power fading away; such setting prompts in Edward Said's terms a contrapuntal reading in which Stevens's silence on the crisis is indicative of a continuity between his past apoliticism and the contemporary moment. The Stevens of the present shares the silence of the Stevens of the past.

This silence underlies the novel's moment of greatest conflict, in which Stevens is asked to dismiss two Jewish female housemaids after being told by Lord Darlington that he feels Jews should no longer be employed on the Estate. Although he admits his 'every instinct opposed the idea', this is overshadowed by the need for 'dignity' which means he must follow Darlington's orders (*RD*: 148), declaring to Miss Kenton that there is 'little more to be said [...] our professional duty is not to our own foibles and sentiments, but to the wishes of our employer' (*RD*: 149). Stevens's response in this moment identifies him as caught in Darlington's politics, which are at odds with the universal recognition of ethics. Both Rich and McPhee relate Stevens in these terms to the work of Hannah Arendt, and her representation of Adolf Eichmann. In these terms Stevens enacts a 'breathtaking yet banal refusal of responsibility' (MacPhee, 2011: 197), a viewpoint echoed by Lydia R. Cooper (2011), whose comparison of Stevens with Kathy H. in *Never Let Me Go* is used to emphasise Ishiguro's focus on how 'the smallest choices may become radical expressions of humanity' (*RD*: 107).

This conventional reading of Stevens's actions does much to emphasise failures of personal responsibility. Derrida's work, however, takes this discussion of responsibility beyond the question of culpability. Instead it asks the reader to consider to what extent Stevens is capable of such responsibility, to challenge the idea that his behaviour is a refusal of political engagement by asking instead whether it needs to be read as his inability to insert himself into political discourse in a juxtapositional relation. For Derrida, answering before the other is central to responsibility which – following from Levinas – is defined as an act of 'exposing of the soul to the gaze of another person' (2008: 26). There is thus a central tension in political responsibility that makes such a term an oxymoron – responsibility which is based on an ethics without limits, yet politics which necessarily must place limits in the name of nation or sovereign (Fagan, 2013: 61). As Darlington demands the latter, Stevens's commitment to the former must inevitably fail. Such failure does not posit Stevens as irresponsible, but rather as what Derrida calls non-responsible, inhabiting a space in which 'one does not yet hear the call to explain oneself [...] to respond to the other and answer for oneself before the other' (2008: 5).

Stevens's non-responsibility starkly distinguishes between responsibility and hospitality. He has shown himself to be a committed host. He is an exemplary butler, who provides nothing but the most open of welcomes to Lord Darlington's guests, including Herr Ribbentrop, the Nazi and German ambassador. Both in public and private, Stevens's hospitality is evidenced by his refusal of any criticism of visitors. When they make him the subject of their amusement, he accepts this without complaint. He is thus a master of a conditional hospitality, limited to those identified as guests. Yet his deference to Darlington is evidence of an exemplary commitment to a set of obligations and sense of duty defined by his status as butler. Stevens cannot translate his relation to others into an allegiance that would question his employer's orders. To do this would be to move beyond hospitality and into the realm of responsibility.

Stevens's dilemma illustrates how such responsibility always requires a decision. As Alex Thompson outlines in *Derrida and Democracy* 'Responsibility, Derrida argues, is only responsible if it is not the unfolding of a programme or the following of a set pattern: that would simply be obeying a rule, and in doing so I could disavow responsibility – I would only be obeying orders, rather than acting in my own name' (2007: 16). Stevens's hospitality is founded purely on a deep-seated sense of proper behaviour, and obligation to a notion of 'dignity' which transcends deference to his employer and yet results in such obligation, the belief that 'a butler of any quality must be seen to *inhabit* his role, utterly and fully; he cannot be seen casting it aside one moment simply to don it again the next as though it were nothing more than a pantomime costume' (*RD*: 169). It is this inability to act in his own name which is the tragic realisation at the end of the novel, Stevens's assertion that his own dignity is fundamentally in question because 'I can't even say I made my own mistakes' (*RD*: 243). Stevens's hospitality is thus a barrier to responsibility rather than a contributor to its development. Darlington's rules and standards function not only to maintain the class relations of the English country house but also to construct a social landscape in which the decision is denied and the responsibility necessary for political action is reserved for those in positions of class privilege. A relentless hermeneutical injustice prevents Stevens from being able to interpret his experiences objectively. Within the context of such limitations, Derrida tells us, no decision is possible: it is not that Stevens is without ethics, but rather that he is trapped in a foundational, universal ethics of law and rules into which the nature of the decision – which rests perversely on undecidability and instability – is never made available.

So it is that the 'small choices' (Cooper, 2011: 107) are not available at all. It is not that rules preclude the decision: in fact the knowledge that comes with rules is necessary for a decision to take place. These rules, however, must be remade anew (see Fagan, 2013: 75), and there must be the opportunity to make this shift: 'the responsible decision must be made by, and with reference to, the Other, not only in terms of the other person, but also in terms of an other knowledge, an-other set of rules or way of thinking' (Fagan, 2013: 79). Yet at various points Stevens is denied the access to such knowledge, declaring 'There are many things you and I are simply not in a position to understand' (*RD*: 149). This 'not knowing, having neither a sufficient knowledge or consciousness of what being *responsible* means, is of itself a lack of responsibility. In order to be responsible it is necessary to respond to or answer to what being responsible means' (Derrida, 2008: 25). Were Stevens to embrace the contradiction of his experiences this would unravel the order on which his understanding of the world relies, and yet through this equally the unravelling of the structures that keep him in a position of servitude without possibility of dissent. As 'there is no responsibility without a dissident and inventive rupture with respect to tradition, authority, orthodoxy, rule, or doctrine' (Derrida, 2008: 29), so Stevens's inability to challenge his employer makes responsibility in Derrida's terms impossible.

Such socialisation is specific to Stevens's role as butler and his place at Darlington, yet it is also part of a wider and notably English and masculine culture, indicated in the novel by Stevens's association of his 'dignity' with the behaviour of his father and his continuance of his duties in the Boer War whilst serving a General who was responsible for Stevens's brother's death. In a profound act of cognitive dissonance, Stevens witnesses Darlington's anti-Semitism yet declares that he has never seen Darlington treat someone differently on account of their race (*RD*: 145). Responsibility is thus also impossible because the very basic recognition of the Jewish housemaids' subjectivity is denied. As Madeline Fagan exposes in her reading of responses to rational ethical theory, post-structuralist criticism of such theories is that they highlight the limits of the 'dominant grids of rational intelligibility' as borne out by the Holocaust, a situation in which ethics is proved to be 'insufficient to an engagement with the other who might exceed these grids' (2013: 19). Such grids rest upon both normalisation and socialisation, meaning that certain Others can neither be seen nor responded to. Stevens cannot be responsible to the housemaids in part because their construction in his 1930s imagination falls outside of the Other to which he relates. They are, in Judith Butler's terms, unintelligible subjects (2004: 30).

Central to this is the notion that to recognise the other one needs first to be able to identify the self, to be a 'subject who says "myself"' (Derrida 2008: 5). In his reading of Patočka, Derrida draws attention to a passage in which the journey to the Good is identified as in the form of '*the soul's internal dialogue*' (2008: 13). Yet Stevens's role drives him to deny his own selfhood to such an extent that it spills over into his life more generally; for instance, in his travels he obscures his own perspective in favour of a book, *The*

Wonder of England; indeed, as Meghan Marie Hammond (2011) has argued, his entire narrative can be read as a series of assumed narrative modes that obscure his lack of personal voice. In this sense Stevens becomes a kind of mimic, revealing via his modest performativity what in Homi K. Bhabha's (1990) terms is an incomplete and destabilised psychological presence. For Fagan, examining the ethics of Levinas and its dialogue with Derrida, the ethical encounter with the other that produces responsibility is disrupted by the presence of what Levinas calls the third person. Fagan argues that this third has been neglected in discussions of post-structuralist ethics, and yet it is the third which both introduces politics and makes responsibility possible by creating the context for a decision (2013: 61). In this encounter Stevens finds himself in the potential of a moment which is both an ethical relation to the other and a political decision mediated by the presence of the third, here taken to be Lord Darlington. Yet Stevens's lack of selfhood makes the decision impossible.

In recounting this unbearable tension between Stevens's hospitality and his failure to be responsible, the novel's romantic and political plots come to serve the same purpose. When Stevens relays Darlington's news regarding the housemaids to Miss Kenton she is horrified, yet her wrath is focused not on Darlington but on Stevens's ability to 'sit there and utter what you have just done as though you were discussing orders for the larder' (*RD*: 148). Stevens's inability to articulate his feelings about the Jewish housemaids is so frustrating to Miss Kenton because it intersects with her desire to see him act in response to her, to make some gesture that would realise the sexual tension in their relationship. As such, his inability to make a decision denies him responsibility, but also love which – as Alain Badiou so eloquently examines in *In Praise of Love* (2009) – relies upon a relation to the other. It is not enough to hold a commitment to responsibility theoretically, one must also be of a mind to enact responsibility 'in action, doing, a *praxis*, a *decision* that exceeds simple conscience or simple theoretical understanding' (Derrida, 2008: 27). Implied in responsibility is thus the need to make a response – 'in answering to the other, before the other and before the law, and if possibly publicly' (Derrida, 2008: 28). Just as Stevens cannot act on his feeling, so it is that he lacks the ability to act on Lord Darlington's prejudice.

Indeed, it is explicitly the lack of the decision which filters into Stevens's relationship with Miss Kenton. Reflecting on the end of their relationship, Stevens locates this as revolving around a 'decision' he makes:

> Naturally – and why should I not admit this - I have occasionally wondered to myself how things might have turned out in the long run [...] [I only speculate over this now because in the light of subsequent events, it could well be argued that in making my decision [...] I was perhaps not entirely aware of the full implications of what I was doing. Indeed, it might even be said that this small decision of mine constituted something of a key turning point; that that decision set things on an inevitable course towards what eventually happened. (RD: 175)

In his acknowledgement that he was not aware of what he was doing, Stevens reveals the lack of knowledge that means his decision is flawed. Within the terms of Derrida's thinking Stevens in fact makes no decision in this moment, instead following the pattern of a decision made many times before, which ceases then to be a decision in each subsequent iteration as it becomes rather a repetition and a reaffirmation that can be predicted in advance. So what sets the inevitable course is, in fact, not the decision but rather the impossibility of the decision.

Beyond realism: *The Remains of the Day* as *example*

Despite recognition of the novel as metaphor, few critics explicitly 'test' *The Remains of the Day* against political events. Those who have most frequently consider the novel in the context of its publication. John Su, for example, argues that Ishiguro evokes the country-house tradition in order to question a nostalgia industry employed by Thatcher in the run up to the Falklands War and in immigration and union control policy (2002: 563), while Christine Berberich sees the Thatcherite return to Victorian values as the novel's 'cautionary subtext' (2011: 118).

Such themes of nostalgia for a lost past, the clinging to a post-imperial dream, have been resurrected in recent criticism surrounding the 2016 UK referendum on membership of the European Union, a trend illuminated by Kristian Shaw's *Brexlit: British Literature and the European Project* (2021). At the centre of liberal shock and horror at the Brexit vote was a question of responsibility. Leave votes were frequently characterised through a trail of comedic interventions which suggest motifs of self-destruction, irresponsible in Derrida's own terms as lacking the knowledge to make a genuine decision (see for example Dawson, n.d.; Warren, 2017). In the discussion that follows, I explicitly do not align myself with those perceptions, yet acknowledging their existence is key to exploring the novel as a parable invested in the claims and interests of such interpretations.

The parallels between Brexit and Stevens's behaviour have not gone unnoticed. Ariel Saramandi's starkly titled 'How *The Remains of the Day* Helped Me Understand Brexit and Trump' (2017) argues that the Leave voter is the inheritor of Stevens's internalisation of the neo-liberal dream. Such a reading aligns with Derrida's own invocation of Europe in the context of responsibility. For Derrida the need to encompass multiple traditions means that European responsibility can exist only in the acceptance of difference – 'If something like Europe exists and can be thought at all, it must be a conception that for structural or principal reasons is open to responding to still more injunctions, including injunctions from other, or non-European, traditions' (Gashé, 2007: 311). In contrast to this, both the Leave voter and Stevens are associated with a resurgence of exclusive English nationalism.

It is this reading that suggests the novel as a marker of an inevitable course, with Brexit as the culminating point. While Saramandi may outline this as a straightforward conflict between neo-liberalism and democracy, reading the novel via Derrida, however, positions this outcome more within the terms of democracy itself. For the novel draws attention to the necessary limits of democracy as a process which rests upon a notion of universal equality and yet has woven within its application a necessary circumscription based upon resemblance which prevents a cosmopolitan consciousness. To be political, one must be partisan, and thus to be political is the enemy of planetary thinking. For the European citizens of Britain unable to vote, this structure was painfully obvious. The democracy in which a Europe might exist is one that rests upon an infinite responsibility that is impossible, revealed by *The Remains of the Day* as an inevitable because recurring pattern.

To end at this point is to read the novel as extended allegory or metaphor, albeit a sophisticated one which crucially draws attention to the socialised and contextual nature of events. And yet the nature of the *example* is such that it always gestures towards a realisation beyond the limits of the real, to the Europe and the democracy that are always *to come*. Where in the novel, then, one might ask, is the departure from representation towards provocation that the *example* implies? Such an extension relies upon two key factors. In the first instance it demands a closer reading of the text that appreciates how the novel prompts an interrogation of the straightforward press representation of unthinking working-class Leave voters by asking readers to consider whether Darlington is any more responsible than Stevens. Into this context comes the specifics of political responsibility as that which rests on the encounter between enemies. Derrida argues that in the two world wars the possibility for face-to-face encounter would be that which creates the possibility of the political and that, after this, such possibility is lost (2008: 19). Yet at Darlington Hall there is no sense of Ribbentrop as an enemy. Stevens is never in conflict with his Jewish co-workers; they remain unseen, as unintelligible, and outside of a space of conflict. Yet, equally there is no conflict between Darlington and his German guests. So it is that Darlington Hall remains an apolitical space and without this encounter the decision and the responsibility that comes from it is impossible not just for Stevens but for everyone.

Not only does the novel put the blame for such irresponsibility squarely at the feet of a society whose performative structures disavow political knowledge and malevolently create a paternalistic society of disenfranchisement, it also illustrates how political intelligence cannot be assumed from any perspective. The knowledge necessary for the decision is impossible for Stevens, but it is also impossible for Darlington. At the novel's denouement we learn how Darlington's involvement in politics culminates with the hosting of a meeting between the prime minister, Halifax, and Ribbentrop in which he is, in the assessment of Lord Cardinal, 'out of his depth' (*RD*: 221), the Nazis 'manoeuvring him like a pawn' (*RD*: 222). Like Stevens, Darlington's ethical encounter with the housemaids, too, is disrupted by a third in the presence of German power. Darlington is thus revealed as naively socialised into a political world where his deference to those with more political standing makes it impossible for him to take a position of criticality. In the same way the lack of knowledge of Leave voters has been challenged more recently with research which shows that Leave and Remain voters are equally ignorant of the EU (Carl, Richards and Heath, 2019). Analyses of the motivations behind working-class voting patterns emphasise this lack of opportunity for a true decision – people who 'did not vote Leave because they thought it would improve their lives' but 'because they just couldn't stand it being the same', and who were motivated not by the issues at hand being debated but by their relation to a national politics from which they felt excluded (Mckenzie, 2017: 278). Yet the wider picture of this lack of true decision is also pointed to as transcendent of class, reflected in the fact that only 25 per cent of people with a postgraduate degree voted Leave compared to more than two-thirds of voters with no qualifications (Hobolt, 2016: 1269). While the latter reflects an inequality of opportunity that is reflected in class background, it is not straightforwardly correlated with it.

As readers, the fact that we pay more attention to Stevens's failure than that of his employer, and that Stevens himself pays more attention to the political motivations of his working-class associates than Lord Darlington's reflects what Gurminder Bhambra has in relation to the European referendum termed methodological whiteness – the scapegoating of white working-class voters for white middle-class voting behaviours in order to detract from the evidence that the largest determining factor in voting patterns was not class but race. In reality, the majority of Leave voters were not working-class but middle-class (2017: 215). Drawing parallels with the election of Donald Trump as President in the US, Bhambra argues that 'to discuss the "left behind" simply in terms of the white working class, and to rationalize their vote for Brexit and Trump in terms of their economic position, is to conflate socio-economic position with racialized identity while claiming to speak only about class and to repudiate identity politics' (2017: 217).

Such awareness takes us away from the stereotype of the Leave voter to the novel as relevant to the perception of a universal failure from both Leave and Remain voters that perhaps reflects Fagan's assertion that responsibility is ultimately impossible. This is indeed what is implied by Ishiguro's statement on the novel that we are in fact 'all butlers' (Yentob, 2021); in discussing his motivation for the novel Ishiguro speaks of his own sense of responsibility as 'this notion that it's up to people like me, ultimately, to *decide* on the big questions, how the country is run, the *decisions* the government makes', and his own awareness of 'how *ignorant* I was about many of the most burning, key, important issues of the day' (Swaim, 1990: 101 – emphasis added) – like Stevens, he suggests that he too lacks the knowledge to make a true decision. The novel thus points towards the need for a wider transformation relation if responsibility is to take place.

In order to realise this potential, the second part of the departure relies upon recognition that Stevens is only a partial correlation to liberal perceptions of the Brexit Leave voter. For while he represents the lack of knowledge and decision implied in critics of Leave voters, he is not a voter at all. In the wake of his failure to decide, Stevens finds himself in a process of deconstruction – for deconstruction is not a conscious method, Derrida tells us, but rather what it is that takes place. Stevens protests too much regarding Darlington's innocence, presents contradictions between events and his perceptions, his narrative uncovering the trace of an alternative which his actions and outward behaviour has denied. In such moments he is evidence of that which escapes, the irrepressible addition which keeps the promise of the *to come* alive: that 'something which would not be recognisable as democracy, but whose promise may be found to be contained within democracy' (Thompson, 2007: 27). This escape is manifested not in Stevens himself but in two other figures in the novel – Miss Kenton and Harry Smith – both individuals who each, in their own way, represent the possibility of a gesture towards a political responsibility and the associated ideal of a true, ethical democracy.

The novel does not indicate specifically what it is that produces Miss Kenton's very different response to both events at the Hall and Stevens; one might speculate that it is partially though not completely bound up with the gendered construction of Stevens's identity and the gendered solidarity between Miss Kenton and the housemaids which potentially forges an ethical relation, so that Miss Kenton draws attention to a politics which is inscribed not merely through class but also through gender, reflective also of the Derridean sense of politics as that which is based on a fraternity that actively absences women, and to which female presence is a threat. Yet it also relates to her position against the specific isolation of his ambivalent class position as butler. Regardless of reason, Miss Kenton's contrasting position illustrates that responsibility is not impossible. Discussing the housemaids, Miss Kenton challenges Stevens with the question 'Does it not occur to you, Mr Stevens, that to dismiss Ruth and Sarah on these grounds would be simply – *wrong?*' (*RD*: 149), declaring the act a 'sin'. In doing so she announces an ethical relation which supersedes her professional allegiances. She offers the possibility to Stevens of a genuine decision, a position taken without obligation, where his politics might emerge. As a result of this conversation, Stevens experiences a crucial awakening: forced to admit that the issue had troubled him greatly, he moves from a position of the acceptance of Lord Darlington's knowledge to one of an explicitly revealed cognitive dissonance: 'I would not say I am not curious [...] However it is not my position to display curiosity about such matters' (*RD*: 222).

In the context of Brexit, then, Miss Kenton marks an opening of an alternative relation to politics that would eschew socialisation for ethical relation. That Miss Kenton does not resign over the incident with the housemaids problematises any suggestion of an easy movement towards absolute responsibility whether by the rebellion of class or of gender. She reveals later that she failed to act on her principles because of her fear of leaving Darlington Hall, politics thus sacrificed to the discourse of economic survival. This, too, resonates with Brexit, where the discourse of economic necessity was frequently invoked as a motivating factor in voting choices. Miss Kenton's own actions are essential in that they reveal Stevens not as anomaly but rather as simply the most obvious limit point of an interaction with the other which is always limited, where friendship is by its very definition exclusive, and thus the structures of relation of which politics is founded equally contingent. Both Stevens and Miss Kenton exist within a world which demands conditional hospitality as a function not only of maintaining the class relations of the English country house, but also to construct a social landscape in which the absolute hospitality necessary for political action is denied to those outside of positions of class privilege. Nevertheless, Miss Kenton is a necessary feature of the *example*. That she is aware of the tension between her economic needs and a wider principle of democracy acts as the gesture towards what might be, an alternative third to Lord Darlington with the potential if not the ability to create the conditions for a decision. So it is, finally, that the significance of the final part of the novel is revealed. For it is a promise that emerges at the novel's conclusion in Stevens's trip to Devon and his encounter with Harry and the explicit discussion of political responsibility. Superficially, this incident might be seen only to reveal an alternative facet of working-class irresponsibility. In particular it might appear to affirm the negative opinions of Lord Darlington's guests regarding the popular vote. Harry is the advocate for a democratic revolution but one which comes in the form of apolitical 'muddle' which drives the town's middle-class doctor from socialism, illustrated when Harry asks the doctor to share his views on 'all kinds of little countries going independent', declaring 'I don't have the learning to prove him wrong, though I know he is' (RD: 192). Thus, while Stevens may be the father of the apolitical voter whose own response to his lack of knowledge is to identify himself as outside of such political responsibility, it is Harry who is the father of the politicised working-class voter, voting without heed for the rules of party politics, muddled because the system has no interest in providing access to the rules of engagement that would allow them to make a decision. Ishiguro makes this explicit by having Stevens at this point in the narrative return to a moment in 1935 when Lord Darlington and a dinner guest asked him to comment on the gold standard. Upon being baffled, Stevens realises that this is indeed the expected response, only to be confronted by another question of the currency situation in Europe which he equally cannot answer, and a third on the situation in North Africa. As the gentlemen laugh at Stevens's inability to respond, so the dinner guest declares:

> we still persist with the notion that this nation's decisions be left in the hands of our good man here and to the few million others like him. Is it any wonder, saddled as we are with our present parliamentary system, that we are unable to find any solution to our many difficulties? Why, you may as well ask a committee of the mothers' union to organize a war campaign. (RD: 196)

Nevertheless, to move to the position of Harry from that of Stevens is to open up a space to the potential of responsibility. Neither Darlington nor Stevens has responsibility. Yet Darlington holds political power, and with this an illusion of a decision that Stevens is unable to access. What distinguishes Darlington from Stevens is not political intelligence but the access to a claim of political responsibility that exists only within the framework of a limited democracy. Stevens himself recognises this in his acknowledgement that Darlington made his 'own mistakes' (*RD*: 243) whereas he did not do even that. What Stevens fails to recognise in his sustained self-deprecation, however, is the social contexts that produce such a difference.

This association of decision with educational opportunity is a wider theme of Ishiguro's – as Hanya Yanagihara has spoken of in her analysis of *Never Let Me Go*:

> One of the most heartbreaking parts of that book is the resignation [...] that their lives are mapped out before them and that they are going to live them and that there is very little possibility of change. And what happens of course when Tommy and Kathy try to change that fate is that they are told that it's impossible. And after a brief moment of rage they go back to accepting it. And the question of course one thinks about as a reader is 'isn't that what happens to all of us'? Those of us who are privileged to have choices perhaps think about it less. But for the majority of the world, for many people in the world they are told what they are going to be and what their hopes are and what their lives are going to be from the moment they are born [...] and it would never occur to them to try to change it because it is dangerous to have those thoughts [...] That is the true horror of that book. (Yentob, 2021)

Harry and the other men refuse acceptance and have 'dangerous' thoughts. Though they maintain Darlington's lack of knowledge, the fact they too are able to make 'their own mistakes' points to an alternative possibility.

So it is that in Derridean terms Harry's muddled politics *is* radical. While he acts without true knowledge (and thus without responsibility or a decision), his idiosyncratic behaviour and explicit demand to reject socialisation and rules represent the opening to that potential. It reflects what Thompson points out in his reading of Derrida's work, as that which lies beyond democracy which is an 'absolute danger' that is 'monstrous, frightening and disturbing' (2007: 29). Thus comes the double bind – for Derrida it is Europe as an idea (if not a practice) that is (in *The Other Heading*) in its cosmopolitan indeterminacy and promise of a universality without singular identity, perhaps the strongest *example* of the democracy to come that we have. Yet in order to create the democracy to come, one must embrace the incongruity of the Brexit vote, the 'worst violence' by which 'the mechanism of negotiation between different injustices would no longer be possible' (Thompson, 2007: 29), the fact that while totalitarianism rests upon the fantasy of unity, democracy rests upon a dissolution of certainty and thus that the unpredictable is not only possible but also desirable. It is the unpalatable awareness that to be democratic must be to fail to be democratic. More specifically in *The Other Heading* Derrida makes this point in relation to Europe, where to be European, Derrida declares, 'one must not be European – I am European […] I do not want to be and must not be European through and through […] If, to conclude, I declared that I feel European *among other things*, would this be, in this very declaration, to be more or less European?' (1992: 83). Europe, then, exists ultimately only in its failure, where it is that failure that signifies its existence. Europe here stands in Derridean terms as an *example* of a possibility of democracy. What may thus frustrate us is that the seemingly counter-intuitive voting patterns around Brexit are on the one hand a depressing reinforcement of the association of political responsibility with class privilege, yet conversely evidence of the transformative possibility of a democracy to break free of ordained laws and codes, a democracy to come in which lies the potential for the decision. In true Derridean fashion, it is not that one such interpretation is correct and waiting to be uncovered, but rather that such voting is simultaneously both, where the ideology may be conservative, but the process at work transgressive. So we must not merely try to understand Harry and the unpalatable and incommensurable vote – we must embrace them, as the necessary hope for the return of exactly what we have lost.

It is in reading the relevance of Harry and Miss Kenton that the novel surpasses what Rich identifies as the lack of praxis implied in Stevens's own awakening, which never itself moves into a field of action (2016: 503). Read today, *The Remains of the Day* offers us the origins of this political landscape; Stevens's professional role and his 'domestic' engagement are ones where the role of 'butler' serves as synecdoche for the British voting public and its emerging political consciousness, simultaneously subject to the destructive forces of repetition and open to the empowerment of transgressive thinking. In doing so, the novel contributes to an understanding that, within the context of the development of political consciousness in Britain, the 2016 EU referendum result is not an aberration but rather represents the concluding point of an inevitable course that has its roots in twentieth-century attitudes towards political responsibility. By the novel's conclusion Stevens has taken a journey towards acknowledging an opening to the need for such responsibility, yet the figures who represent this – Miss Kenton and Harry Smith – do not take readers universally towards liberalism. If there is comfort in such understanding, it is perhaps that such tensions are the very foundation of democracy, and the possibility of a democracy that is yet to come. Yet remaining unseen, in such politics nevertheless exists the hope of the resurrection of what that politics has itself destroyed. The provocation of the novel's *example* is to retain the possibility of responsibility, and the ethical relation to the other that it signifies, even when to do so means to embrace outcomes that seem ironically in contradiction with the beliefs we might most obviously consider synonymous with such a reality.

Conclusion

The Remains of the Day marks an early instance of a concern for the intersection between ethical imperative and political contingency that shapes many of Ishiguro's later works – novels such as *Never Let Me Go*, and *Klara and the Sun* (2021) in which the question of the responsibility for the other is pitted against the limitations of legislative and social norms. Ishiguro presents a genealogy of British politics in which events are shaped by the contingent nature of democracy and a rule of law normalised to the advantage of the maintenance of existing power structures. In doing so, the novel offers a reading of political responsibility that speaks not only to both its pre- and post-Second World War setting and the Thatcherite context of its publication, but also tp recent political events regarding membership of the European Union. Ishiguro, then, offers us in his novel an 'inevitable course' to the present moment.

However we describe that moment in terms of literary criticism – as a moment of new sincerity, metamodernism, post-postmodernism, or transglossic literature – in which we turn again to fiction for social-political resonance, it is a vital time to consider again Ishiguro's most famous work. In *The Gift of Death* Derrida asks the reader to consider 'history *as* responsibility' (2008: 5). Derrida's question 'What would responsibility be if it were motivated, conditioned, made possible by a history?' is motivated by his assertion that 'the classic concept of decision and responsibility seems to exclude from the essence, heart, or proper moment of responsible decision all historical connections' (2008: 7). Through the use of the Second World War as parable, Ishiguro upholds Derrida's invocation of history as an *example* pushing us towards imagining a political responsibility that would challenge this political circumstance. As in so many things, Ishiguro's novel is thus a prescient forebear of our contemporary desire for a more accountable politics. Despite all its bleakness, it is a novel, Ishiguro exclaims, in which there nevertheless remains 'a little bit of optimism' (Yentob, 2021). While responsibility is impossible, the novel tells us, it is in continuing to strive in hope for its existence – even when the consequences of that striving are unsavoury – that we keep its possibility alive. We focus, then, always, on what remains, even at the end of the day.

References

Badiou, Alain (2009). *In Praise of Love*, translated by Nicolas Truong (London: Serpent's Tail).
Berberich, Christine (2011). 'Kazuo Ishiguro's *The Remains of the Day*: Working through England's Traumatic Past as a Critique of Thatcherism', in Sebastian Groes and Barry Lewis (eds), *Kazuo Ishiguro: New Critical Visions of the Novels* (London: Palgrave Macmillan), 118–129.
Bhabha, Homi K. (1990). 'DissemiNation: Time, Narrative, and the Margins of the Modern Nation', in Homi K. Bhabha (ed.), *Nation and Narration* (Abingdon: Routledge), 291–322.
Bhambra, Gurminder K. (2017). 'Brexit, Trump, and "Methodological Whiteness": On the Misrecognition of Race and Class', *The British Journal of Sociology*, 68:S1, 215–232.
Butler, Judith (2004). *Undoing Gender* (New York: Routledge).
Carl, Noah, Lindsay Richards and Anthony Heath (2019). 'Leave and Remain Voters' Knowledge of the EU after the Referendum of 2016', *Electoral Studies*, 57, 90–98.

Cooper, Lydia R. (2011). 'Novelistic Practice and Ethical Philosophy in Kazuo Ishiguro's *The Remains of the Day* and *Never Let Me Go*', in Sebastian Groes and Barry Lewis (eds), *Kazuo Ishiguro: New Critical Visions of the Novels* (London: Palgrave Macmillan), 106–117.

Dawson, James (n.d.). 'Jeremy Clarkson Calls Brexit Voters "Idiots" and "Coffin-Dodgers" in pro-EU Tirade', *Joe*, www.joe.co.uk/news/jeremy-clarkson-brexit-idiots-coffin-dodgers-eu-215102 (accessed August 2021).

Derrida, Jacques (1978). *Edmund Husserl's 'Origin of Geometry': An Introduction*, translated by John P. Leavey Jnr (New York: Nicholas Hays).

—. (1992). *The Other Heading: Reflection on Today's Europe* (Bloomington: Indiana University Press).

—. (2008). *The Gift of Death and Literature in Secret*, translated by David Wills (Chicago: Chicago University Press, 2nd edn), 1–120.

Fagan, Madeline (2013). *Ethics and Politics after Poststructuralism: Levinas, Derrida and Nancy* (Edinburgh: Edinburgh University Press).

Gashé, Rodolphe (2007). 'European Memories: Jan Patočka and Jacques Derrida on Responsibility', *Critical Inquiry*, 33:2, 291–311.

Hammond, Meghan Marie (2011). '"I Can't Even Say I Made My Own Mistakes": The Ethics of Genre in Kazuo Ishiguro's *The Remains of the Day*', in Sebastian Groes and Barry Lewis (eds), *Kazuo Ishiguro: New Critical Visions of the Novels* (London: Palgrave Macmillan), 95–105.

Hobolt, Sara B. (2016). 'The Brexit Vote: A Divided Nation, a Divided Continent', *Journal of European Public Policy*, 23:9, 1259–1277.

Holmes, Chris and Kelly Mee Rich (2021). 'On Rereading Kazuo Ishiguro', *Modern Fiction Studies*, 67:1, 1–19.

Ishiguro, Kazuo (1989). *The Remains of the Day* (London: Faber and Faber).

—. (2021) *Kazuo Ishiguro: Remembering and Forgetting*, Imagine, BBC One, 28 March.

James, David (2010). 'Artifice and Absorption: The Modesty of *The Remains of the Day*', in Sean Matthews and Sebastian Groes (eds), *Kazuo Ishiguro: Contemporary Critical Perspectives* (London: Continuum), 54–66.

MacPhee, Graham (2011). 'Escape from Responsibility: Ideology and Storytelling in Arendt's *The Origins of Totalitarianism* and Ishiguro's *The Remains of the Day*', *College Literature*, 38:1, 176–201.

Mckenzie, Lisa (2017). 'The Class Politics of Prejudice: Brexit and the Land of No-hope and Glory', *The British Journal of Sociology*, 68:S1, 265–280.

Naas, Michael (1992). 'Introduction: For Example', in *Jacques Derrida, The Other Heading: Reflection on Today's Europe* (Bloomington: Indiana University Press), vii–lix.

Rich, Kelly M. (2016). 'Troubling Humanities: Literary Jurisprudence and Crimes against Humanity in Ishiguro's *The Remains of the Day* and McEwan's *Atonement*', *Law, Culture and the Humanities*, 12:3, 496–508.

Saramandi, Ariel (2017). 'How *The Remains of the Day* Helped Me Understand Brexit and Trump'. *Electric Lit*, 11 October, https://electricliterature.com/how-the-remains-of-the-day-helped-me-understand-brexit-and-trump/ (accessed August 2021).

Shaw, Kristian (2021). *Brexlit: British Literature and the European Project* (London: Bloomsbury).

Su, John J. (2002). 'Refiguring National Character: The Remains of the British Estate Novel', *Modern Fiction Studies*, 48.3, 552–580.

Swaim, Don (1990). 'Don Swain Interviews Kazuo Ishiguro', in Brian W. Schaffer and Cynthia F. Wong (eds), *Conversations with Kazuo Ishiguro* (Jackson: University Press of Mississippi), 89–109.

Thompson, Alex (2007). *Deconstruction and Democracy* (London: Continuum)

Tolkien, J.R.R. (1947) 'On Fairy Stories'. Andrew Lang Lecture, University of St Andrews.

Vorda, Allan and Kim Herzinger (2008). 'An Interview with Kazuo Ishiguro', in Brian W. Schaffer and Cynthia Wong (eds), *Conversations with Kazuo Ishiguro* (Jackson: University Press of Mississippi), 66–88.

Warren, Jack (2017). 'BBC Viewers OUTRAGED as Richard Dawkins Brands Brexit Voters "IGNORANT" in Outrageous Rant', *The Express*, 10 March, www.express.co.uk/news/uk/777247/BBC-outra48.ge-Richard-Dawkins-Brexit-voters-ignorant-rant).

Yentob, Alan (ed.) (2021). *Kazuo Ishiguro: Remembering and Forgetting*, BBC One, 28 March.

5

Klara in the junkyard: on loneliness in *The Unconsoled*

Bruce Robbins

'How can you *like* being lonely?'

'I do, I just do'.

(U: 171)

In the final scene of *Klara and the Sun* (Ishiguro, 2021) Klara has a conversation with Manager, now retired from the store where Klara was displayed and sold. The meeting happens in a junkyard. Klara, no longer able to move, has been in the yard since her teenage purchaser went off to college and her career as an AF, or Artificial Friend, ended. Manager asks whether, until being deposited in the junkyard, Klara had stayed with the same family. Klara says yes. Manager says, 'So it was successful. A successful home.' Klara replies, 'Yes. I believe I gave good service and prevented Josie from becoming lonely.' To which Manager responds, 'I'm sure you did. I'm sure she barely knew the meaning of loneliness with you there' (*KS*: 300).

Manager is being courteous, but, under the circumstances, barely knowing the meaning of loneliness is more than a polite phrase. *Klara and the Sun* does not explicitly ask big existential questions about what loneliness means, where it comes from and whether it can really be alleviated by the acquisition of an expensive new piece of technology. But one might say that it sidles up to such questions by making us wonder about Klara herself. Is it possible that Klara does not feel lonely? She has been abandoned in the desolate junkyard after a novel's worth of surprisingly compelling relationships, first in the store and then in the family that purchased her. Although she is a robot and has no appetite for food or sex, she does have feelings, and people, trying to imagine those feelings, worry that she may well be suffering from loneliness. A 'kind yardman' has offered to transport her to an area of the yard where there are other decommissioned AFs. Klara declines, 'content with my special spot' (*KS*: 299). She declines again when Manager mentions the same possibility 'in case you'd like some company' (*KS*: 302). Two refusals within three pages – the point is made, and emphatically. Klara was designed to provide company, but she herself does not seem to need any.

Klara's inhuman status marks her off from the humans around her in more than one way. As a machine, she falls victim to their casual prejudice and cruelty. At one point, as in *Never Let Me Go* (2005), the non-human being is designated as a candidate to be sacrificed bodily in favour of the health of a human. On the positive side there is also the possibility that her invocation of the sun, key both to her technology and to her non-human belief system, really did save Josie's life, as she seems to believe. That feat would overshadow her advertised function of preventing Josie from feeling lonely. Klara's apparent immunity to loneliness is only one sign of her difference. It seems an especially important one, however, given the sharp attention Ishiguro's works give both to loneliness and to its antithesis, belonging. Ishiguro's decision to create a being who is capable of being kind *without* belonging suggests that he may be trying out a hypothesis: that belonging may not be, as it seems, the proper model of social life and the sole prescriptible antidote for loneliness.

The scene in the junkyard at the end of *Klara and the Sun* rhymes with the final scenes of *The Remains of the Day* and *The Unconsoled*. In the latter two cases these are the scenes that come closest to explaining the novel's title. Hence each is an obvious place to look for some condensation of the novel's meaning. Both are scenes of exclusion and solitude – extremely painful solitude. In both such consolation as is available for the protagonist's loneliness is provided by strangers they are not likely to see again. Exiled as Ryder and Stevens are from sustaining familial intimacy, it does not seem like much consolation. A moralising reader would no doubt see the loneliness as well-deserved punishment for fatal personality flaws or for the choice each has made to value the wrong things – service to strangers, professional duty, public acclaim – over the right ones, which are private and personal. In previous writings about Ishiguro

I have tried to suggest that there is an opposite case, admittedly a counter-intuitive one: that Ryder and Stevens are not simply wrong in their attribution of value, or – to put this more precisely – that Ishiguro has an under-acknowledged if only partial investment in their way of seeing, and that this investment becomes visible when you notice how sceptical he is of the private, personal and (in *The Remains of the Day*) patriotic commitments to which their own commitments are contrasted. Other readers of Ishiguro have noticed – it is hard *not* to notice – that family intimacy as he presents it is quite dysfunctional. I have tried to push this point farther, proposing that Ishiguro lays out elements of an ethical case in favour of the professional, impersonal, cosmopolitan commitments that are set against intimacy and that lead both figures into their final solitude. The difference is that Klara's solitude does not seem painful to her.

This absence of loneliness, although Klara too has provided 'service' to strangers, may be usefully taken as a way of highlighting what humans, by contrast, would and already do feel when they are treated as social discards, junked by the system after they have served their profitable purpose. That may have been Ishiguro's intention, and if so it can certainly be applauded. From my perspective, however, it can also be seen as a new twist in a career-long argument about caring and cosmopolitanism, a twist with the potential to revalue both the earlier novels and the stilted, somewhat robotic voice that has been one of Ishiguro's signature effects. That lonely voice is clearly more to him than an object of pity or an instrument of satire. There is a certain desire in it.

Ishiguro has suggested that in writing *The Buried Giant* (2015) he was thinking about Rwanda, South Africa and the former Yugoslavia, sites of recent atrocity (see Cain, 2015). For those of us who ask ourselves what is to be done in the wake of mass collective violence, it may seem inevitable to channel such references into a concern with the ambiguities of memory and forgetting, ambiguities with which *The Buried Giant*, like contemporary humanitarianism, is very directly concerned. Is it better to commemorate atrocity even if remembering is likely to lead to further violence? Are there ways of remembering that avoid this risk? Or should we be grateful, finally, for the all-too-human weakness that little by little allows our memories to slip and fade, even if the slippage also means the impossibility of holding anyone accountable? But Ishiguro also seems interested in other perspectives on violence. If the bones of the slaughtered can be found beneath England's green and pleasant land as well as in Rwanda or the former Yugoslavia, one bleak and universal moral that Ishiguro might seem to be drawing is that society is founded on violence, that civility merely disguises that violence, and – to stretch the point, but not too far – that belonging as such is inextricable from cruelty. The dizzying temptations of this dark view are the other side of Ishiguro's Orwellian fascination with the notion that there exists a basic human decency. Revelations of decency in characters from whom we have not been led to expect it, almost as shocking as the revelations of cruelty for which Ishiguro is better known, satisfyingly thicken the emotional texture of *Klara and the Sun*. In *The Buried Giant* the verbal courtesy that is such a distinctive fact about Axl and Beatrice, and about other people they meet on the road, people who like them are both humble and civil, seems the very antithesis of extreme cruelty. The same holds for the distinctive courtesy of the porters in *The Unconsoled* when they offer hospitality to Ryder and again when they cluster around the dying Gustav. And yet it turns out that Axl has concealed or forgotten a bloody past of his own.[1] And it turns out that the porters themselves, who display no signs whatsoever of cruel intention, can be held responsible for Gustav's death.

The scene of the Porters' Dance is worth recalling in detail.[2] Gustav consents to perform the dance only when 'virtually every person in the room [is] chanting his name, and even those standing out in the square seemed to be joining in' (*U*: 399). It is at this point that Gustav gives his grandson 'a weary smile' and, although he seems genuinely weary, surrenders to the wishes of the crowd: 'Being by some years the eldest of the porters, Gustav appeared to have more difficulty clambering up onto the table, but many hands reached forward to help him up' (*U*: 399). The dance is all about bearing the weight of suitcases, which is the work of porters. Its principle is to make the bearing of heavy weight appear effortless. Gustav is especially good at it, and perhaps for this reason, or simply to increase their entertainment, the crowd covertly adds extra weight to the new suitcase with which Gustav is expected to perform. He pretends not to notice it, then notices it with 'dismay' (*U*: 401). The crowd takes this as a joke and roars its appreciation. But Gustav's expression remains 'troubled, and for an instant it occurred to

Boris that his grandfather was not entirely faking his concern' (*U*: 401). No one else notices. They laugh and continue to egg him on. Hoisting up the new, much heavier suitcase, Gustav bends his knees, 'whether because of infirmity or out of showmanship was not clear' (*U*: 402). Again, more weight is added: this time, a heavy piece of machinery concealed in a golfing bag. Whether Gustav is ready to give up or not, we are told that 'the crowd had no intention of letting him do so yet' (*U*: 403). The scene is drawn out almost unbearably. Boris tries to get his grandfather to stop, the crowd keeps shouting 'Good old Gustav!', urging him on, reassuring Boris that he shouldn't worry, 'Your grandfather's magnificent' (*U*: 405). No one but Boris (and Ryder) seems to notice that Gustav is in fact suffering: 'His face became strangely flushed. His jaw clenched furiously, his cheeks grew distorted, the muscles in his neck stood out. Even in the heavy din, the elderly porter's breathing seemed audible' (*U*: 405). Finally, 'something inside him seemed to suddenly to snap'; he recovers, but he knows he is 'not well' (*U*: 406; 423). He embraces his grandson and gives him what turns out to be some parting advice on how to live. The crowd continues to celebrate. A few pages later, racked with pain, he asks to see his daughter one last time before he is taken to the hospital. Soon afterwards his death is reported.

The principle of coerced and excruciating entertainment is roughly the same as what we see, earlier in the novel, when Ryder goes to see Miss Collins and runs into an old friend from his student days in England, Jonathan Parkhurst. Parkhurst says that he has left England because their circle expected him 'to be the clown all the time'; and, when he returned, they welcomed him with a 'braying noise': 'I can't tell you how awful it was. And I could feel myself turning into that pathetic clown I came here to get away from' (*U*: 302). He goes on, 'Okay, here I don't have to do all those faces and funny voices, but at least that all worked. It may have been intolerable, but it worked, they all loved me, my old university friends, poor sods, they must believe I'm still like that' (*U*: 303–304). This is apparently how one makes oneself loved. He is not really like that, he says. What is he like, then, to those around him now? He is unloved. 'Very lonely, and very dull' (*U*: 404). The choice seems to be between belonging by playing the clown and being lonely. If so, then the choice is between loneliness and cruelty. Clownishness is always cruel to someone, if only to the clown. But there are no innocent victims. Parkhurst, the object of that cruelty in England, with sublime unconsciousness here passes the cruelty on to Ryder:

> 'Then finally one of them says: "What about Ryder? Anyone heard of him lately?" Then they all explode, making the most disgusting noise, something halfway between a jeer and a retch [...] Then they all start to laugh and then they all start to mimic piano-playing, you know, like this' – Parkhurst put on a haughty expression and played an invisible keyboard in a highly precious manner – 'they all do this, then make more retching noises'. (U: 304)

The fact that Ryder too seems unconscious of the cruelty of this bit of surplus narration does not mean the cruelty is not there and does not affect him. On the contrary the existence of so much gregarious cruelty suggests an aetiology for Ryder's anti-social unconsciousness – call it his loneliness – as well as a way of looking at his own moments of cruelty, most dramatically his cruelty to Boris.

The most obvious objection to this line of argument – the argument that Ishiguro sees cruelty as constitutive of belonging at the level of society in general, or what *The Unconsoled* calls 'this city' or 'the community' – is that for Ishiguro there is as much cruelty inside the intimacy of private relationships as in the larger community around them. Gustav's cruelty to Sophie when she discovers her dead hamster and he ignores her sobbing; the Hoffmans' cruelty to their son Stephan, walking out on his performance at the concert; Ryder's cruelty to Boris (more than once); Sophie's deliberate abandonment of Ryder and Boris as they are walking at night towards an unknown destination and then her long hesitation to go in to her dying father, whom she has rushed to see – all these encourage us to decide that what Ishiguro is illustrating is the inexplicable perversity of the human heart, or something of the sort. He may well be, but such generalisations are as banal as they are irrefutable, and, appended to a work as ambitious as *The Unconsoled*, they are also strangely incongruous. Why take so many pages to say something so simple and so disappointing? Why go to the trouble? If for Ishiguro human perversity is universal, then decency is unattainable by any social rearrangement, however creative, and there is no higher end for human creativity, including the novelist's, than getting everyone to see and admit it.

This conclusion seems irreconcilable with Ishiguro's stubborn commitment to decency and, for that matter, with the puzzle-solving, technical-fix, social engineering impulse that his alternative-world fictions share with the bestselling utopias of the late nineteenth century. Both of these commitments are crowd-pleasers. Yet both also suggest the existence in Ishiguro of what I have called a cosmopolitan project: the quest for a decency beyond the limits of belonging as it actually exists, a decency embodied in relations that are impersonal and perhaps even inhuman. Even if this project does not dominate Ishiguro's fiction, it seems worth bringing into relief the utopianism that counterbalances his more obvious attention to the dystopian aspects of the present. He deserves credit for his contradictions.

At the opening of the scene in Sophie's apartment when Ryder is so shockingly cruel to Boris, pretending not to hear him when he asks what game they should play, and this after Boris calls him Papa and says how wonderful the handyman's manual is, Ryder has a thought that does not let him off the hook, but is certainly intriguing: 'the thought struck me that I was perhaps expected to behave as if I were familiar with the apartment. On the other hand, it was equally possible that I was expected to behave like a guest' (*U*: 283). He is uncertain as to whether he belongs or not. One might therefore conclude that his anger, which might otherwise seem evidence of the inexplicable perversity of the human heart, makes more sense as an expression of that uncertainty: do I belong, or not? Some readers will refuse this uncertainty. They will conclude that he is simply delusional. Of course he belongs; he is merely acting as if he did not. But if one does not jump to this conclusion, if one instead takes the novel as deliberately holding open an uncertainty about Ryder's belonging, then Ryder's anger at his intimates becomes something more than an individual symptom. It generates the speculation that perhaps, in Ishiguro's world, you cannot belong well in private unless you can also belong well in public, and 'the community' does not make it easy to belong well in public. The community is at least part of the problem.

In a 2001 essay entitled 'Very Busy Just Now: Globalization and Harriedness in Ishiguro's *The Unconsoled*', I offered a frame for this uncertainty about belonging. I proposed that one could make sense of Ryder's wavering between cruel emotional withdrawal and helpless entrapment in nightmarish proximity to seemingly distant figures, like the porter who suddenly makes absurdly disproportionate claims on his time and attention, by putting it in the context of the mid-1990s. The mid-1990s was a moment when, with the borders of Europe in the long and sometimes bloody process of being redrawn, the usual guidelines seemed suddenly to have disappeared that once helped Europeans separate off (for better or worse) legitimate from illegitimate claims on *their* time, attention and resources. It was the dramatic moment of military intervention in Kosovo, but also of dramatic non-intervention in Chechnya. This argument still seems valid to me. Since then, as the pressure of non-Europeans seeking to escape poor and violence-prone countries has increased, as the institutions for dealing with them have failed along with the categories for evaluating their claims (can it be that only those escaping violence count as refugees, with some claims, while those escaping poverty are migrants, with no claims at all?), this situation has persisted and even intensified. The inhabitants of the relatively prosperous metropolitan north are now even less clear than they used to be as to who they must let in and who they must not or shall not let in, and on what grounds. They are more confused than they have ever been as to when and where and whether to release their sympathy, to expand their budgets, to send in their bombers – when and where and whether a particular set of atrocities or a generalised state of inequality and misery demands so-called humanitarian intervention, or not. Are there natural, legitimate, defensible borders within which they can and should restrain their care and concern, and the state policies that reflect them? If so, where are they? And if not, who knows who belongs and who does not?

The Unconsoled catches the ordinary person's indifference to the news of distant suffering in a telling bit of dialogue between Ryder and the novel's villain, the hotel manager Mr Hoffman. Hoffman refers to bad news. Ryder replies, '"There's been so much bad news lately." Hoffman asks, "So much bad news?" I gave a laugh. "I mean the fighting in Africa and so on. Everywhere, bad news." I gave another laugh. "Oh, I see. I was of course referring to the bad news about Mr Brodsky's dog"' (*U*: 118). Like a true villain – and it is noteworthy that this novel includes one – Hoffman acts out a malignity that cannot be reduced to a single motive.[3] And yet much can be traced back to his taking the concerns of the local community as if they were all that counted in the world, as in the tragi-comic mistake he makes about the 'bad news' – a mistake that counts as backhanded evidence for Ishiguro's own cosmopolitan concern for fighting in Africa and other matters of comparable global significance. In the beginning of Hoffman's biography, as he narrates it, there is his misrepresentation of himself to his wife, when he allowed her to believe that he enjoyed from the community a respect for his musical accomplishments that he knew to be baseless. Trying to please 'the community' – more precisely, trying to save the community from 'loneliness' (*U*: 113) – is also Hoffman's rationale for trying to rehabilitate Brodsky, which explains his, and the community's, hilarious over-reaction to the dog's death. As it happens, Hoffman tries to get Brodsky drunk on the night of the concert just as, at the hotel, he enacts a systematic passive-aggressive persecution of the sleep-deprived Ryder. He behaves badly in public as well as in private. He is consistently cruel to his son, and he does his best to stop Brodsky and Miss Collins, now in their old age, from reconciling. The reuniting of that couple would arguably have given the novel a genuine if only partial happy ending, more important to the reader than anything that does or does not happen to Ryder. But in the end Brodsky and Miss Collins are not reconciled, and that too can be laid to the account of the local community, which demands fidelity.

'Oh, how I hate you!' (*U*: 499) Miss Collins tells Brodsky as he lies on the floor of the concert hall. But the reason for the outburst of hatred is less Hoffman's efforts at sabotage than the fact that Miss Collins too takes service to the community as her highest value:

> You'll never be a *proper* conductor. You never were, even back then. You'll never be able to serve the people of this city, even if they wanted you to. Because you care nothing for their lives. That's the truth of it. Your music will only ever be about that silly little wound [...] At least I, in my small way, can say I did what I could. That I did my best to help the unhappy people here. But you, look at you. You've only ever cared about that wound. (*U*: 499)

As Brodsky sees it, Miss Collins has pronounced that he must 'go alone. To some dark lonely place' (*U*: 500). He is condemned to loneliness by Miss Collins not because of Hoffman's machinations or his own alcoholism but because his music does not serve the community.

Showcasing an unreliable narrator can make it seem as if the rest of the social world is populated by reasonable people whose perspectives are more or less reliable. It makes the narrator's unreliability seem the point of the story. That is not the case here. Other characters turn out to be just as unreliable. Miss Collins has sometimes seemed to be the only adult in the room, and yet here it is she who is unreliable. As the scene is presented, Brodsky's failure to win back his place in the community has two causes, and neither of them is his narcissistic obsession with his wound. The first is the fact that he loses his balance, while using an ironing board as an impromptu crutch after his wooden leg is removed, and crashes on to the stage. The second is the fact that he takes his interpretation of the music 'too far' – too far for his audience, and even for the musicians. Neither of these causes reflects badly on Brodsky. If they reflect badly on anyone, it is the 'provincial audience' (*U*: 492).

In spite of the local community's over-the-top expressions of grief at the untimely demise of Brodsky's dog, as if the dog had been an assassinated national hero, it seems clear that Ishiguro does not want to get easy laughs from a smug, one-sided satire of the provinces. He does not take for granted that the cosmopolitan characters, Brodsky and Ryder, self-evidently have a superior understanding of music and life (Brodsky himself is more level-headed about the death of his dog). But it is also clear that Ryder does appreciate Brodsky's provocative musical experimentation. More important, the terms of Ryder's appreciation seem to resonate with Ishiguro's own probable thoughts on the bold modernist experiment he undertook in writing *The Unconsoled*, especially after the huge mainstream success of the more conventional *The Remains of the Day*. They resonate with his hypothetical expectation that, like Brodsky, he would be perceived by the readers who loved *The Remains of the Day* as, this time, having gone 'too far'. Too far from the values and sentiments of ordinary people, the people who, after the concert, will proclaim Brodsky's performance 'tasteless' and 'immoral' (*U*: 502).

The fact that the community sees itself mirrored in its chosen music is not ridiculed. For a novelist, it cannot help but recall the bygone times when the novel, too, seemed the inevitable place where a society articulated and debated its deepest commitments. Here the issue seems to be the cold of modernity versus the warmth of local tradition. Ishiguro cleverly evades any neat antithesis between the philosophies of Brodsky and Christoff, the two Slavic-named outsider rivals for the city's affections, that would enable readers to take sides. In the same way he also evades points of controversy between them which readers could understand well enough to have an opinion – hence incomprehensible phrases like pigmented triads and crushed cadences. Instead, he keeps the focus on musical modernity as such. Do ordinary people really want an inventive modernity? Or do they want an affirmation of their pre-existing values and emotions? Christoff is accused of 'stifl[ing] natural emotion': 'How can people like this, untrained, provincial people [...] understand such things?'; 'To them it's just crashing noise, a whirl of strange rhythms' (U: 190; 186; 185). Christoff seems right. One member of audience at the cinema, discussing Christoff's music, remarks that '"cold" is the word that had sprung to his mind'; Ryder suggests 'dryness' (U: 102). The common thread here is *inhumanity*. The inhabitants, who have not resigned themselves to 'being just another cold, lonely city' or, again, a 'cold modern city' (U: 107), seem to require from the music that represents them a human warmth that they do not find in it.

If they are right, then Ishiguro could not expect a warm reception for *The Unconsoled*. It seems unlikely that he was not recalling or anticipating a similar characterisation of his own carefully restrained prose and penchant for cold, emotionally blocked narrators, whether butlers or carer clones or Artificial Friends. When Ryder says what he likes about Brodsky's music, Ishiguro seems to be talking almost directly about the coldness of his own fiction, its unnatural detachment from ordinary emotions, and in particular what he is trying to do in *The Unconsoled*:

> He was almost perversely ignoring the outer structure of the music – the composer's nods toward tonality and melody that decorated the surface of the work – to focus instead on the peculiar life-forms, hiding just under the shell. There was a slightly sordid quality about it all, something close to exhibitionism, that suggested Brodsky was himself embarrassed by the nature of what he was uncovering, but could not resist the compulsion to go yet further. The effect was unnerving, but compelling. (U: 492)

It has been easy for readers to notice what is sordid and embarrassing in the depths of Ishiguro's fiction. But the peculiar life-forms hiding deep under its surface include cold, somewhat inhuman beings who, however offensive and even misshapen they may seem, contribute to the aspirations of cosmopolitanism and belong to the discourse of utopia. These include the basic form of Ryder's relations with his local admirers. Like the author who created him, Ryder is a celebrity. His brief but harried visit to the unnamed Central European city resembles the book tours that take famous, often jetlagged writers away from home to peddle their wares. In a time of desperate inequality, a famous writer on tour, surrounded by fawning strangers, will inevitably come across as a figure of privilege, hence not a figure who instinctively attracts the reader's sympathy (that at least was my experience when I tried to teach the novel).[4] Yet novels are not easy to sell, and this is all the truer for novels that, like *The Unconsoled*, voluntarily surrender relatable characters and compelling plots in favour of a radical redesign of the space/time of storytelling. From the novelist's point of view, the issue is an everyday material one: will I be able to sell enough copies so that I can eke out a living and write another novel? And if, in trying to write another novel, I am eventually thrown back on my own personal experiences, can I avoid writing about the experience of having strangers come up to me at readings and, while flattering me shamelessly, press demands that show they give a great deal more importance to their own lives than to mine? The porter who takes his bags up in the elevator wants Ryder to add something about porters to his speech and, before that, to speak to the porter's daughter, from whom he is estranged and who is sitting in a café in the town centre, not far away at all. On the night of the big performance, when Ryder has barely managed to get in one practice session, the hotel manager is still trying to get him to look at his wife's albums. For Ryder this is somewhere between comedy and nightmare. For Ishiguro it sounds like an opportunity to do some venting.

For the reader, however, it may be closer to a radically democratic answer to George Eliot's celebrated question: 'But why always Dorothea?' What about minor characters? Do not they have the right to a story of their own? Strangers coming up to the famous writer with inappropriate requests stand in for minor characters who have their own claims to narrative space. Here the comedy of manners shades into a kind of modernist sublime, a crystallisation of the impossibility of responding to everyone. In earlier work

(Robbins, 2001), I argued that Ishiguro is testing the supposedly natural limits on caring for strangers, a burning question for humanitarianism in the 1990s.[5] From this perspective, the novel's stretching and shrinking of time and space can be interpreted as a denaturalising of the grudgingly accepted ceiling on public concern. When Sophia says there is so little time, the reader is made to share her anxiety – objectively, a phenomenon more associated with the 'time bind' of women than men. How can anyone possibly satisfy all the conflicting demands on their time? It is physically impossible to participate in in so many events at once, to do this for that person and that for this person while also practising and researching local conditions and giving an interview and being photographed and taking Boris to their old apartment to look for a lost toy. But, as if dabbling in political theory, the novel cancels that impossibility. Time can be stretched, and space can be compressed. The considerable distance travelled by tram and car, which has taken Ryder far out of the city and into the country while he is supposedly in charge of Boris, can somehow be reversed by opening the door of a cupboard, so that Boris, left alone for what must have been many hours, is discovered, one hundred pages later but somehow only steps away, still sitting in front of his cheesecake. Boris says 'you've been ages' (*U*: 265), exactly as if it has only been five minutes. Here Ishiguro is no longer reflecting or generating anxiety. He is allowing us to imagine transcending that anxiety. We can imagine living a rearranged life in which caring is no longer governed by the logic of scarcity. The zero-sum premise that dictates that we think in terms of so-called 'compassion fatigue' is suspended in favour of a utopian fantasy where temporal abundance becomes an emotional abundance that allows for an unprecedented reimagining of social arrangements. The projected endpoint of this argument, of course unrealised here, would be something like genuine democracy on a global scale.

The Unconsoled, unlike some of Ishiguro's other novels, is not an explicit political fantasy. It only plays with the ground rules that would have to change in order for such a fantasy to become more plausible. But, in doing so, it addresses democracy as we know it, making it clear how far the actually existing version remains, even at the local level, from democracy in a more genuine sense. At one point Ryder finds himself riding on a tram. He does not have a ticket. The ticket inspector approaches. He starts to explain that there are 'special circumstances'. The ticket inspector responds: 'Not having a ticket is one thing. But you know, you really let me down last night' (*U*: 170). Hearing this, Ryder gradually recognises her as a girl he knew in primary school. He does not remember any promise he might have made to get together the night before.

When Ryder finally does visit the apartment of the ticket inspector, who wants to show him off to friends who do not believe she knows such a celebrity, he is mysteriously unable to open his mouth and tell them who he is. It is not funny. It is anxiogenic enough to make one want to pop a pill. Yet it also makes a kind of sense. While he is inexplicably silent, the guests tell a story about seeing Miss Collins and Mr Brodsky at the zoo, where efforts have been made to bring the long-estranged couple back together. Fiona wants to show off her very important friend. And there has been a certain amount of comedy, from the first scene onward, aimed at Ryder's importance being mysteriously ignored by those who supposedly value it most. Yet this scene encourages the irreverent thought that whether Brodsky and Miss Collins get back together is actually more important to the community, to the novel, and even to us, than whether the celebrity pianist gets to reveal who he really is. The locals think they care, but they do not. Who he is not really important to them; and it is not clear they are wrong. There is a kind of democratic mini-rebellion here.

It is the accumulation of such rebellions that helps explain why the novel's atmosphere is so dreamlike – which is not the same as nightmarish. Every culture has its rules, written and unwritten, dictating the particular obligations its members owe to particular other members: what spouses and friends, parents and children can legitimately expect from each other, the very different things that are to be expected from participants in a business transaction, and so on. They may not be *good* rules, judged by a higher standard, but they are how that culture works. In this novel those rules seem to have been quietly suspended. As a result, you – the visitor from elsewhere – cannot be certain as to what others expect from you or what your proper obligations to them are. Confronted with a ticket inspector, you would seem obliged to present a ticket, and no more than that. But perhaps you are obliged (or were obliged) to show up at the ticket inspector's home for a social gathering the night before. What if any ticket inspector on a tram might also be a long-lost friend, with the expectation that she would be treated as such? That is not life as we know it.

Disguised by a carefully non-colloquial formality of speech that might otherwise be attributed to the literary conventions of foreignness, *The Unconsoled* shows you a wild and wonderful unhinging of social hierarchy. In the novel's opening sequence, as mentioned above (the scene cannot be mentioned too often), an elderly porter mentions to the pianist that he is worried about his adult daughter and asks Ryder to go find her in a nearby café and sound her out. Given that Ryder's relations to the porter have been restricted to having his bags carried up in the elevator, this request seems excessive, to say the least. But Ryder agrees. And when he eventually finds the daughter, she greets him as if she has been expecting him. She says she has good news about a house in the woods, just the sort of house they have been looking for. Ryder gradually recognises her. It appears that she and he might already be a couple. Perhaps they are even married.

Yes, men who are conspicuously missing some of the faculties necessary for ordinary social interaction are notorious, in literature and in life. But pause a bit before going diagnostic. If Ryder and Sophia are indeed married, then the porter is Ryder's father-in-law. And in that case, it would *not* be abnormal for him to propose a mediatory chat between the pianist and his daughter. That is the maddening but also utopian undecidability that organises so many pages. The principle is clear, democratic and utopian: what if, having your bags carried (or your ticket inspected or your breakfast served or your garbage collected), you could not determine whether the person offering you that service should be treated not politely, but the way you would want to treat a family member or a friend? Ishiguro's invented city is a great deal more democratic than any city in which Ishiguro or his readers have actually lived.

If readers do not reject Ryder as a figure of privilege and instead allow themselves to see the world through his eyes, they may well lose patience with his inability to say no to all the presumptuous people who have no right to the favours they request. The hotel manager wakes Ryder from a deep sleep on what seems to be the morning after his arrival and asks him to come down to the lobby. Why? So that he, the hotel manager, can greet him. Ryder does not tell him what you or I might have told him, what he deserves to hear. He does not hang up. He answers that he will be down before long. The hotel manager says fine, but he will remain standing in the lobby until Ryder arrives. Ryder gets up and goes, seemingly oblivious to this textbook display of passive aggression.

On the other hand the people who ask Ryder for unreasonable favours, right down to the day of the big concert (when Ryder suddenly remembers he has not practised, or even chosen what pieces he will play), include those to whom he is closest. And his failure to comply sometimes turns out to be a kind of success. When Ryder does finally steal time to practise for the concert, in an unlikely shed on a hillside, he ends up unintentionally fulfilling another untimely and inconvenient request: that he provide piano accompaniment as Brodsky buries his famously deceased dog. This turns out to be the only concert that he gives. The musician is outside, listening while he shovels. And we are told that the music leaves him consoled.

This novel is magical because it invents a unique form for a key ethical and political uncertainty of our time: the anxiety-producing question of how much we owe to invisible strangers, a question which also obliges us to re-evaluate the relative priority we give to our near and dear ones. Everyone has a story, porters and ticket inspectors as much as celebrity pianists. Everyone's story deserves to be told. If you are a novelist, everyone has a claim on you, and a pressing one. In this sense, to repeat, Ryder stands in for his author. Ishiguro has created a protagonist who embodies both the truism that you cannot satisfy everyone (hence the anxiety) and the moral imperative dictating that you cannot *not* try.

That effort is why *The Unconsoled* is as much a utopian dream as an anxious nightmare. It is pervaded by the unkept promise of democracy. I mean democracy not just in the cosmopolitan sense (my point in the earlier essay) – that is, in the insistence that distant obligations ought to be as real as immediate local ones. *The Unconsoled* is also radically democratic in the domestic sense. It experiments with representing a world in which there would be nothing abnormal about friendly and intimate equality between a world-famous pianist and the porter carrying his bags in the elevator or the woman demanding his ticket on a tram. Knowing we have not got there yet is the source of an anxiety that is worth having. Even to imagine the goal, however, is to experience something very different from anxiety. It is a foretaste of a different sort of belonging – of a happy ending that the novel does not deliver, but that is built into it nonetheless.

Stephan Hoffman, much-abused son of the hotel manager and another key player in the happy ending that does not quite happen, says afterwards, commenting on how the audience has received Brodsky's music, 'They didn't want it, it startled them. It was much more than they'd ever bargained for'; it 'reminded them of everything they're afraid of' (U: 522; 523). The same might be said about *The Unconsoled*. The obvious contrast in Ishiguro's oeuvre is with the reception of *The Remains of the Day*. Within *The Unconsoled*, the contrast is with the speech that is reported to have been given, not by Ryder but by a local, which 'made us all feel good about ourselves and our city and now everyone's enjoying themselves' (U: 516). And yet Stephan's own performance, which Ryder admires for its modernity, is loudly applauded by the locals. It seems possible that cosmopolitan modernity and local values might after all be reconciled. 'After all', Ryder thinks after the opportunity for him to perform has been lost, 'if a community could reach some sort of equilibrium without having to be guided by an outsider, then so much the better' (U: 524). Ishiguro is not ready to relegate community to the junkyard of concepts. Loneliness, which modern music like *The Unconsoled* itself teaches us to live with, is not a simple denial of community. *The Unconsoled*, then, is part of the same enterprise as *The Remains of the Day*.

As I read it, the imagination of a loneliness that would not be painful, as in the quotation that serves as epigraph to this chapter, is not a banal affirmation of individualism, as if the point – a familiar one – were to avoid at all costs committing oneself to any cause. For Ishiguro the uncommitted are in no way morally superior. His point, I think, is double: that it might be possible to care about more others – more rather than fewer others, in an expanded community – and that it might be possible to do so in a manner that does not commit one to the forms of cruelty, cruelty to oneself as well as to non-members, that *The Unconsoled* shows to *belong* to belonging as we know it, belonging in its conventional and constrained forms. In this sense Klara is not an exemplary victim, but a kind of hero. Like Ryder she is unnaturally detached. Like Ryder she is a rescuer of others, but this time in a novel that offers less resistance to the project of rescue. In that sense she also rescues *The Unconsoled*, allowing us to see it less as an indictment of the delusional self-aggrandisement of the rescuer and more as an argument in favour of cosmopolitan caring, kindness without loneliness, even if one ends up in a junkyard.

Notes

1 One might say that *The Buried Giant* lays out in a mythic, diachronic version – as a narrative – a statement about cruelty as the price of belonging that is synchronic in *The Unconsoled*.
2 In retrospect, the scene may well be remembered largely as a sort of mock-heroic parallel to the main plot. The porters, although competence in their job is more readily available than competence in concert-level piano performance, take their work too seriously just as Ryder takes his too seriously, and the result in both cases is unfortunate; Gustav dies, and Ryder is expelled from his family. But this reading underplays the community's cruelty – the high price it exacts for the privilege of belonging. The parallel extends further in the sense that the Porters' Dance too is of course a form of art, and art in its relation to the community's demand for work. Recalling Ryder's fear that his parents might not have someone to help them with their luggage gives another, more serious, twist to this motif.
3 It is interesting to note how Ishiguro nuances his own recourse to old-fashioned villainy. When Brodsky sees through Hoffman's villainy, he calls him 'that bell boy, that hotel janitor', and then 'that cleaner of hotel lavatories' (*U*: 458). Suddenly we are in a realm of class and class contempt that has seemed as alien to the novel's life-form as difficulties of translation.
4 As someone who has taught the novel to generally resistant undergraduates, I would say that their first impulse is to hold fast to a pathological view of Ryder, a view for which the novel of course offers ample evidence. They are drawn to the idea of Ryder as another in a long list of self-important, self-centred men who are out of touch with their feelings, hence cruel and destructive to those around them. The time is not ripe for the idea that the importance attributed to him by the community might somehow be deserved. If there is a side of the novel that is instinctively enjoyed, it is the repeated demonstration that the community does not in fact treat him with much respect after all.
5 More abstractly, I argue that 'The temporal limits on caring, which can be experienced without leaving the kitchen, become a way of confronting

experientially the *geographical* limits on caring, the global borders of solicitude, which are harder to experience or make into stories' (Robbins, 2001: 431).

References

Cain, Sian (2015). 'Writer's Indignation: Kazuo Ishiguro Rejects Claims of Genre Snobbery', *The Guardian*, 8 March. www.theguardian.com/books/2015/mar/08/kazuo-ishiguro-rebuffs-genre-snobbery (accessed August 2021).
Ishiguro, Kazuo (1995). *The Unconsoled* (London: Faber and Faber).
—. (2021). *Klara and the Sun* (London: Faber and Faber).
Robbins, Bruce (2001). 'Very Busy Just Now: Globalization and Harriedness in Ishiguro's *The Unconsoled*', *Comparative Literature*, 53:4, 426–441.

6

Novel dysfunction in *When We Were Orphans*

Andrew Bennett

Neither the presentation nor the plotting of *When We Were Orphans* (2000) properly stacks up. In interviews Ishiguro has commented on what he calls the 'peculiar elision' of the governing geopolitical premise and promise of its plot (Hunnewell and Ishiguro, 2008: n.p.) – that in finding his parents, who have supposedly been kidnapped and held for more than two decades in the Chinese sections of Shanghai, the celebrated detective Christopher Banks will be able to resolve an international crisis and prevent in turn: regional war; invasion; civil war; communist revolution; the end of the British empire; and the coming global catastrophe of the Second World War. In this respect, at least, the novel follows quite closely the absurdist redemption narrative of Ishiguro's previous novel, *The Unconsoled* (1995), in which the protagonist-narrator's much anticipated piano recital is deemed, improbably, to promise an unspecified form of salvation both for individuals and for the inhabitants in general of the unnamed Central European city in which the concert will take place.[1]

In *When We Were Orphans* Banks 'starts off relatively sane, then starts to go pretty insane', Ishiguro explains in an interview with Brian Shaffer soon after the publication of the novel: 'it's necessary to have these justifications for why the narrator is so unreliable', he concedes, because 'there is no logical or rational relationship [...] between his wanting to solve the mystery about his parents and his wanting to avert the Second World War'. It is, Ishiguro goes on, 'a gap that simply cannot be filled with any kind of reason or logic; it's a purely emotional response': the 'really interesting areas' in the novel involve an 'internal world' and an 'emotional logic', he says

(Shaffer and Wong, 2008: 164; 165).[2] Like many of the thoughtful, carefully worded, precisely phrased comments that Ishiguro makes on his own work – statements that are characteristically, in equal measure, clarifying and guarded – Ishiguro's explanation for the flaw in the novel's narrative logic is intelligently argued and entirely reasonable. His novel is 'internal' – affective and psychological – in focus rather than, in any simple sense, about the solving of a crime and its effectiveness in resolving national and international conflicts; the apparent *illogic* or unreason of plotting accords, on another level, with the *logic* of a certain affective or mental state or condition.

But the logic of or justification for the novel's curious plot is also addressed in another comment by Ishiguro where the emphasis falls a little differently. Here Ishiguro explains that in plotting the novel he wanted to exploit the conventions of early twentieth-century detective fiction, according to which the external problem of evil within a community can be identified with an individual and comprehensively expunged, expelled or excised by the detective. The detective sets out not only to solve the crime but to 'root out single-handedly all the evil in the world', as a 'silver-haired' guest at a London party in the summer of 1923 comments – in a phrase that Banks himself picks up and reuses when he begins fully to register the responsibility involved in 'rooting out evil in its most devious forms' (*WWWO*: 16; 13; 30). Ishiguro's aim, he tells us in this interview, was to explore larger-scale questions of 'evil and suffering' in the context of 'modern technological warfare' – in the context of a world in which 'nationalism and racism had gone bananas' and in which 'bloodshed and suffering seemed to be unlimited in potential'. So, he said to himself: 'let's look at someone who believes that everything that's gone bad in the world, in his personal world as well as the larger world, comes from an evil criminal element that needs to be unmasked. Let's bring him into the chaos of the twentieth century and the brink of another world war. Let's see how he copes. Let's see how long he can hang on to his little vision of how to deal with the problems of life' (Shaffer and Wong, 2008: 159). While this account also points to a psychological explanation, it is primarily historical in focus: the detective's worldview is challenged by the specific 'chaotic' circumstances of the twentieth century. In this sense the two interviews offer overlapping but slightly competing accounts – an explanation from the perspective of emotion and psychology, and one from a genre/historical perspective – to explain what might be described as the novel's structural 'design-flaw' (a flaw and not a flaw; a flaw that is designed, built in, intended). While each of the explanations is reasonable and coherent in its own terms, the fact that Ishiguro offers two slightly different rationalisations – and the fact that each is incomplete in itself – is telling. But *what* it tells us is perhaps more difficult to pinpoint.

I have begun by highlighting this discrepancy between Ishiguro's two accounts of his novel – and the fact that the novel needs at least two – because the inconsistency might alert us to other problems or questions, other productive or energising structural flaws or difficulties in the novel. The incoherence of the narrative and causal logics of *When We Were Orphans* is not just indicative of the extent of the famous detective's delusions, or of the cognitive disturbances resulting from the world-historical crisis that he records, but ultimately points to the narratological anomalies of the novel itself. The problem is not just internal or characterological, in other words, but structural, external and authorial – aesthetic, in a sense. That the narrative itself fails to identify a coherent causal link between the disappearance of Banks's parents, on the one hand, and the Sino-Japanese war that is engulfing Shanghai in the autumn of 1937 and the coming conflagration of the Second World War on the other, points not just to a local 'failure' of plotting but to a more fundamental failure of the novel to *work* in the way that its readers might reasonably expect. As Brian Finney puts it in a perceptive early discussion of the novel, Ishiguro's strategy is to 'progressively break the reader's dependence on the conventions of traditional fictional realism' (Finney, 2002: para. 22). The flaw in logic – one that is self-evident, unhidden, apparent and at the same time obscure and easily overlooked – cannot easily be accounted for simply as an effect of the narrator-protagonist's psychological condition; nor can it simply be understood within a historico-generic framework as a critique of twentieth-century colonialism or as an analysis of a world falling apart. But I want to propose that the plotting anomaly, the structural flaw, in *When We Were Orphans* – what makes it not work, its novel dysfunction – is, nevertheless, just what makes the novel work, what makes it a powerful and compelling 'work' of fiction.

This is not, in fact, the only way in which Ishiguro's novel may be said to work by not working. We might think of the book's mildly dysfunctional title: 'We'? Who is this we? What kind of collective is it? Are *we* involved, you and I? 'Were'? When is this 'were'? Are we, then, *not* now orphans? Has our – or has their – orphanhood ended? *Can* an orphanhood end? What, anyway, is an orphan?[3] Or we might think of the novel's dysfunctions of genre – it is, after all, impossible to miss or to dismiss the novel's telling distortions of the classic detective mode to which it pays homage by shameless reproduction and relentless satire. But is it a detective novel or a pastiche of one (or is it indeed something entirely different)? And we might notice the provocative but uncertain suggestiveness of names in the novel: is Uncle Philip somehow related to the Philip Pirrip of Dickens's *Great Expectations*, to which Ishiguro's plot seems to owe so much? (But how?)[4] What are we to make of the orphan-immigrant Jennifer's insistence that the orphan-immigrant Christopher Banks should look at the archetypically 'English' Windrush valley in Gloucestershire in the final chapter (*WWWO*: 306–7), and how might we relate it to HMT *Empire Windrush* – that icon of British colonial immigration – docking at Tilbury ten years earlier in June 1948? Is Banks's surname supposed to remind us of the financial institutions whose presence in Shanghai 'underscored' the city's 'internationalism and its sheer materialist rapacity', as the historian Michael Miller puts it? (Miller, 1994: 240).[5] And is his mother's christian name really an allusion to Diana Spencer – 'Princess Di' – as one critic suggests (Bain, 2007: 257)? And so on ...

But I want briefly to describe three other ways – respectively narratological, hermeneutic and intertextual – in which *When We Were Orphans* manages failure, manages to fail.[6] First, there is the narrative question. Like every other first-person narrator in Ishiguro's novels – that is, like every narrator except for the mistily vague, hardly individualised, third-person narrator that predominates in *The Buried Giant* – Christopher Banks has serious problems in his role as narrator because he has serious, and repeatedly foregrounded, problems with his memory and therefore with the credibility of his account of himself and his life-events. 'I am sure these impressions are not accurate', he tells us in an early example of what builds up to a candid catalogue of memory defects that develops over the course of the novel, 'but that is how the evening remains in my mind' (*WWWO*: 13). His memory of his voyage to England is, he ambiguously comments, 'quite clear' (so at the same time entirely clear and somewhat unclear: 'quite clear' means both) (*WWWO*: 27). He says that he finds himself 'less certain about some of the details' (*WWWO*: 68); and then comments a little later that 'this is how, admittedly with some hindsight, I have come to shape that memory' (*WWWO*: 87). 'I cannot remember a great deal about the first part of the morning [...] I do not remember now if we shook hands', he says (*WWWO*: 100–101). Given the narrator's status as 'the one who is supposed to know' (to adapt Jacques Lacan's definition of the analyst (Lacan, 1981: 230–243)), Banks's inability to remember, to know, his own past, his inability accurately to retrieve the history that he is recounting, undermines his sole responsibility *as* a narrator: to know, and to tell us what he knows; to tell us what happened and how he feels about it. This is fundamental: if you can't know the story you are telling, then what are you doing telling it? As it is in his other novels, it is part of Ishiguro's accomplished failure in *When We Were Orphans* to present the story through a faulty, failing storyteller, a narrator who somehow doesn't fully know the story he is telling. 'That's what my early books are about', Ishiguro comments in a 2008 *Paris Review* interview: 'people who think they know' but find out they don't (Hunnewell and Ishiguro, 2008: n.p.). The failure of storytelling is precisely the point of Ishiguro's storytelling – his own, that is to say, and, rather differently, that of his unfailingly fallible narrators. In that sense Ishiguro's narrator-protagonists are 'their own Socrates', as he puts it – Socrates being the person who argues with people who think they know something and through the force of sheer logic 'demolishes' their belief in what they thought they knew (Hunnewell and Ishiguro, 2008: n.p.).

Another prominent novel dysfunction in *When We Were Orphans* concerns its meaning-making efficacy. The novel stages a radical disruption of its own meaning-making potential – of, indeed, the very hermeneutic *stuff* that readers might reasonably expect to encounter. As Brian Finney comments, the narrative 'continually offers the reader a plurality of meanings and interpretations while remaining uncommitted' (Finney, 2002: para. 14). Prominent among the strikingly suggestive motifs in *When We Were Orphans*, for example, are blindness, on the one hand, and severed body-parts, on the other. Repetition, in both cases, alerts the reader to potential significance, and in both cases a key resource of literary fiction – the recurrent deployment of an image or 'symbol' across a narrative to generate, without explicitly stating it, a sense of purpose, intention, significance or meaning – is both offered and concertedly disrupted or undone.

Thus, although it is deployed far more deftly than it is in the heavy-handed symbolism of Todd Jackson's actual, ocular blindness in the novel's sister-film, the prewar Shanghai-based Merchant Ivory-branded *The White Countess* (2005), the word-concept 'blind' is deployed in *When We Were Orphans* in at least two highly resonant but competing ways. On the one hand, there is the self-consciously 'literary' use – almost comically pointed up, overdetermined, and critic-triggering, so to speak – of the metaphor of the window blind. Gesturing towards a 'slatted sun-blind', Banks's Japanese childhood friend Akira explains that 'We children' are like the 'twine' that keeps 'the slats held together': it is 'we children', he says preposterously, childishly, that in effect bind 'not only a family, but the whole world together'. 'If we did not do our part', Akira explains, 'the slats would fall and scatter over the floor' (*WWWO*: 73). The simile seems carefully designed – almost over-designed, rhetorically overdetermined – to guide the reader towards an interpretation of the novel as a whole. Akira makes it clear that part of what he means by 'doing our part' relates to national identity, to being or not being Japanese or English 'enough'.[7] Christopher later relays the idea to Uncle Philip (the secret communist sympathiser and activist), who seems to the young Christopher to understand and sympathetically to gloss it, while seeming to the reader slyly to ironise the boy's fear, thus undermining it. 'People need to feel they belong. To a nation, to a race. Otherwise, who knows what might happen?', Uncle Philip asks: 'This civilisation of ours, perhaps it'll just collapse. And everything scatter, as you put it' (*WWWO*: 76–7). Not a 'real uncle' at all, as we later learn (*WWWO*: 74), Philip is himself precisely intent on 'scattering' both the hegemony of Western imperialism and Christopher's family. Like the communist doubleagent that he is, Philip obliquely or equivocally satirises the boy's anxiety, questioning it while appearing to affirm it, while all the time working to make it come about, but not in the way or for the reason that Christopher imagines. In this sense, through the figure of 'Uncle' Philip, the text undermines the efficacy of the metaphor, presenting metaphoricity, the work of figurative language itself, as misleading or dysfunctional – as, in effect, coming apart and scattering on account of the pressure exerted on it by a kind of double or triple agency.

The metaphor of the window-blind also crops up at various other points in the novel. It occurs next, momentarily and perhaps ironically, as a literal window-blind in a melodramatic scene from Part Two in which the young Banks and Akira steal into the 'small, sparse, tidy' room of Akira's family servant, Ling Tien: 'The window was covered by a sun-blind, but the light was leaking in brightly at the edges' (WWWO: 95). The literalness of the blind's seemingly random mention at this dramatic point in the narrative can be seen to undermine the efficacy of metaphorical language. The comment both prompts and resists interpretation, an effect that is emphasised by the 'bright' light 'leaking' at its edges. Here it is not the binding function of the blind's twine that is important but the blind as a barrier to light, and indeed to enlightenment.

The metaphor of the blind's twine is more fully recycled by the adult Banks in Part Three when he is investigating 'one of the most dispiriting crimes' he has ever encountered – a multiple child-murder committed in Somerset in the autumn of 1936, an unspeakable, 'horrific', 'ghastly' crime that makes him feel, in an almost Conradian or Marlovian way, that he is 'looking right into the depths of the darkness' (WWWO: 134–135).[8] Unconsciously echoing his childhood friend's claim, Banks tells the policeman with whom he is working that the two of them are 'like the twine that holds together the slats of a wooden blind' and that if the two of them 'fail to hold strong, then everything will scatter' (WWWO: 135). The deployment of Akira's metaphor in this very different context seems designed once again to undermine as much as reinforce its literary and symbolic efficacy. By transposing the twine metaphor from a statement about family and national identity in the context of early twentieth-century Shanghai to something altogether darker and more existentially disturbing in 1930s rural Somerset, Ishiguro questions whether the inbuilt readerly compulsion to link two such different contexts can ever be properly assuaged. And are detectives not anyway supposed to shed light on things, rather than shielding things from light or from view? Can the metaphor operate effectively and coherently in these two contrasting contexts, or is Banks's adult use of it an illegitimate and incoherent distortion of its original sense?

Such questions are posed even more urgently when the 'twine' of the metaphor is extracted from the blind metaphor entirely and figured not as a form of societal unity and cohesion but as a form of imprisonment – as a bind rather than a blind. Traversing the war-torn Chapei district of Shanghai in Part Six, Banks notes the 'twine' that binds the hands of a Japanese PoW who he assumes, seemingly without reason, is his friend, Akira (*WWWO*: 252). The recurrence of twine in this quite different context again provokes but concertedly resists associations with the twine that holds the window-blind together, thereby raising further questions about the coherence of the metaphor, and indeed about the reliability and viability of figurative language – and about interpretation as such.

But the problem is further complicated by the fact that the word 'blind' is also employed in its other literal sense – not as a window-covering at all but as the condition of sightlessness. Returning to Shanghai during the Sino-Japanese war in 1937, Banks meets Inspector Kung, the original detective on the case of his missing parents. His memory apparently jogged by his opium pipe, Kung recalls hearing that Banks's parents were being held in a house that stands opposite one belonging to a well-known but blind actor, Yeh Chen (*WWWO*: 218, 219). Banks therefore comes to the improbable, not to say causally incoherent, conclusion that finding the blind actor's house will untangle the whole mystery of his parents' disappearance, some twenty years earlier, and thereby apparently resolve the coming global crisis and avert the Second World War. The first part of this, at least, is just how conventional detective novels work: by acting on unlikely clues, seemingly random hunches, contingent and apparently tangential coincidences. The second part – the idea that solving the 'case' will resolve societal conflict more generally – is also at work in classic or Holmesian detective fiction, of course, and can indeed be said to be a psycho-social driver of such writing, its motivation and a significant element in its attraction for readers; but it is usually articulated in ways that are more muted and less direct, and that therefore seem more plausible. Ishiguro's deconstruction of the detective fiction genre in *When We Were Orphans* involves, in part, an exaggeration and literalisation of this reassuring fiction of the famous detective. The following sixty densely wrought pages involve an increasingly surreal quest through the Chinese slums of Shanghai – now a devastated war zone – to find the blind man's house. Literal or ocular blindness therefore has a weird centrality within the narrative-hermeneutic structure of this section, and indeed of the novel as a whole. And yet, while the allusion prompts our interpretative work, it appears to take us, as it seems to take Banks, precisely nowhere – or on a wild goose chase. Despite its hermeneutic suggestiveness, the figure of the blind actor in fact plays no part in the eventual resolution of the mystery surrounding the disappearance of Banks's parents, since the search for his house turns out to be a blind alley or dead end. If 'blind' is a key signifier in *When We Were Orphans*, it is one that points, most of all, to the failure of metaphor or symbolism and to our own failure to interpret a text – which involves not so much our blindness to it as its constitutive resistance, in the end, to the production of meaning.

A conventional reading would, of course, work to bring the two literal senses of the word 'blind' – a window covering and the condition of sightlessness – into formal congruity and would attempt to make something of the word's intrinsic metaphoricity. The two quite different uses of 'blind' would be seen as alluding, in a unified and 'meaningful' way, to the question of sightedness and its absence (a window-blind can, after all, serve not only to keep light out but also to prevent an interior – or indeed an exterior – from being seen). And the use of the dual word/motif may seem to fit with the literary convention whereby a repeated word, phrase or image generates a series of associations and thereby a certain interpretation. In particular the lexical item 'blind', in both of its senses, might alert the reader to its reverse association with the magnifying glass, the classic or stereotypical signifier of the ocularly privileged detective in classic detective fiction. The magnifying glass appears repeatedly in the novel – starting early on when Banks is given one by his schoolfriends (*WWWO*: 8) – but almost exclusively as a comic exaggeration of a familiar, not to say stereotypical or clichéd, signifier of classic detective fiction (and particularly of Sherlock Holmes, who is himself slyly and wryly referenced at various moments).[9] The critical sightedness of the detective is thus foregrounded within a mode that emphasises the character's ability, through the use of a profession-specific prosthesis, precisely to *see* (and therefore to know) that which others cannot.

And yet if classic or Holmesian detective-figures precisely *see* – literally and figuratively – what others cannot see by artificially making the non-visible visible, they can be said to be visually impaired in another metaphorical sense: Banks's examination of the otherwise hardly visible detail through the magnifying glass can be said to distract him from the larger and more important visual thing – to blind him from seeing the bigger contextual, political and historical picture.[10] 'My great vocation got in the way of quite a lot, all in all', Banks eventually confesses to Jennifer as the novel ends (*WWWO*: 309). It is Banks's idea that he will evict evil from the world, an idea that involves a kind of distorted 'proximity' to Sherlock Holmes and other 'fictional antecedents' that blind him to what Brian Finney calls 'the ubiquity of evil in the modern world' (Finney, 2002: para. 32). And yet it is precisely this deft move between different levels of symbolism that the novel resists if, as I am trying to suggest, the arbitrarily or contingently paronomastic word/motif 'blind' fails, in the end, to amount to a signifier of hermeneutic coherence and closure. The window-blind and the twine that binds it have only a tenuous, uncertain connection with a blind actor or with a detective's prosthetically enabled micro-scrutiny of empirical visual evidence, or in turn finally with a more generalised ethical or geopolitical blindness. However hard we work as reader-interpreters of the book (styling ourselves literary-hermeneutic detectives, perhaps, our metaphorical magnifying glass being the interpretative tools that enable us to conduct a particularly attentive form of close-reading), at some level the symbolism itself fails us, fails to work – even while we necessarily fail *it* in our valiant and principled quest for interpretative closure.

The problem, I want to suggest, is only complicated further by intertextuality, the final instance of novel dysfunction that I want to examine. In addition to its 'symbolic' signifying aspect, the blind word/motif may be identified as having a specific intertextual resonance. Ishiguro has confessed in interviews that his knowledge of Shanghai – the city in which his grandfather worked as a business executive in the early decades of the century and the birthplace of his father – is fabricated out of books rather than from direct knowledge, and his handwritten research notes for the novel on the nineteenth- and early twentieth-century history of Shanghai run to more than one hundred pages.[11] Although Ishiguro comments in an interview that it is easy to 'get bogged down with too much information about a historical or real place' and that too many details can 'get in the way of building your world' (Shaffer and Wong, 2008: 191), his research notes include details of the complex political, social and cultural contexts of the multi-cultural and multi-national colonial city, as well as names of streets, politicians and gang leaders; the shops, parks, cafés, restaurants, bars and brothels; the transport and education systems; and so on. And much of the material makes its way into his novel in direct and, more often, indirect and allusive ways.

One of the books on which Ishiguro took detailed notes in preparation for writing *When We Were Orphans* is a remarkable volume on the city by Harriet Sergeant first published in 1991, which Ishiguro sums up as offering a 'vision of S'hai as a corruptor of every sort of political idealist + soldier [...] who cares'.[12] Sergeant's book weaves memories and historical reportage into a detailed evocation of 1920s and 1930s Shanghai, and it is possible to identify in it specific candidates for the sources of certain features of Ishiguro's novel. The following passage, for example, in which Sergeant records the experience of a certain Mr Lord during the Japanese invasion of Shanghai in 1937, bears a marked resemblance to a notable moment in *When We Were Orphans*. When Sergeant interviewed him, the uncannily Ishigurian Mr Lord was aged 101 and living in England in the Home Counties (Sergeant, 2002: 68). He recalled his time as a British insurance company employee during what Sergeant calls 'the first salvo of the Second World War' (Sergeant, 2002: 184):

> On another occasion, Mr Lord was checking a claim in a Chapei warehouse when shelling shattered the walls and the roof began to cave in. Mr Lord jumped through a window into a next-door store room, explaining, 'I didn't know what was on the other side and I didn't care'. When the shelling quietened down he decided to leave by a hole in the wall. It led into the living room of a Chinese family. At a table sat an old man eating his breakfast; in the corner his wife crouched on a commode. Mr Lord shook his head. 'I popped back again pretty sharpish, I can tell you.' (Sergeant, 2002: 307)

Rather like Mr Lord, Christopher Banks, a professionally successful and notably privileged British national, is apparently invulnerable, immune to physical danger in the Shanghai war zone when he returns to the city in the autumn of 1937. And the brutality, devastation and surreal domesticity and cultural otherness of Mr Lord's experience are directly echoed in Ishiguro's evocation of what Sergeant calls this 'new kind of war' (Sergeant, 2002: 190). Searching for his parents in the 'warren' of war-torn Chapei, Banks comes across what he calls 'pockets of domesticity' as he makes his way through 'holes' blasted in the walls of the houses (*WWWO*: 257; see 240–242, 247). He finds a family 'cowering back into a dark corner: several children, three women, an elderly man', with, around them, 'the bundles and utensils of their existence'; he tries to communicate with the family, 'only to be met by uncomprehending stares' (*WWWO*: 248). In both cases what stands out is the surreal domestic banality of the scene, its sheer quotidian familiarity and literal uncanniness (the unhomely homeliness of its dramatically framed *Unheimlichkeit*), in the context of extreme violence, terror and destruction. And in both cases the savagely dissociated weirdness of the scene is emphasised by the insouciant colonial professionalism with which the insurance agent and the detective go about their work, largely oblivious to – or at least strangely detached from – the suffering of the indigenous Chinese inhabitants of a bombed-out, uninhabitable yet inhabited warscape. The sheer *oddness* of chasing up on, trying to solve or resolve, an insurance claim or a murder case amongst so much military-colonial mayhem is particularly striking. What does one insurance claim settled, or one murder-case solved, resolve amongst so much carnage? After all, as both insurance companies and armies will be the first to tell you, acts of war largely indemnify both the actants of destruction and those who would otherwise be liable for financial restitution within the context of peacetime norms of legal responsibility. In both cases the sheer uncanny unreasonableness of the scenes foregrounds the societal and ethico-political dilemma.

In the closing paragraphs of Sergeant's book there is a striking line about Shanghai's brutality and glamour, its sophistication and decadence, its privilege and its sordid colonial exploitation that links with Ishiguro's concern with blindness in *When We Were Orphans*: 'Individuality and anarchy, extraordinary vitality and bestial poverty, black humour and blind indifference; the city attracted and appalled in equal measure', Sergeant writes (Sergeant, 2002: 336). Taking the book as one of Ishiguro's sources, we might say that in this sense, too, *When We Were Orphans* coheres around the question of metaphorical ethico-political blindness – to be about the so-called 'black humour' involved in the 'blind indifference' of Christopher Banks and his imperialist British and Japanese friends and acquaintances to the suffering of the indigenous Chinese inhabitants of semi-colonial Shanghai (despite Banks's shocked and uneasily empathetic encounters with bombed-out Chinese families in the Chapei district). Prominent references to the window-blind and to the blind actor can in this sense be understood to originate in the figurative use of 'blind' in the phrase 'blind indifference', in what can be taken as an encapsulation and condemnation of a whole ethico-political system – a whole socio-cultural national and trans-national organisation of quasi- or semi-colonial oppression and exploitation. The word/motif 'blind', in other words, can be read as a disguised and transformed version of Sergeant's comment on the ethical and political blindness of an imperialising and unquestionably racist Western occupation.[13] And yet it is a version that is so dispersed, scattered and dislocated as to be effectively hidden or disguised.

Sergeant's book is also a possible source for the scene in chapter 12 of *When We Were Orphans*, in which, on his return to Shanghai in September 1937, Banks witnesses the fighting nearby in the Chapei district of Shanghai while at a party on the 'penthouse floor of the Palace Hotel': when a 'thunderous explosion' rocks the room, people at the party send up 'a few ironic cheers' (*WWWO*: 154, 159). Banks is handed a pair of opera glasses to get a better view of the scene, and comments, as if at a spectacle put on for the benefit to the party guests, 'So that's the war. Most interesting. Are there many casualties, do you suppose?' (*WWWO*: 160, 161). But then as the partygoers turn from the battle raging outside to a troupe of 'Eurasian' dancers entering the room to perform, he senses 'with a wave of revulsion' that it is 'as though for these people, one entertainment had finished and another had begun' (*WWWO*: 162). For her part, Sergeant describes the way that, as the Japanese invasion began in early August 1937, foreign businessmen and Chinese inhabitants of the international concession ventured out on to rooftop spaces 'for a better view' of the battle in something of a carnival atmosphere: 'People cheered and booed as the Chinese bombers missed three times, their loads landing harmlessly in the Whangpoo or on the Hongkew wharf', she writes (Sergeant, 2002: 298). But if we identify this as a potential source for Ishiguro's novel we are only reminded of the ways in which historical representation

Novel dysfunction in When We Were Orphans   139

is complicated, reframed and distorted in Ishiguro's fiction – and how, rather than closing down interpretation, such sources serve rather to open it up.

But in its multiple depictions of severed body-parts – of limbs that are literally war-torn, blown apart – Sergeant's book offers one more possible source for a striking and uncertainly symbolic detail in Ishiguro's novel. Sergeant's account is striking, and quite singular in its detailing of first-hand accounts of human mutilation. When wayward Chinese bombs land on the International Settlement during the Japanese invasion of 1937, separate eyewitnesses accounts recorded by Sergeant offer details of a man with 'both legs cut off and his right arm hanging in shreds'; 'a man's hand lying on the ground'; 'corpses [...] torn to pieces'; a detached human leg being carefully 'placed' on the ground; 'blood everywhere [...] and arms, legs and heads separated from their bodies'; and 'severed limbs and blood, as if someone had spilled a tin of tomato paste' (Sergeant, 2002: 300–301, 304). One unnamed man who is standing on a hotel balcony when an explosion occurs is said to have received 'a box on the cheek from a severed hand flying up from the street' (*WWWO*: 304).[14] Strikingly similar images of severed limbs appear in displaced, surreal and ambiguously meaningful ways as a highly sinister motif in Ishiguro's novel. They occur first in the nightmarish and overtly sinophobic Gothic fantasy sequence from Banks's childhood in Part Four, when Akira tells him that he has discovered that the family's Chinese servant, Ling Tien, collects human and monkey hands and has found a way to turn them into spiders. The two boys furtively enter Ling Tien's room to examine the collection. Although they fail to locate either the hands or the spiders, the boys steal a 'lotion' that, according to Akira, Tien uses for his ghoulish metamorphoses. The gothic, nightmarish, bizarre and surreal childhood fantasy seems to recur in a dreamlike, displaced form in later sections of the novel. At one point Banks investigates a triple murder that appears to him to have a 'very significant bearing' on his parents' case, in which the victims have 'all had their arms and legs cut off' (*WWWO*: 169). Later on, when Banks and Sarah Hemmings start their planned elopement from Shanghai, more-or-less oblivious to the destruction of the Japanese invasion in nearby Chapei, Sarah mentions having incongruously brought along her teddy bear, Ethelbert, whose arm has fallen off (*WWWO*: 222). And then perhaps most literally and tellingly, as Banks enters a bombed-out house in the war zone, he sees the corpse of a woman whose arm has been 'torn off at the elbow' (*WWWO*: 270). There is a sense in which one might see the multiple mutilations of the actual historical conditions in war-torn Shanghai in Sergeant's account as being translated and transformed into Ishiguro's fictional representation of the city – thematic pieces of this and other books are torn off, like severed limbs. The fact that Sergeant's account of severed hands and limbs is concentrated exclusively around a stray bomb that falls on the otherwise protected International Settlement emphasises the fact that Banks's account of his experience of the city is haunted by imperial precarity, by a sense of the fragile, always inherently unstable (in-)security that the inhabitants of the international zone in Shanghai enjoyed up until the late 1930s. The so-called 'International Settlement' is anything but settled, permanently settled, in other words.[15] As Ishiguro comments in his notes on Sergeant's book, its 'recurring theme' is of Shanghai as 'an ephemeral city that thought it was solid': 'this brash, arrogant place vanished only a few years after it was at its height', he remarks.[16] But we can say once again that there is a fundamental gap, an ontological distance, between the significance of the severed limbs in Sergeant's historical account – in which they stand metonymically (*literally* metonymically, we might say), for the indiscriminate violence of modern urban warfare – and their adoption and adaptation as a literary device in the playful and surreal grotesquerie of Ishiguro's fiction.

Sergeant's claim about Western 'blind indifference' and her description of violently detached body-parts, then, offer explanatory intertextual resources for some of the striking events and images in Ishiguro's novel. And yet the scattering and transformation of these motifs also, and at the same time, scatters and distorts any sense of cohesion. The novelistic adaptation and translation of historical elements, intertextually sourced from other books, at the same time resists interpretative closure. In this respect, and in terms of plot, narrative authority, language (or naming), genre and symbolism, *When We Were Orphans* obstinately fails to add up, succeeds in failing to work in the way that novels are conventionally supposed to work. It is a failure that somehow – but in a radically distorted way – reflects or reproduces in its literary *form* the historical geopolitical collapse that it records. And this perhaps reminds us to be wary of concluding that in any simple sense Ishiguro's novel allows for interpretative resolution or that it offers any form of literary redemption for historical disaster or atrocity. *When We Were Orphans* is, after all, a novel finally about a 'sort of emptiness' that, as the middle-aged protagonist-narrator confesses in its final sentence, ends up filling his hours (*WWWO*: 313). The novel's resolution, such as it is, is itself kind of empty. As Elizabeth Weston has commented, the novel forces the reader to 'read without hope of consolation and without formulas' (Weston; 2012: 347). But we should also refrain from looking to the novel's middle-aged author for some kind of resolution to or wisdom about our contemporary crises and anxieties. After all, neither Kazuo Ishiguro nor any other novelist is necessarily equipped to advise us on our societal, technological, cultural or economic dilemmas.[17] And yet, returning to the interviews with which we began, we could say that it is precisely by failing in novelistic terms – precisely through its 'peculiar elision[s]' – that Ishiguro's book may be seen to be presenting, non-redemptively, a powerful 'vision' of someone dealing, and, tellingly, *not* dealing, with the 'problems of life' that are generated and brought sharply into focus by what the blind bar-keeper and one-time US diplomat Todd Jackson in *The White Countess* refers to as the 'mistrust, deceit, hatred, viciousness, and chaos' that characterises the world outside his bar (Ishiguro, 2005: 1:10:06–10).

Notes

1 As Ishiguro comments in an interview, there is 'a clear parallel between Christopher Banks's saving the world and Ryder's saving the town' (Shaffer and Wong, 2008: 164).
2 Tim Christensen argues that 'The vague yet persistent suggestion throughout this scene that the resolution of Banks's personal crisis will somehow also resolve a crisis of British imperial authority might strike the reader as strange' but that 'Ishiguro is merely foregrounding a problem of what he has termed "emotional logic"' (Christensen, 2007: 205): my suggestion would be that there is no 'merely' about it – that the illogicality cannot be dismissed and is structural, in fact, to the novel.
3 See Brian Finney's comment on the 'proliferation' of orphans in the novel (Finney, 2002: para.15). For Ishiguro's own explanation of the

metaphorical 'orphan condition' denoted by the title – orphanhood as a metaphor for 'coming out of that bubble [of childhood] in an unprotected way' (see Shaffer and Wong, 2008: 168).

4   See, for example, Luo (2003: 57–61), on the resonances of Dickens's novel in *The Unconsoled* and *When We Were Orphans*.

5   See also Ling (1982: 46), on money as 'Shanghai's *raison d'être*'.

6   See Rebecca Karni's wide-ranging Chapter 3 above for a similar account of the ways that Ishiguro's novels 'resist, even as they invoke, expectations on the levels of form, content and genre'.

7   Ishiguro is here reflecting a key dimension of immigrant-colonial communities in early twentieth-century Shanghai. Historians such as Robert Bickers have written about the socialisation of British expat and especially settler children into British habits, expectations and mores through education and other means. As Bickers comments, 'Not forgetting one was British lay at the core of the new identity acquired by recruits [to the International Settlement] and by children. Children were educated to be British, not cosmopolitan' (Bickers, 1999: 97).

8   Bain points to a later allusion to Conrad's *Heart of Darkness* in Uncle Philip's eventual explanation of the earlier events in chapter 22 (Bain, 2007: 256).

9   For Ishiguro's comments on '[t]he business of the magnifying glass' in *When We Were Orphans*, see Shaffer and Wong (2008: 187). The first sentence of the novel refers to the address of the 'small flat' in which Banks lives, 'Number 14b Bedford Gardens in Kensington' (*WWWO*: 3), the numerical specificity of which both chimes with and differs from Holmes's famous address at 221b Baker Street; and, in case we are in any doubt, we are told that the magnifying glass that Banks is given is made in Zurich in 1887 (*WWWO*: 8), which might allude both to Sherlock Holmes's first appearance in print (in the 1887 novel *A Study in Scarlet*) and to his death at the Reichenbach Falls in Switzerland in 1891 (as recounted in 'The Adventure of the Final Problem' (1893)). For other references to Conan Doyle, see Karni (2015: 344).

10 Another telling moment of apparently significant visuality involves the song 'I Only Have Eyes for You', which the shopkeeper seems to believe is a secret code when Banks goes to the record shop, as agreed, to elope with Sarah Hemmings (*WWWO*: 221). The song itself introduces further hermeneutic intrigue or blind alleys: the shopkeeper tells Banks that it is from a recent batch of records sent from England and that it is sung by Mimi Johnson. While the singer seems to be an invention, the song itself originally featured in the 1934 Busby Berkeley musical comedy *Dames* and was subsequently used in, and as the title of, a Merrie Melodies cartoon short released in 1937 – the very year in

which this scene from the novel is set. Having uncovered this detail, however, what are we to do with it?
11 Ishiguro, n.d. The folder begins with some notes from a conversation with Ishiguro's father Shizuo, dated 4 May 1997, and is followed by Ishiguro's handwritten notes on nine books. Most of the notes are undated, but the notes on Christopher Cook's *The Lion and the Dragon* (1985) date from 13 September 1995. Compare Ishiguro's comments in an interview from 2001: 'I have a pretty large collection of books at home about Shanghai during this period. I found that stuff written there at the time was the most interesting; the guidebooks published gave local histories' (Shaffer and Wong, 2008: 190).
12 From the first page of notes on Sergeant's book in Box 26.3 (Ishiguro, n.d). Ishiguro's notes start at p. 115 and end at p. 240 of Sergeant's 350-page book (they do not include any of the specific passages discussed below).
13 Compare Ishiguro's comment on pp. 137–165 of Sergeant's book (a section on 'The Abattoir of All Human Joys' in chapter 4, 'The British'): 'This chapter good on a) racism b) capitalism unregulated; the priorities of business ruling unchallenged by an enlightened vision of humanity'.
14 Sergeant's book is more detailed and shocking than other accounts but compare Barbara Baker's generalised description of the outbreak of war in 1937: 'Streets became sticky with blood and strewn with the debris of severed limbs' (Baker, 1998: 170).
15 'The most important element' in the 'mental set-up' of the Western inhabitants of Shanghai, according to one almost-contemporary commentator/historian, Ernest O. Hauser, 'was fear': 'Out here, on the frontier of the White Man's empire, three generations of taipans had lived precarious lives. They had held their few square feet of mud against the four hundred million Chinese [...] It had been a short time between shots, always, and the intervals had become shorter of late. The Shanghai man was afraid' (Hauser, 1940: 269). Security is an illusion, in other words, and is already fundamentally breached: once the Sino-Japanese war starts in August 1937, however, death 'struck anywhere, within the settlement and without' (Hauser, 1940: 313). *The White Countess* perhaps more immediately and viscerally depicts the destruction of the Western 'concessions' during this period – and, like Ishiguro's novel, is no doubt prefigurative of the events depicted in the early pages of that other notable British novel of war-torn Shanghai and the end of Empire, J.G. Ballard's *Empire of the Sun* (1984). Ishiguro's semi-historical novel is also, in complex and displaced ways, itself inevitably indebted to Ballard's semi-autobiographical novel, which is set during and after the Japanese invasion of Shanghai in 1941 (there is

a tick beside Ballard's novel in a photocopy of Sergeant's bibliography included in the Harry Ransom archive materials, seeming to indicate that Ishiguro has already read it).

16 Ishiguro, n.d. (note on p. 210 of Sergeant, *Shanghai*).

17 In an (unpublished) interview at the Oxford Literary Festival on 3 April 2019, for example, Ishiguro commented that after a person wins the Nobel Prize, 'everybody wants your opinion on everything', even on things that 'you know nothing whatsoever about', which is 'a very dangerous tendency' (Ishiguro, 2019). Ishiguro's own take on the resolution or otherwise of the ending to his novel is somewhat equivocal. In the 2001 interview with Brian Shaffer, he comments that Banks has been 'handed this broken thing at a certain point' in his life and he has to 'fix' it: by the end of the novel he 'hasn't fixed it, but at least he's kind of gotten rid of it'; the question of whether Banks has acted 'correctly or incorrectly' and whether his life 'ends on a hopeful note or not' is 'almost irrelevant' since he has been given a 'compulsive task' that he has to 'see [...] through to the end, until it's resolved in some way' (Shaffer and Wong, 2008: 170–171).

References

Bain, Alexander M. (2007). 'International Settlements: Ishiguro, Shanghai, Humanitarianism', *Novel*, 40, B240–264.

Baker, Barbara (ed.) (1998). *Shanghai: Electric and Lurid City* (Hong Kong: Oxford University Press).

Bickers, Robert A. (1999). *Britain in China: Community, Culture and Colonialism 1900–1949* (Manchester: Manchester University Press).

Christensen, Tim (2007). 'Kazuo Ishiguro and Orphanhood', *The AnaChronisT*, 13, 202–216.

Finney, Brian (2002). 'Figuring the Real: Ishiguro's *When We Were Orphans*', *Jouvert*, 7, https://legacy.chass.ncsu.edu/jouvert/v7is1/ishigu.htm (accessed June 2021).

Hauser, Ernest O. (1940). *Shanghai: City for Sale* (New York: Harcourt, Brace and Company).

Hunnewell, Susannah and Kazuo Ishiguro (2008). 'Kazuo Ishiguro: The Art of Fiction No. 196', *The Paris Review*, 184. www.theparisreview.org/interviews/5829/the-art-of-fiction-no-196-kazuo-ishiguro (accessed May 2021).

Ishiguro, Kazuo (2000). *When We Were Orphans* (London: Faber and Faber).

—. (2005). *The White Countess*, Sony, 21 December, directed by James Ivory.

—. (2019). Bodley Lecture and Award of Bodley Medal, Sheldonian Theatre, 3 April. Author's notes.

—. (n.d.) Ishiguro Papers. Harry Ransom Center, Austin, Texas.

Karni, Rebecca (2015). 'Made in Translation: Language, "Japaneseness", "Englishness", and "Global Culture" in Ishiguro', *Comparative Literature*, 52:2, 318–348.

Lacan, Jacques (1981). *The Seminar of Jacques Lacan, Book XI: The Four Fundamental Concepts of Psychoanalysis*, translated by Alan Sheridan (New York: Norton).

Ling, Pan (1982). *In Search of Old Shanghai* (Hong Kong: Joint Publishing).

Luo, Shao-Pin (2003). '"Living the Wrong Life": Kazuo Ishiguro's Unconsoled Orphans', *Dalhousie Review*, 83:1, 51–80.

Miller, Michael B. (1994). *Shanghai on the Metro: Spies, Intrigue, and the French between the Wars* (Berkeley: University of California Press).

Sergeant, Harriet (2002). *Shanghai* (London: John Murray).

Shaffer, Brian W. and Cynthia F. Wong (eds) (2008). *Conversations with Kazuo Ishiguro* (Jackson: University of Mississippi Press).

Weston, Elizabeth (2012). 'Commitment Rooted in Loss: Kazuo Ishiguro's *When We Were Orphans*', *Critique*, 53, 337–354.

7

Empathy and the ethics of posthuman reading in *Never Let Me Go*

Peter Sloane

In a seminar on what is often held to be Kazuo Ishiguro's most moving, even most human(e) fiction, *Never Let Me Go* (2005), I asked my students for their initial emotional responses. Predictably, words like tragic, futile and unethical summed up the general sentiment to this admittedly dark speculative dystopia about bioethics, bio-harvesting and 'the socially underprivileged' (Whitehead, 2011: 63). I polemically suggested that they had misread; *Never Let Me Go* is not a tragedy at all, but rather a farce, predicated on the misconception that the subjects of the novel, the therapeutic clones, are human, when they are at best posthuman, and at worst simply non-human. That is to say, *Never Let Me Go* employs narrative techniques and the very form of the novel to manipulate readers into empathising with the narrator, Kathy H. – a clone 'carer' who stoically nurses her friends as they undergo mandatory 'donations' of organs until they finally 'complete' – and through her a range of non-human characters who, though humanesque, are simply facsimiles of human beings; unwittingly succumbing to a category error, my students had read the posthuman as human, and had thus attributed to the novel an unwarranted degree of empathy by invoking categorically inappropriate ethical systems.

Richard F. Storrow also takes what might be considered a humanist approach to the posthuman text and narrator, passionately claiming that 'Embracing Kathy's story forces us to conclude that human clones are every bit as human as the rest of us if only because their lives are likewise defined by love and loss and hope' (2009: 270). Exploiting the nurturing word 'embracing' which simultaneously foregrounds the text's absence of parental love and echoes Kathy 'clutching' a 'pillow to stand in for' a baby that she can never have, Storrow's impassioned claim seems a little specious. This rather romantic idea of a person derives from a problematically Western understanding of humanism which is the subject of intense and increasing scrutiny. As Myra J. Seaman notes, 'Posthumanism observes that there has never been one unified, cohesive "human", a title that was granted by and to those with the material and cultural luxury to bestow upon themselves the faculties of "reason", autonomous agency, and the privileges of "being human"' (2007: 246–247). Love and loss and hope, then, fulfil only certain geographically, temporally and culturally specific criteria of personhood. Jeff Wallace articulates the fact that, 'under the rubric of an implicit universalism, humanism can be a narrowly Western version of liberal-humanist individualism' (2010: 693). In the wake of posthuman, post-structural, postmodern and postcolonial theory, the idea that the Western subject stands as a kind of archetypical proxy for the human subject broadly construed has been aggressively decentred in what Thomas A. Shannon refers to as the 'postgeneration' (2005: 269).

Despite her ostensibly more sceptical stance towards the credibility of a universally valent definition of 'human nature', Seaman comes to a similarly passionate conclusion about *Never Let Me Go*, arguing that, 'For the reader, the clones' experiences and responses to those experiences regularly confirm their humanity, but within the posthuman world of the narrative, their humanity must be proven [...] The clones who are the central figures of the novel are shown, through the narrative, to meet that requirement as fully as any humans' (2007: 266). Seaman's argument is more rhetorically sophisticated; clones are produced from humans, and so need to demonstrate certain behaviours that, while always arbitrary and conventional, are nonetheless vital to species categorisation. That is to say, the requirements are not only fluid but so diverse and malleable as to be, essentially, meaningless, leading to the inevitable conclusion that neither clone nor human is 'human', but that each participates in a common, but inarticulable humanity. Storrow and Seaman raise the troubling implication that our moral obligation to empathise with fictional characters, and by extension real-world entities, is predicated on their being 'like us', sharing a common 'human nature'. Indeed, if Seaman identifies the problematic fact that intra-diegetically the clones must repeatedly prove their humanity, she overlooks some of the more worrying indications that she too requires the clones to continually affirm and prove that they are human in the extra-diegetic sense. One might even suggest that this is precisely the question that the novel (and the more recent *Klara and the Sun*) poses: must something be human in order to be worthy of our identification and empathy, and, perhaps more importantly, social justice?

Attempting to answer this requires engaging with progressively more imperative issues about novel reading and readers' responses to fictions, especially those that feature non-standard human characters, being received by, perhaps, in an ever more bioengineered 'postgeneration' society, non-traditional human readers. Informed by Suzanne Keen's argument that, despite the fact that readers are endowed with the capacity 'to convert their emotional fusion with the denizens of make-believe worlds into actions on behalf of real world others', they 'rarely decide to do so' (2010: 168), this chapter's concerns with empathy are broader, highlighting the pervasive anthropocentricism evidenced in critical responses to novels, and the ways in which this reflects a more systemic unwillingness to empathise with the non-human *qua* non-human. How then do humans read posthuman texts and posthumans read human texts? If we agree with Donna Haraway's prescient polemic that 'we are *all* chimeras […] *all* cyborgs' (1991: 150 – emphasis added), perhaps *Never Let Me Go* offers a rich simulated socio-political space in which, rather than attempting to empathise with posthuman characters by tracing intersections with their humanity, the reader is encouraged to recognise their own posthumanity, to acknowledge not that *they are like us*, but that *we are like them*, and that we share constitutive differences which paradoxically unite.

This chapter examines a range of novels that explore the scientific creation of posthumans, notably *Frankenstein* (1818), *Brave New World* (1932) and *Where Late the Sweet Birds Sang* (1976), to provide a continuum within which to situate a more focused discussion of Ishiguro's novel, in turn interrogating whether the presence of affective response in the reader is either a sufficient or necessary condition to confer the nebulous status of 'human' on to other entities. Indeed N. Katherine Hayles has suggested that 'the age of the human has given way to the posthuman', that 'the concept of the human has given way to its evolutionary heir' (2016: 247), while

Nancy Armstrong, seeing a comparable paradigm shift in literature, proposes that the contemporary novel 'confront[s] us with forms of human life so innovative as to make it next to impossible for us to recognize ourselves in them' (2014: 442). With the aid of Martha Nussbaum's work in *Frontiers of Justice* (2006), this chapter is also an attempt to think through the literary implications, the ethics of reading in a world in which the human subject is, demonstrably, becoming a more fluid species. Much influential criticism of Ishiguro's novel assumes a human reader, and so, as I will argue below, participates in both the anthropocentrism and human exceptionalism which it attempts, at least in principle, to challenge. I argue here that the novel as a form has always posed questions about human nature and human identity; that empathising in and with novels does not extend to real-world altruism; and that Armstrong exemplifies a strand of criticism which assumes a human reader (ourselves) of the posthuman (other), placing an implicit bias on reading as a human. Armstrong powerfully demonstrates her thesis, that 'novels featuring an apparently damaged, subhuman, or insufficiently individuated human being prepare us to attempt the kind of sympathetic identification that novels have traditionally offered readers. They do so in order to turn a critical eye on all such person-to-person relationships' (2014: 442). However, the contemporary novel aspires to more than simply 'person-to-person' relationships: both text and reader are undergoing an epistemological and even ontological resituating in relation to the refiguration of the humanities to the posthumanities in what Francis Fukuyama somewhat anxiously refers to as the '"posthuman" stage of history' (2003: 7). Indeed one might consider Ishiguro to be advocating for a neo-humanism, a recognition of species fluidity alongside a commitment to extending both empathy and rights to the traditionally post- or non-human.

Posthuman fictions

Armstrong's claim that the contemporary novel challenges the reader to the degree that it represents a 'sea change in the traditional subject of fiction' is persuasive (2014: 442). That said, much earlier fiction grapples with questions of the limits of the human and the efficacy of the novel as a catalyst for both sympathy and real-world altruism.

We might consider *Frankenstein* the first text to construct an imaginary scenario within which to explore the ethical and theological implications of the scientific production of a humanoid non-human. If, as Storrow has suggested, cloning is conceived to be an 'an affront to human dignity' because human clones 'lack a connection to two genetic parents' (2009: 259), this affront is exacerbated by the monster's uncanny virtue of being composed of many corporeal 'parents' but of being born of none of these. The literary and cultural resonance of Shelley's ground-breaking work of Gothic science fiction is immeasurable, while it is also adduced as an allegory for the dangers of unregulated scientific endeavour. Michael Mulkay draws attention to the novel's frequent use in popular press, and in official discourse shortly after the advent of the biotechnological revolution in the latter part of the last century, quoting a prominent newspaper's (*The Sun*, 1987) claim that 'The Government admits that the prospect of Frankenstein-style experiments is unlikely, but it wants to stop any genetic tinkering with embryos which would predetermine characteristics' (1996: 161). Mulkay shows that *Frankenstein* has been used as an exemplum of the potential harms of genetic engineering to support a 'proposal to establish strict control over the activities of scientists engaged in research on human embryos' (1996: 161). This intersection between science fiction and real-world regulation of the sciences supports Amit Marcus's hypothesis that science fiction and clone narratives 'can provide insights pertinent to the ethics of human cloning in actuality' (2012: 407).

These precautions reflect initial widespread religious, scientific, political and public fears about genetic modification, cloning, new eugenics and even 'designer babies'. But the uncertainty also represents more abstract and philosophical worries about whether 'the eugenic or dysgenic effects of genetic engineering could ever become sufficiently widespread to affect human nature itself' (Fukuyama, 2003: 80). Wallace sees Fukuyama as representing a 'popular' as opposed to a 'critical' strand of posthumanism, describing his position as a 'reactionary' response to biotechnology perceived as a threat to the 'integrity of human nature' (2010: 692). Indeed, despite never offering any kind of precise definition of human nature, Fukuyama anxiously asserts that 'human nature exists, is a meaningful concept, and has provided a stable continuity to our experience as a species', proposing that the 'most significant threat posed by contemporary biotechnology is the possibility that it will alter human nature and thereby move us into the "posthuman" stage of history' (2003: 7). Such amorphous and seemingly irrational fears over the potential harms of genetic engineering abated somewhat around the turn of the millennium, shortly after the completion of the human genome project, with one 'major recent advance [being] the emerging consensus on the acceptability of stem cell research' (Singer, 2000: 283). However, there remains an unease in the twenty-first century about genetic manipulation, and the science seems to have stalled in the face of strict regulation and nebulous public repugnance.

Frankenstein is also fascinated with the ways that texts and reading influence behaviour and foster community. Reading is a recurring and highly potent motif at every level of the narrative: Victor Frankenstein frequently expounds excitedly upon his avid, obsessive reading which, inevitably, leads to or facilitates his own monstrous transgression. But, where Victor reads the sciences and to a degree loses what we might think of as his humanity, it is from the arts that the monster develops some insight into the human condition, recalling that Goethe's *The Sorrows of Young Werther* and Milton's *Paradise Lost* evoked in him 'an infinity of new images and feelings', finally provoking the fundamental question of the novel: 'Who was I? What was I? Whence did I come? What was my destination?' (2012: 89). The monster is forced in his exposure to human literature to acknowledge simultaneously his radical physical and experiential alterity, and the fact that his difference does not render him incapable of inter-species empathy. Without evolutionary or cultural history, ancestors or the possibility of genetic progeny, his situation gives rise to a series of unique existential uncertainties. However, as a posthuman he is still able to respond to human texts, and, to have an expectation that literature is the place to seek a sense of community and fellow feeling. The monster is a compassionate posthuman reader with a clear concern for a species that is not his, and with a powerfully acute, preternaturally perceptive awareness of his own difference, each of which is mediated by the precariousness of his position as the single member of his species (hence the desire for a mate).

A similar scenario occurs in *Brave New World*, a novel peopled entirely with clones produced through a procedure known as 'Bokanovsky's Process'. The Director observes gleefully that they, the World State, have traversed 'the realm of mere slavish imitation of nature into the much more interesting world of human invention' (Huxley, 2007: 10). Jean Baudrillard has called cloning the 'delirious apotheosis of a productive technology' (2002: 97), and this jubilant, celebratory mood is shared by the Director. Tellingly, reading plays a crucial role in the novel, in terms of its major plot points but also its conceptual matrix. Bernard Marx, the novel's absurd hero, recounts finding a volume of Shakespeare, recalling with reverence the 'words and the strange, strange story out of which they were taken (he couldn't make head or tail of it, but it was wonderful, wonderful all the same)' (2007: 114). The genre-standard counterpoint to the high-living World State Marx, John the Savage, raised in nature in the reservations outside the city walls, is equally taken with Shakespeare. During one scene John recites *Romeo and Juliet* for Marx and Helmholtz, the novel's intellectual, who suffers a bout of what Marx refers to as 'obscene' laughter, before declaring, '"But fathers and mothers!" He shook his head. "You can't expect me to keep a straight face about fathers and mothers. And who's going to get excited about a boy having a girl or not having her?"' (2007: 162). In this passage a posthuman product of selective breeding and cloning, living in a society that operates on a basis of 'all for all' in sexual terms, reads a definitively human text and finds it comedic precisely because the interpersonal relationships portrayed, the fascination with romantic love and monogamy, are socio-culturally ridiculous in the context of the World State. The passage draws our attention to the politico-historical and cultural specificity of what we think of as both human value and human essence. The posthuman reading of the human presented in both texts reveals some interesting things about the nature of being human, and the inherently contingent and constructivist nature of what might traditionally be thought of as Human Nature.

Clones are the subject of Kate Wilhelm's novel of environmental catastrophe and worldwide famine *Where Late the Sweet Birds Sang*. As flu strains and plagues ravage the population, a research group led by David Sumner begin researching animal cloning and fertility, at which point they realise that the men and women in their commune of around two hundred have become sterile. The impetus naturally shifts to perpetuating their own species. In this novel, unlike *Frankenstein* and *Never Let Me Go*, clones are not sterile – they only become less sterile by the fourth generation. After overseeing the production of the first successful batch of clones, David remarks to his uncle Walt that 'They're inhuman, aren't they' (2006: 47). However, the clones rapidly develop their own sense of community, one that is aggressively distinct from that of their human creators. As the clone W-1 says to David, 'we realized that each of you is alone. We're not like you David [...] sexual reproduction is not the only answer. Just because the higher organisms evolved to it, it doesn't mean it's the best. Each time a species has died out, there has been another higher one to replace it [...] You pay a high price for individuality' (2006: 60). There is a suggestion here that what makes human beings distinct is also what leads, inevitably, to their decline. Jerng remarks on the text's preoccupation with individuation, concluding that 'the question of individuation is used to distinguish clones from humans: clones are depicted as beings who are unable to individuate [...] The humans are distinguished by these traits because they are reared within the parent–child relationship, which provides a site for this form of maturation and separation' (2008: 369–370). So crucial is this differentiation that the clones form a committee and decide that they are a separate species. After David attempts to sabotage the cloning operation, he is brought before the clones, who tell him that 'We agree now that there is still the instinct to preserve one's species. Preservation of the species is a very strong instinct, a drive if you will'; David replies with alarm that 'You are not a separate species' (2006: 66). David is banished, and, later, while surveying the destruction of the cities, the clones remark that it was 'done by savages', 'another species, extinct now' (2006: 90).

A similar technique is used by Michel Houellebecq in *La Possibilité d'une île* (2003), which develops the conceit of Samuel Beckett's *Krapp's Last Tape* (1958). Houellebecq's central character, Daniel1 records his life, his memories, his consciousness, which is then reflected upon in a post-apocalyptic future by Daniel24, his own clone around a thousand years in the future, who looks back less than favourably on his human forebear's exploits. Perhaps, though, this is because Daniel1's obsession with sex, and his existential anxiety are almost cosmically anachronistic: Adams suggests in his review of the novel that 'In the absence of the necessity of sex and death, the post-human clones have found that all human emotion has, over the centuries, become extinct' (2005a). It is hard to dispute the idea that, due to the manner in which clones are conceived, gestated, birthed and raised, their sense of communal identity, their means of reproduction and their unique cultural heritage, Frankenstein's monster, Daniel24, and the clones in Wilhelm's novel are in fact a distinct variety of intelligent life. Daniel24 certainly thinks so, commenting on the remaining humans that 'For them I feel no pity, nor any sense of common belonging; I simply consider them to be slightly more intelligent monkeys' (2006: 17). However, *Where Late the Sweet Birds Sang* turns away from its more interesting premises; Molly, individuated after spending time outside the community, is exiled and has a child with another clone. Eventually, that child leads a group of fertile females away, reproduces sexually, only to return after twenty years to discover that the clone community has died out. One might argue of course that the novel, written during the Cold War, enacts the failure of both the communist and capitalist ideals, showing that neither radical communitarian politics nor radically individualistic politics is tenable. It also makes some interesting points about obsolescence and species differentiation that have resurfaced in two recent films, Alex Garland's *Ex Machina* (2015) and Spike Jonze's *Her* (2013): in each of these films it is the AI, the synthetic human consciousness that outstrips, outgrows and eventually abandons its less capable human ancestor.

One concern raised by the humans in these texts, and *Never Let Me Go*, is that something is lost in the manner of duplication, and, further, that the thing that is lost will have a profound impact on human society and development. That may be the soul, human dignity or simply 'human nature'. Importantly, whatever is intuited or assumed to be missing also often leads to scientifically produced human or humanlike forms being considered simply non-human, even inhumane, and generally being excluded from basic human rights or comparable non-human rights. Baudrillard addresses some of the reasons for this in 'Clone Story', in which he draws a comparison between the mechanically reproduced clone and the printed text. He refers to Walter Benjamin's suggestion that what is lost in a 'work that is serially reproduced, is its *aura*, its singular quality', suggesting that this 'is what happens to us with cloning, no longer at the level of message, but at the level of individuals' (2002: 99). Something is lost, according to Baudrillard, in the human subject, something that replicates, re-enacts, even paradoxically duplicates that which is lost in the mechanical reproduction of works of art or literature. Copying seems to disinvest, to render something empty, missing some profound, and profoundly intangible, quality. For Baudrillard, in cloning, 'the subject is also gone, since by identical duplication' the key 'mirror stage [is] abolished in cloning, or rather it is parodied therein in monstrous fashion' (2002: 97). However, fabrication, replication and simulation are central to the contemporary experience of being human, and may in fact represent a future that will be, inevitably, more mechanised, more bioengineered, more complex in the figuration of reproduction. These fears then seem to belong to a past age.

Never Let Me Go

Never Let Me Go shares concerns (family, friendship, service, failure) and a narrative perspective that are central to Ishiguro's other novels; like them, it is narrated by a person who 'looks back over his or her life in old age' (Shaffer and Wong, 2008: 114). Tragically, in this case old age for the narrator Kathy H. is thirty-one: she opens her memoir by telling us that she's 'been a carer now for over eleven years', but that she will only be a carer 'until the end of this year' (*NLMG*: 3), after which, presumably, she will become a donor, and will 'complete', or die, usually after the fourth organ removal. *Never Let Me Go* is interested in memory, fabrication, a fetishisation of the modernist aesthetic of the unreliable narrator and, foremost, a preoccupation with dignity which recurs in Ono (*An Artist of the Floating World*), Stevens (*The Remains of the Day*) and Ryder (*The Unconsoled*). There is a further refinement in this novel: it is *human* dignity that is in question, because human dignity is precisely what is assumed to be missing in cloned humans, Baudrillard's and Benjamin's 'aura'. Indeed policy on cloning has been directly driven by this vague concept, with UNESCO's Universal Declaration on the Human Genome and Human Rights recommending a ban on 'practices which are contrary to human dignity, such as reproductive cloning' (UNESCO, 1997).

In an interview with Tim Adams of *The Guardian* Ishiguro said that the novel, which takes place predominantly in a clone boarding school called Hailsham, is an allegory for childhood and parenting: 'Hailsham is like a physical manifestation of what we have to do to all children [...] It is a protected world. To some extent at least you have to shield children from what you know and drip-feed information to them. Sometimes that is kindly meant, and sometimes not' (Adams, 2005b). Trauma is a recurring theme of Ishiguro's works, and, with memory, a related theme, has become the standard point of critical reception. I have argued elsewhere (Sloane, 2018) that trauma does not account for, or mitigate, some of the more reprehensible behaviour that Ishiguro's narrators confess to in their reflective narratives (Nazi appeasement in *The Remains of the Day*, support for the Imperial Japanese ideology of prewar Japan in *An Artist of the Floating World*). This holds true for Kathy, too, who is remarkably passive towards, and even participates in, a brutal programme of organ harvesting. Yet, despite the horrors masked by the façade of care, in comparison to earlier incarnations of clone rearing, Hailsham is indeed something of a sanctuary, one that nurtures and protects the clones in ways which were advanced. As the 'guardians' Madame and Miss Emily inform Kathy and her friend Tommy near the novel's end, 'there are students being reared in deplorable conditions, conditions you Hailsham students could hardly imagine. And now we're no more, things will only get worse' (*NLMG*: 255). While the word 'reared' at once recalls the 'hatcheries' of *Brave New World* and betrays some less admirable sentiments, indicating perhaps that underneath a surface of empathy is a fear and recognition of the clone's radical otherness, there is none the less a degree of care that one might think of as an allegory for protecting children from the very many bad things happening in the world.

The novel's title offers a key to understanding what it has to say about empathy. It is taken from the fictional song of the same name, one that Kathy listens to and is absorbed by. The song, as Kathy remarks, is 'slow and late night and American' (*NLMG*: 69). Kathy listens to the song over and over, and in one crucial scene she is observed by Madame while she dances, lovingly, desperately grasping a pillow. Later, when Kathy and Tommy track down the old school managers after Hailsham is closed, Kathy tells Madame that she 'imagined it was about this woman who'd been told she couldn't have babies. But then she'd had one, and she was so pleased, and she was holding it ever so tightly to her breast, really afraid something might separate them, and she's going baby, baby, never let me go' (*NLMG*: 266). Madame, however, misinterprets Kathy's reasons for dancing in the manner that she does, and so imposes on to the performance of the posthuman something that is misplaced and which involves a degree of socio-cultural awareness about both society and their place within it from which the clones are precluded:

> When I watched you dancing that day, I saw something else. I saw a new world coming rapidly. More scientific, efficient, yes. More cures for the old sicknesses. Very good. But a harsh, cruel world. And I saw a little girl, her eyes tightly closed, holding to her breast the old kind world, one that she knew in her heart could not remain, and she was holding it and pleading, never to let her go. That is what I saw. It wasn't really you, what you were doing, I know that. But I saw you and it broke my heart. And I've never forgotten. (*NLMG*: 266)

Indicated here, explicitly in the line 'it wasn't really you', is the fact that empathy is not an emotion that has to do with the subject that is empathised with, but rather the subject empathising: in that sense empathy is a purely theoretical construct, a function of the imagination, as opposed to a transitive, outwardly directed one. Ishiguro presents us with a song that itself is problematic – it is about a romantic love that is the illusory product of American popular culture, one that perhaps gives rise to a conception of human nature as involving 'love and loss and hope' and which thus contributes to the distinctively contemporary and distinctively Western conception of the human being. Further, the work of art is merely the catalyst for one response from posthuman and sterile Kathy, and a second response from human Madame, while the misalignment provokes a third response from the reader. There is even a degree of insensitivity here: Kathy has never known an 'old kind world'; for her the world has, and always will be 'harsh, cruel'. Given this, the young girl that is the subject of Madame's empathy cannot be Kathy, and so the affective bond is doubly illusory. Perhaps Madame even, mirroring Kathy's fantasy, imagines that Kathy is the child that she might have had, and the child that she may have found herself unable to nurture, to protect. Importantly, the tape is a clone of an original recording. This fact is foregrounded when Kathy's tape goes missing, and her friend Tommy finds another, identical copy, notably while they are on a trip to Norfolk to try to locate their 'originals', something that poses a fascination for the clones. At the centre of the misunderstanding is the 'me' of the song's title: for the human subject it is about autonomy, individuation, a being in a cultural, political and social world that is constructed for and around it. For the posthuman subject, the clone, that 'me' has an altogether different status, and requires an act of imagination to make relevant, to facilitate empathy.

Empathy, then, in its relation to the work of art, initiates a response that is only tangentially related to that work and the subjects depicted therein. Not only does this imply that the novel is about misreading, as many of Ishiguro's ambiguous and often deceptive first-person novels are, it also exploits the feeling generated in the recipient, that is to say the reader. The novel as a form manipulates the fundamental human capacity for empathy, especially, as Keen notes, first-person fiction, which 'more readily evokes feeling responsiveness' (2010: 215). Indeed there is a tendency in discussions of empathetic responses to read too much into the implication that what is being empathised with is necessarily human. In their introduction to *Rethinking Empathy through Literature,* Hammond and Kim begin by suggesting that the collection 'challenges common understandings of empathy', only to then define empathy studies as investigating 'how "thinking with" or "feeling with" another happens' (2014: 1) within or because of literary texts. Keen is perhaps guilty of precisely this anthropocentric assumption: although she concedes that 'Humans feel empathy. We aren't the only animals to do so', she also defines empathy as 'a vicarious, spontaneous sharing of affect, [that] can be provoked by witnessing another's emotional state, by hearing about another's condition, or even by reading' (2010: 6, 208). Underlying this definition of empathy is a presupposition, even a requirement, that it is a person, 'another', that facilitates or even necessitates 'feeling responsiveness'. However, popular culture shows us that human beings empathise with, and enjoy the consoling and valorising illusion that they empathise with, all manner of fictive quasi-sentient entities, including orphaned deer, Buzz Lightyear toys, Minions and even, in Quentin Dupiex's recent film *Rubber* (2010), a somewhat psychotic car tyre. Keen argues that 'narratives in prose and film infamously manipulate our feelings and call upon out built-in capacity to feel with others' (2010: 209), but that evocation is not dependent upon, or does not necessarily entail, that the recipients are human.

Anne Whitehead develops Keen's work, also disputing Nussbaum's claim that reading is 'productive of an empathetic sensibility, and such a sympathy [is] an inherently moral virtue' (2011: 55). She also shares Keen's dissatisfaction with Nussbaum's hypothesis that empathy generated in and for fictional worlds can 'result in altruistic' behaviour in the real world. To suggest that it can is to place 'too great a burden on both empathy and the novel' (Keen, 2010: 168). In *Poetic Justice* Nussbaum does indeed make some bold claims for the novel as a tool for simulating scenarios and stimulating change: 'The novel constructs a paradigm of a style of ethical reasoning that is context-specific without being relativistic, in which we get potentially universizable concrete prescriptions by bringing a general idea of human flourishing to bear on a concrete situation, which we are invited to enter through the imagination' (1995: 8). This pre-empts Marcus's (2012) conviction that science fiction 'can provide insights pertinent to the ethics of human cloning in actuality'; both argue that the act of reading fosters a sense of ethical engagement that extends beyond the page. As a result, Nussbaum proposes, as Whitehead sees it, 'literature is central to the functioning of a healthy democratic society' (2011: 54). Both Keen and Whitehead are interested in *failed empathy*, and its tendency to 'lament the inefficiency of shared feelings in provoking action that would lead to positive social or political change'; and *false empathy*, which emphasises the 'self-congratulatory delusions of those who incorrectly believe that they have caught the feelings of suffering others' (Keen, 2010: 159).

Much emphasis is placed on the benefits of reading in *Never Let Me Go*; the clones are encouraged to read, particularly Victorian fictions, 'a lot of nineteenth-century stuff by Thomas Hardy and people like that', especially, as Whitehead remarks, Nussbaum's personal favourite George Eliot (*NLMG*: 97). Whitehead argues that this is a practice employed by the guardians of Hailsham to make the clones more human, and perhaps even more sensitive and empathetic carers. But she asks rhetorically whether 'the Victorian novels that the clones read, articulate entirely misleading and inappropriate hopes and desires', that they produce 'false hope' (2011: 72). Whitehead sees in Kathy a remarkable 'lack of maturity or growth [which] is in particularly marked contrast to the Victorian novels that she herself reads, both at Hailsham and the Cottages, which offer her a range of variations on the themes of self-development' (2011: 70). Evident here is that the novels do not in fact reflect the manner in which clones mature or fail to mature; they are, as Kathy herself tells us in relation to sex education, 'more or less useless' (*NLMG*: 97). If that is the case, then the *Bildungsroman* would be an alien narrative that would not inspire empathy in characters that clearly in the text do not mature or develop in any meaningful sense. However, this estrangement from standard narratives is also true of John the Savage and Marx in *Brave New World*: Shakespeare is entirely 'strange' to them, and the world and emotions he describes largely redundant. This is why Helmholtz is inspired to write new literature that reflects his condition. Keen and Whitehead read Nussbaum through *Not for Profit*, and *Poetic Justice*, two works that deal largely with the importance in empathetic, socio-political and therapeutic settings that involve human beings and the relationships that texts establish, a nexus of concern between text, reader and society. Whitehead suggests that the novel is about the 'complex entanglement of human relations', and in her logic novels necessarily exclude the post/non-human.

Hailsham is in fact a special case, and the education that the 'students' receive is a vital ingredient in the project; it is an experiment to prove that 'if students were reared in humane, cultivated environments, it was possible for them to grow to be as sensitive and intelligent as any ordinary human being' while also fostering a universal sense that clones should 'take their place in society' (*NLMG*: 256). Part of the assessment process involves the art and creative writing classes at the school, where paintings and poetry would be produced, and some taken away by the guardians (I shall discuss this more below). The project is overseen by Madame (Marie-Claude) and Miss Emily. Late in the novel, when Kathy and Tommy visit these two after Hailsham has been closed, Miss Emily remarks that 'Marie-Claude worked hard for our project. And the way it all ended has left her feeling somewhat disillusioned. As for myself, whatever the disappointments, I don't feel so badly about it. I think what we achieved merits some respect. Look at the two of you. You've turned out well' (*NLMG*: 251). What is suggested here is that there is a set of human-posthuman entanglements, empathetic connections between Madame, Miss Emily and the students of Hailsham, ones that at least are suggestive of a powerful bond of care.

However, Kathy recalls an incident in which Marie-Claude came into direct contact with the students and Kathy saw her 'shudder', thinking that the custodians were 'afraid of us in the same way someone might be afraid of spiders' (*NLMG*: 85).[1] Miss Emily admits that:

> 'We're *all* afraid of you. I myself had to fight back my dread of you all almost every day I was at Hailsham. There were times I'd look down at you all from my study window and I'd feel such revulsion ...' She stopped, then something in her eyes flashed again. 'But I was determined not to let such feelings stop me doing what was right. I fought those feelings and I won'. (*NLMG*: 264)

Crucial here is that the guardians recognise that the clones are not human, but that it is still the *right* thing to care for and to try to help them, not because they are human, because that is not the case, but because they are posthuman, but sentient. The winning here involves overcoming not a theoretical response to the clones as we the reader might have at a distance mediated by text, but a feeling of visceral repulsion in direct contact, a contact that the novel precludes between reader and subject. As Whitehead and Keen both suggest, the novel enacts a kind of nexus of care, but not one that necessarily extends into extra-textual altruism. The visceral response is something of an evolutionary defence, as Nussbaum proposes, 'The core objects of disgust are reminders of mortality and animality, seen as pollutants to the human' (2004: 99). Leon Kass, as Jean Bethke Elshtain notes, discusses shuddering in relation to failed clones of Dolly the sheep, but asks some deeper questions, suggesting that we should be mindful of those things we find '"offensive," "repulsive," or "distasteful"', that 'repugnance may be the only voice left that speaks up to defend the central core of our humanity. Shallow are the souls that have forgotten how to shudder' (2005: 167). If shuddering is an indicator of some profound sense of ethical or moral repugnance, one that is not abstract, then the guardians' response to the clones might in fact indicate that they are uncannily, frighteningly other, non-human.

In their discussions with Madame and Miss Emily, Tommy and Ruth develop an awareness of the truth about their situation, and about their relationship with human beings. As Madame notes, there is a fear, and a double standard: 'It's one thing to create students, such as yourselves, for the donation programme. But a generation of created children who'd take their place in society? Children demonstrably superior to the rest of us? Oh no. That frightened people. They recoiled from that' (*NLMG*: 258–259). However, of central importance to this chapter and the reading of posthuman texts that depend on empathy is the continued suggestion, in the novel, that being human is the criterion for care. As Madame remarks, 'However uncomfortable people were about your existence, their overwhelming concern was that their own children, their spouses, their parents, their friends, did not die from cancer, motor neurone disease, heart disease [...] they tried to convince themselves you weren't really like us. That you were less than human, so it didn't matter' (*NLMG*: 259). At stake here is the empathetic and ethical value of the novel as a form, not simply because it might not, as Keen and Whitehead argue in contradistinction to Nussbaum, extend to the real world, but because it is predicated on the presence of human beings. The question raised in this text, peopled with characters that are not human in vital ways, is why it is imperative to prove human status to accord value and justice and basic rights to another species. Nussbaum, thinking through the implications of John Rawls's seminal work of political ethics, *A Theory of Justice* (1971), recalls his statement 'that animals lack those properties of human beings "in virtue of which they are to be treated in accordance with the principles of justice" (504)' (2006: 331). The properties are however held by clones: 'a capacity for a conception of the good and a capacity for a sense of justice' (2006: 331). Regardless of whether the entity that possesses these capacities is human, Nussbaum argues, it is unjust not to accord full rights to them. Of course, today, animal rights and social justice are top of the agenda, but these should not involve demonstrating similitude to human behaviour as the determining criteria: empathy is to empathise, not to be empathised with.

Sex and sexual reproduction are perhaps the single most common theme in speculative fictions: as with *Where Late the Sweet Birds Sang*, Margaret Atwood's *The Handmaid's Tale* (1985), Orwell's *Nineteen Eighty-Four* (1949), Marge Piercy's *Woman on the Edge of Time* (1986) and numerous other important examples hypothesise dilemmas which arise from, or result in, changes to human reproduction. Questions of procreation, however, provoke more pervasive unease about asexual reproduction, as Stephen E. Levick remarks, 'by removing the sexual glue heretofore necessary for human reproduction, [reproductive cloning] may fundamentally undermine the family as the most fundamental basis of society' (2004: 226). After being informed that they cannot reproduce, *Never Let Me Go*'s clones are told that 'sex affects [human] emotions in ways you'd never expect': 'people out there were different from us students: they could have babies from sex [...] even though, as we knew, it was completely impossible for any of us to have babies, out there, we had to behave like them. We had to respect the rules and treat sex as something pretty special' (*NLMG*: 82). This meditation is remarkably reminiscent to Helmholtz's rhetorical question as to 'who's going to get excited about a boy having a girl or not having her?' As a result of her inability to feel and think about sex as a reproductive as opposed to simply a pleasurable act, Kathy is ostensibly excluded from what has traditionally, in conventional and patriarchal societies, been conceived of as a fundamental component of being human. Simulacra that they undeniably are, they must *perform* humanness, behave 'like' a 'them' which defines a category that is irretrievably other by the same logic. This is troubling; if we return to Seaman's suggestion that 'The clones who are the central figures of the novel are shown, through the narrative, to meet that requirement as fully as any humans'; they may well be simulating human behaviour in the way that, for example, Data in *Star Trek: The Next Generation* tries and fails, the female extra-terrestrial of Jonathan Glazer's *Under the Skin* (2013), Deckard and the replicants in *Blade Runner* (1982) and *Blade Runner 2049* (2017), and the Cylons in *Battlestar Galactica* manage more successfully. *Never Let Me Go* takes the concept of performativity beyond the question of gender, provocatively suggesting that those aspects of being human which appear most fundamental, intransient, pancultural are subject to cultural and discursive remodulation.

Perhaps the most tragic part of *Never Let Me Go* is the idea of 'deferment'. In Hailsham, the artworks that the clones are required to produce serve two purposes: they are either sold or swapped with other inmates, or, more exceptionally, taken by Madame for what in the text is referred to as her 'gallery'. A consoling rumour develops among the clones that exceptional works are selected for inclusion in this mythical gallery because they 'reveal their souls'.

However, and much to the profound disappointment of Kathy and Tommy, Madame corrects them: 'Well, you weren't far wrong about that. We took away your art because we thought it would reveal your souls. Or to put it more finely, we did it *to prove you had souls at all*' (*NLMG*: 255). Kathy and her peers also come to believe, possibly because of Kathy's own propensity for circulating fantastic rumours, that if two clones 'could prove they were properly in love that they can get their donations put back for three years' (*NLMG*: 151). Once more this fabulous word 'love' reappears, with the implication that it is (1) definitional of humanity and (2) sufficiently sacred to confer, however temporarily, life and rights on the non-human. Again, here, it is not enough that the pictures demonstrate a worldview, an intelligent and affective response to the world, but they are used to put on 'large events all around the country [...] "There, look!" we could say. "Look at this art! How dare you claim these children are anything less than fully human?"' (*NLMG*: 256). This insidious assumption that humanness is a necessary condition for empathy and rights manifests in readings of texts which feature posthumans, such as *Never Let Me Go*, scholarship of which takes for granted that the clones are sufficiently similar to us to warrant empathy *by virtue of that similarity.*

After leaving Hailsham, Tommy spends his spare time sketching what Kathy refers to as 'fantastic creatures'. He tells Kathy, 'It's like they come to life by themselves. Then you have to draw in all these different details for them. You have to think about how they'd protect themselves, how they'd reach things' (*NLMG*: 176). Kathy is impressed, if a little confused:

> The first impression was like one you'd get if you took the back off a radio set: tiny canals, weaving tendons, miniature screws and wheels were all drawn with obsessive precision [...] For all their busy, metallic features, there was something sweet, even vulnerable about each of them. I remembered him telling me, in Norfolk, that he worried, even as he created them, how they'd protect themselves or be able to reach and fetch things, and looking at them now, I could feel the same sort of concerns. (*NLMG*: 184–185)

It seems important, here, that the guardians of Hailsham refer to Tommy, Kathy and the clones as creatures, rhetorically asking, with sincere emotion: 'Poor creatures. What did we do to you? With all our schemes and plans?' (*NLMG*: 249). Tommy, however, is sensitive to the needs of a species that are at once imaginary but to him viable: in creating, he accepts responsibility to ensure that the creatures are capable of self-care. His concerns are with their needs, drawing attention not to any use function they may have as machines but to the needs of the imaginary created animal and how it can serve its own ends in its pursuit of the good. Importantly, in a shared moment of posthuman bonding, Kathy can also 'feel' and therefore share both Tommy's concern and the plight of the creatures. This reflects Steven Pinker's more inclusive notion of empathy as 'the ability to put oneself into the position of some other person, animal, or object, and imagine that sensation of being in that situation' (quoted in Hammond and Kim, 2014: 8). Tommy's artwork gestures towards such an inclusive and non-anthropocentric conception of empathy, one not predicated on 'person-to-person' compassion. Indeed there is a profound intimacy to this moment in which Tommy shares with Kathy, reveals to her his vulnerable progeny and in this moment he entrusts to her not simply their care but his too, as he moves toward completion.

Of course, tragically, Tommy's own creatures are used to draw our attention to the awful fact that the clones cannot protect themselves, and even more troublingly for certain critics demonstrate no desire to do so. Whitehead comments on Kathy's 'frustrating passivity' when she does not seek 'any form of reprisal from the system' (2011: 73). It is conceivable, however, that genetic engineering has rendered them passive, incapable of revolt because they have not been designed to 'protect themselves'. Tommy's creatures represent perhaps both literary representation, fantastic textual creatures in the small pages of a book, and the possibility of genetic manipulation. He however also manages here, as he does elsewhere, to intuit the brutal reality of his passivity, his coded inability to rebel, and so ensures that his creations will be capable of resisting similar fates.

Ishiguro poses questions about artistic expression in the broadest sense. This notion of having souls, and having souls and experiencing 'real love' as a fundamental criterion for being conferred the status of personhood, is of course a hangover from early Greek philosophy and its fascination with metempsychosis (a key word in *Ulysses*

(1920), and played on in David Foster Wallace's *Infinite Jest* (1996) in the character Madame Psychosis), and Judaeo-Christian beliefs which were instrumental in the formation of Western civilisation. Nussbaum proposes, convincingly, that a *capabilities* approach to social justice, one grounded in the idea of flourishing, both human and non-human, might enable a broader definition, and so application, of justice. As she notes, 'A truly global justice requires not simply looking across the world for other fellow species members who are entitled to a decent life. It also requires looking, both in one's own nation and around the world, at other sentient beings with whose lives our own are inextricably and complexly entwined' (2006: 406). This brings to mind Whitehead's phrase concerning the 'complex entanglement of human relations'. If we return to Nussbaum's, Whitehead's and Keen's comments about narrative empathy, we might think more about the ways in which the novel form can facilitate inter-group empathy with a range of new varieties of human life. That is to say, there is something a little reductive about concluding with Hayles that we have always been posthuman; technology is radically affecting the nature of being human, and literature can provide an empathetic bridge to newer forms of *homo* life.

Indeed many theorists and writers have seen an inevitable move towards an eventual bifurcation of the species. As Diane B. Paul remarks, 'H.G. Wells describes a future in which humanity has split into two species [...] Peter Sloterdijk anticipates a division of humanity into genetic engineers and the genetically engineered [...] Lee Silver predicts that in the distant future the species will break into two, the "genrich" and the "normal"' (2005: 134). Although these may be in the very distant future, society already contains a host of radically different experiences, ones that, in some cases, question the possibility of humanity being a single species. Literature is at the forefront of bridging these existential and empathetic spaces, between different cultures and histories and sexualities. As Jerng notes, much speculative fiction bears out 'Paul John Eakin's concern that "normative models of personhood" will be used to judge others as "lacking in the very nature of [their] being"' (2008: 371). If human narratives involve love, the sanctity of sex, childbirth, developing and radical independence, self-development, then they exclude lives that do not touch upon these co-ordinates. Literature, the novel, must be more open to non-standard narratives, if it is to remain relevant and perhaps even an important spur to social justice as the ways of being human and posthuman multiply.

Now, in the posthuman world, literary fiction may provide an invaluable vehicle to acknowledge the many sub-species that genus *Homo* seems on the brink of fragmenting into. As Armstrong proposes, 'By forcing us to feel beyond the present limits of personhood, for all we know, contemporary novels may be developing a generation of readers with an emotional repertoire more attuned to the demands of our time' (2014: 464). That is not by conferring or refusing to confer the status of human being, and therefore empathising in that way, but, as Nussbaum argues, by recognising that flourishing and the desire to flourish, having preferences as Peter Singer suggests, warrant justice, and equality. However, we as readers need to also acknowledge that our responses, at a distance, outside the text, away from possible contamination, give us an illusion about our capacity for real-world empathy. We witness Frankenstein's 'breathless horror and disgust' (Shelley, 2012: 36) on first seeing his creation; Madame 'shudder' at the feelings of 'dread' and 'revulsion' on coming into direct contact with the clones that she so deeply cares for; David's assertion that his clones, of himself and his family, were 'inhuman'. It should suggest to us that literature presents an imaginative access to empathy only, and that, in actuality, we would likely share in the responses of these characters: how many times do we recoil from racial or sexual slurs in a canonical work of fiction, from the idea of slavery, of anti-Semitism, and from the comfort of an armchair sit securely in the knowledge that we would never behave like that, with such inhumanity. Another possibility is that we recoil at the uncanny horror of self-recognition – in these characters we see mirrored our own fragility as a species and are forced to recognise our kinship with the posthuman. This then is the ethic of posthuman reading, which might then be more appropriately described as neo-humanism.

Note

1 This scene is perhaps inspired by *Gulliver's Travels*, when Gulliver is tiny in Brobdingnag and his master's wife 'screamed and ran back [when

first seeing him], as women in England do at the sight of a toad or a spider' (Swift, 2003: 35).

References

Adams, Tim (2005a). 'The Book of Daniels', *The Guardian*, 30 October, www.theguardian.com/books/2005/oct/30/fiction.michelhouellebecq (accessed May 2021).
—. (2005b). '"For me, England is a mythical place": An Interview with Kazuo Ishiguro', *The Guardian*, 20 February, www.theguardian.com/books/2005/feb/20/fiction.kazuoishiguro (accessed May 202).
Armstrong, Nancy (2014), 'The Affective Turn in Contemporary Fiction', *Contemporary Literature*, 55: 441–465.
Baudrillard, Jean (2002). *Simulacra and Simulation*, translated by Sheila Faria Glaser (Ann Arbor: University of Michigan Press).
Elshtain, Jean Bethke (2005). 'The Body and the Quest for Control', in Harold W. Baillie and Timothy K. Casey (eds), *Is Human Nature Obsolete: Genetics, Bioengineering, and the Future of the Human Condition* (Cambridge, MA: MIT Press), 155–175.
Fukuyama, Francis (2003). *Our Posthuman Future: Consequences of the Biotechnology Revolution* (London: Profile Books).
Hammond, Meghan Marie and Sue J. Kim (eds) (2014). *Rethinking Empathy through Literature* (London. Palgrave Macmillan).
Haraway, Donna J. (1991), 'A Cyborg Manifesto: Science, Technology, and Socialist Feminism in the Late Twentieth Century', in Donna J. Haraway (ed.), *Simians, Cyborgs and Women: The Reinvention of Nature* (New York; Routledge), 149–181.
Hayles, N. Katherine (2016). 'The Life Cycle of Cyborgs: Writing the Posthuman', in Sherryl Vint (ed.), *Science Fiction and Cultural Theory: A Reader* (London: Routledge), 247–257.
Huxley, Aldous ([1932] 2007). *Brave New World* (London: Vintage).
Ishiguro, Kazuo (2005). *Never Let Me Go* (London: Faber and Faber).
Jerng, Mark (2008). 'Giving Form to Life: Cloning and Narrative Expectations of the Human', *Partial Answers: Journal of Literature and the History of Ideas*, 6:2, 369–393.
Keen, Suzanne (2010). *Empathy and the Novel* (Oxford: Oxford University Press).
Levick, Stephen E. (2004). *Clone Being: Exploring the Psychological and Social Dimensions* (Oxford: Rowman and Littlefield).
Marcus, Amit (2012). 'The Ethics of Human Cloning in Narrative Fiction', *Comparative Literature Studies*, 49–3, 405–433.

Mulkay, Michael (1996). 'Frankenstein and the Debate over Embryo Research', *Science, Technology, & Human Values*, 21:2, 157–176.
Nussbaum, Martha C. (1995). *Poetic Justice* (Boston: Beacon Press).
—. (2004). *Hiding from Humanity* (Princeton: Princeton University Press).
—. (2006). *Frontiers of Justice* (Cambridge, MA: The Belknap Press of Harvard University Press).
Paul, Diane B. (2005). 'Genetic Engineering and Eugenics: The Uses of History', in Harold W. Baillie and Timothy K. Casey (eds), *Is Human Nature Obsolete: Genetics, Bioengineering, and the Future of the Human Condition* (Cambridge, MA: MIT Press), 123–152.
Seaman, Myra J. (2007). 'Becoming More (than) Human: Affective Posthumanisms, Past and Future', *Journal of Narrative Theory*, 37:2, 246–275.
Shaffer, Brian W. and Cynthia F. Wong (eds) (2008). *Conversations with Kazuo Ishiguro* (Jackson: University of Mississippi Press).
Shannon, Thomas A. (2005). 'Human Nature in a Post-Human Genome Project World', in Harold W. Baillie and Timothy K. Casey (eds), *Is Human Nature Obsolete: Genetics, Bioengineering, and the Future of the Human Condition* (Cambridge, MA: MIT Press), 270–316.
Shelley, Mary ([1818] 2012). *Frankenstein*, edited by J. Paul Hunter (New York: W.W. Norton).
Singer, Peter (2000). 'Recent Advances: Medical Ethics', *BMJ: British Medical Journal*, 321:7256, 282–285.
Sloane, Peter (2018). 'Literatures of Resistance Under U.S. "Cultural Siege": Kazuo Ishiguro's Narratives of Occupation', *Studies in Contemporary Fiction*, 59:2, 154–167.
Storrow, Richard F. (2009). 'Therapeutic Reproduction and Human Dignity', *Law and Literature*, 21:2, 257–274.
Swift, Jonathan (2003 [1726]). *Gulliver's Travels* (London: Penguin).
UNESCO (1997). Universal Declaration on the Human Genome and Human Rights, Paris: UNESCO.
Wallace, Jeff (2010). 'Literature and Posthumanism', *Literature Compass*, 7/8, 692–701.
Whitehead, Anne (2011). 'Writing with Care: Kazuo Ishiguro's "*Never Let Me Go*"', *Contemporary Literature*, 52:1 (Spring), 54–83.
Wilhelm, Kate ([1976] 2006). *Where Late the Sweet Birds Sang* (London: Orion).

8

Nocturnes, hope and 'that croony nostalgia music'

Yugin Teo

Ishiguro remarked in 2000 that nostalgia, in its purest form as 'a profound emotion', is 'to the emotions what idealism is to the intellect' – a way of 'longing for a better world' (Ishiguro, 2000a). Ishiguro's preoccupation with nostalgia, the aching sense of desire and longing for home or the past, in many ways matches his concerns with memory. Christopher Banks's return to Shanghai in *When We Were Orphans* (2000) was not so much about rooting out evil as it was to retrieve lost objects, people and moments from his past. Banks's departure from Shanghai as a child bears echoes of Ishiguro's own departure from Nagasaki to England at the age of five, departing without the chance to bid a genuine farewell to home.

Nocturnes (2009), when compared with the scholarly attention received for his novels, seems to have been neglected to some extent. This could be due in part to the lack of sustained exploration of the psychological and emotional arcs of Ishiguro's characters in contrast to his novels (Wong, 2019: 171–172), which can be attributed to the use of the short-story form in the collection.[1] Ishiguro's previous novels depict intense nostalgic moments that complicate the boundaries between individual history and the imagination, and this is true for *Never Let Me Go* (2005) and *When We Were Orphans*. The Judy Bridgewater music tape that Tommy bought in Cromer to replace the one that Kathy had lost stirs up feelings of 'nostalgia' for Hailsham and the Cromer trip (*NLMG*: 159). The implausible voice of Christopher Banks's old friend Akira in war-torn Shanghai advocates for nostalgia as a way to remember a 'better' world (*WWWO*: 263). The childhood longing for a better world carries with it a utopian impulse, one that is in further evidence within

Nocturnes. Scenes of nostalgia often lead to 'imaginary utopian spaces' (Waugh, 2011: 16) in Ishiguro's novels; however, he structures his examination of these themes differently in the collection. Ishiguro employs the musical forms and themes from jazz standards in the Great American Songbook to explore the complicated relationship between the fleeting quality of nostalgia, and the persistence of memory and loss. Unlike the use of nostalgia as a tool in resisting forgetting in *Never Let Me Go* (Teo, 2014: 91–92), in *Nocturnes* nostalgia seems to have a less combative and more restorative function of longing and desire. It is certainly tempting to consider Ishiguro's collection of stories as an ode to the Great American Songbook, and a straightforward portrayal of nostalgic longing. This would however miss the more subtle (but crucial) discussions on time, imaginary homelands and utopia that lie just beneath the surface. This chapter examines Ishiguro's unique exploration of nostalgia through the five stories, and his meditations on fleeting utopian moments in the vignettes featured in the collection. Beginning with the concept of home, the discussion first examines the desire to return to a more innocent and stable time, triggered by the characters' dissatisfaction with the present. This will be followed by an analysis of the utopian spaces generated through nostalgic reminiscence, as well as Ishiguro's development of a critical and reflective form of nostalgia through the stories in the collection. The study finishes by looking at how Ishiguro utilises the form of the short-story collection to highlight further the powerful and yet elusive qualities of nostalgia.

Longing for home

Nostalgia, a word described by Svetlana Boym as 'pseudo-Greek' and coined by a Swiss student named Johannes Hofer in 1688, comes from *nóstos* describing a 'return home', and *álgos* which indicates 'longing' (Boym, 2011). Boym goes on to define nostalgia as 'a longing for a home that no longer exists or has never existed'. The sense of longing for home in nostalgia carries with it elements of the mythical, the imagination and memory. In this chapter I take a more expansive interpretation of what returning home means. In Boym's seminal *The Future of Nostalgia* (2001) she describes modern nostalgia as a mourning of the loss of 'an enchanted world with clear borders and values' as well as a longing for 'a home that is both physical and spiritual' (2001: 8). The concept of home in *Nocturnes* can be linked to specific places, such as Janeck's memories of his mother's record collection in the former communist bloc in 'Crooner', but in other stories home refers to a specific period of time such as Ray's university days with Emily and Charlie in 'Come Rain or Come Shine'.

The stories in the collection exhibit alternative expressions of the concept of home: a world that is idealised and reshaped through memory and imagination. These 'imaginary homelands', as described by Salman Rushdie (1991: 10), are indicative not of an idealised physical home country but of a particular time, place or feeling from the past. Rushdie comments that writers who are 'exiles or emigrants or expatriates' are 'haunted by some sense of loss', and that, in responding to the urge to look back, it will not be a return to the exact country or place of origin, but versions that are fictions and homes 'of the mind' (1991: 10). The return home for a number of characters in *Nocturnes* is tinged with nostalgia for a more innocent, happier or safer time, but these are memories that have been affected by loss and mediated through the imagination. Both Janeck and Tibor, Italian-based musicians from the stories 'Crooner' and 'Cellists' that bookend the collection, are emigrants from behind the former Iron Curtain (N: 197). Janeck, working as an itinerant guitarist among the café orchestras at Venice's iconic Piazza San Marco, recognises the American singer Tony Gardner, and immediately thinks of his late mother and her love for his records. Within the first-person narrative, Janeck thinks back to the 'communist days' when it was difficult for his mother to find American records, and how years later working in Warsaw, Janeck would seek out those records on the black market and spent a few years finding replacements for his mother's worn copies (N: 6). This reflection, built around poignant memories of her mother's love for music and his relationship with her, thinly veils a sense of loss for his mother through his determination in making amends for damaging one of her treasured Tony Gardner records. In a period of over three years, he found replacements for all her worn-out Gardner records, including the one that he damaged, and brought them to her 'one by one' each time her went to see her (N: 6). This sense of repetition and ritual of bringing her a Gardner replacement from the black market extended beyond just replacing the damaged record and became a means by which Janeck reconnected with his mother each time he returned to visit. The narration's emphasis on not only the time frame of this quest but the persistent energy where he 'kept getting them' so that he could 'bring her another' (N: 6) brings a psychological insight into the strength of feeling regarding his relationship with his mother, as well as the importance placed on this particular fragment of home: a home of childhood memories.

Home carries with it associations of hearth and of safety. For the characters in *Nocturnes*, the concept of home is intertwined with ideas of family life, relationships, experiences of the Cold War and foreign cultural artefacts, including American popular music. The blurb on the dustjacket of *Nocturnes* describes the characters encountered in the stories as ranging from 'young dreamers to cafe musicians to faded stars, all of them at some moment of reckoning', connected by the 'struggle to keep alive a sense of life's romance' (Ishiguro, 2009). These narratives of dreamers and old stars represent the confluence of idealism, disappointment and longing, in particular, a longing for a time that is perceived to be a happier one; being in exile or being a migrant compounds this emotion further. Through this collection of stories Ishiguro creates a utopian environment, an 'imagined community of dreaming strangers' (Boym, 2001: 256), who simultaneously long for home and long to be away from home.[2] In 'Crooner', Janeck, an emigrant musician in Venice, recalls poignant childhood memories triggered by his encounter with Tony Gardner. Tibor, another emigrant in 'Cellists' based in a different Italian city, is an ambitious musician who is proud of his classical training pedigree until his meeting with Eloise McCormack.

The urge to return to a place of stability is apparent in 'Come Rain or Come Shine'. The London-based couple Emily and Charlie are going through 'a bit of a sticky patch' (N: 43), and, on one of his visits from Spain to see them, Ray is tasked by Charlie to make himself seem inferior to Charlie in order that Emily will reappraise Charlie's worth and become reconciled with him. Charlie is aware that Ray has a unique connection with Emily through their shared love of popular jazz standards and the Great American Songbook.

Ray is, for Charlie, the epitome of the nostalgic past. He asks Ray to avoid engaging in music-related conversations with Emily, whilst also asking Ray to do the impossible by being his 'natural self' (N: 63). Charlie views nostalgia from a purely functional perspective – as a tool to get Emily into a happier frame of mind whilst allowing for the more negative aspects of nostalgia to manifest themselves. Emily would realise that Ray had not progressed in life as much as she and Charlie have, and Charlie would come out in a better light. Towards the end of the story, we find that Charlie's plan is flawed, as Emily's intellectual and emotional connection with Ray is very much grounded in music, and to avoid the subject is to risk rousing Emily's suspicions that not everything is as it seems. Emily puts on a Sarah Vaughan record, which Ray insists he no longer remembers, saying that he does not listen to that kind of music any more. Sarah is stunned by this, insisting that '[t]hings can't change that much' (N: 83). Sarah's response underlines the subtleties of nostalgia's power, representing a flawed hope that certain things dating back to the past would, somehow, remain the same. Her instincts prove to be right in this instance however, as Ray tries to keep to the promise he made to his best friend in not engaging with Sarah on 'that croony nostalgia music' they both still love (N: 63). Ray's comment moments later about the difficulty in 'know[ing] where to settle [...] [w]hat to settle to' (N: 85), encapsulates the sense of restlessness that they both experience; for Sarah, in not really knowing if Charlie is still the right person for her, and for Ray, in being uncertain about which country to settle in. Both characters in different ways long for a version of home, but are unsure of how to reach it, or know what it might look like.

Space, nostalgia and utopia

The perception of nostalgia as a yearning for the past that holds one back from living in the present carries with it a strong element of truth, but this sentiment does tend to gloss over the fallible aspect of memory, and the irrecoverable nature of the past. The past that is yearned for by the remembering subject is mediated through time and imagination. Linda Hutcheon asserts that nostalgia is not about the past 'as actually experienced' but is about the projection of an idealised present into the past (2000: 20). This relates to the utopian aspect of nostalgia that addresses the 'longing for a better world' spoken about by Ishiguro (Ishiguro, 2000a). Pickering and Keightley argue for the wider acceptance of nostalgia as a 'contradictory phenomenon' that retains both 'utopian impulses' and 'melancholic responses to disenchantment', with both dimensions mutually informing each other (2006: 936; 921). This allows for a positive quality of nostalgia to be made manifest, where the desire to return to an idealised past can be seen as a search 'for ontological security in the past', and the desire not to return but 'recognize aspects of the past' becomes the basis for 'renewal and satisfaction in the future' in the midst of present uncertainty (Pickering and Keightley, 2006: 921). Varying dimensions of nostalgia are also reflected in Boym's conceptions of restorative and reflective forms in her 2001 book. In Ishiguro's story cycle the characters' dissatisfaction with the present leads to their longing and struggle for a sense of 'life's romance' mentioned in the book's dustjacket. However, what they long for is not the actual past that happened, but one that has been 'idealized through memory and desire' (Hutcheon, 2000: 20).

Citing Mikhail Bakhtin, Hutcheon notes that the ideal life that is not being lived in the present gets projected into the past, and consequently nostalgia is often not really about the past, but about one's dissatisfaction or disillusionment concerning the present (2000: 20). Hutcheon observes that this process 'exiles' and distances us from the present, whilst drawing closer an imagined and idealised past that feels more 'complete, stable, coherent, safe' (2000: 20). The nostalgic past occurs as utopian spaces in Ishiguro's fiction. These spaces are revealed as representations of imaginary homelands for the characters in *Nocturnes*, facilitated through musical themes that trigger happy memories of childhood and youth, forgotten romance and faded dreams. Patricia Waugh defines these 'imaginary utopian spaces' in Ishiguro's writing as worlds 'produced out of nostalgic longing' that are 'necessary lies' we tell ourselves in order to survive (2011: 16). She argues that these spaces can sustain the remembering subject, and provide consolation, but warns of their potential of keeping past injustices hidden (2011: 16). This describes a duality to nostalgia in *Nocturnes*, where at times it seems to represent utopian longing, and at other times indicates the inability to move on from the past. Music is utilised to establish utopian spaces in the story cycle, allowing for characters who seek solace and consolation to find a site of stability. These spaces, and how each character negotiates their way within them, constitute a unique meditation on nostalgia's power, typified by a yearning to return to a happier or more familiar time. 'Cellists', narrated from the perspective of one of the piazza café musicians, tells the story one summer seven years ago of Tibor, a classically trained Hungarian cellist who was attending the unnamed Italian city's Arts and Culture Festival.

Aside from getting to know members of the café band, the story centres on his encounter over a brief period with Eloise McCormack, an American music enthusiast who views herself as a virtuoso despite not having progressed with the cello beyond the age of eleven. Believing her pretence of being a virtuoso musician, Tibor takes up her offer of tutoring him to unlock his hidden potential. After one of these sessions, while they are having refreshments in a café, their conversation leads to an interesting observation Eloise makes about Tibor's playing. Despite Tibor's insistence that he does not love a German girl he once knew, Eloise insists that he must have experienced romantic love, as he played a passage in a Rachmaninov piece in a manner evoking 'the *memory* of love', along with its associations of 'desertion, abandonment' (N: 205). Eloise observes further that the movement is usually played with joy by most cellists, but that Tibor interprets this movement like 'the memory of a joyful time that's gone for ever' (N: 205). The narrative does not expand further on this point, nor does this particular subject return again in the story (apart from the poignant farewells toward the end). This might be reflective of some of the limitations of the short-story format for Ishiguro's writing style, or issues that Ishiguro has had in engaging with his usual themes in the collection. None the less, this scene between Tibor and Eloise, and Eloise's words mentioned above in particular, crystallise the collection's meditations on nostalgia. Tibor's playing summons these utopian spaces, evoking the bittersweet act of remembering past romantic love or a happier time that is 'gone for ever', along with the associated pain of displacement and exile. This bittersweet quality of nostalgia is a refrain that runs through many of the stories in *Nocturnes*; it is reminiscent of the phrase 'music and nightfall' in the collection's subtitle, where the imminent sunrise is indicative of the fleeting nature of pleasure. This powerful sentiment is evocative of *ukiyo-e*, the traditional style of Japanese art that seeks to capture the 'transient pleasure-seeking world' that the painter Masuji Ono is surrounded by in *An Artist of the Floating World* from 1986 (Teo, 2014: 119). In the novel Ono's mentor Seiji Moriyama sets his goal of capturing the 'transitory, illusory qualities' of the beauty in pleasure houses after dark, a beauty that will 'vanish with the morning' (*AFW*: 150).

The vignettes, depicted through the short-story form, offer a meditation by Ishiguro on the elusive and fragmentary nature of the nostalgic utopian spaces depicted. Nostalgia, according to Boym, is an act of defiance against the linear flow of 'modern' time: the remembering subject '[refuses] to surrender to the irreversibility of time', yearning for childhood or a time of 'slower rhythms' (Boym, 2011). This rebellion against the modern concept of time interrupts its irreversible flow and generates utopian spaces. But, despite these acts of resistance, the elusive quality of the fictionalised and nostalgic past remains. Following a comical and absurdist turn of events at Charlie and Emily's home in 'Cone Rain or Come Shine', Raymond finds himself at his wit's end trying to explain his actions to Emily. Emily decides to put on some music that she knew Ray would be familiar with. It is a Sarah Vaughan record, and, after a brief moment protesting that he is no longer interested in that style of music, Ray agrees to Emily's request to dance to 'April in Paris' outside on the terrace. As we have known all along, Ray had been lying to Emily in order to keep a promise he made to Charlie. He is in fact very familiar with the track and knows that it is at least eight minutes long. As Ray holds Emily closely, his senses are 'filled with the texture of her clothes, her hair, her skin' (*N*: 86). The song and the intimacy of the dance create a temporary utopian space where '[they] were safe' as they '[danced] under the starlit sky' (*N*: 86). This space of safety is an idealised present, and Ray is very much aware that this moment lasting eight minutes, like all nostalgic moments, is fleeting. He observes at the end of the story that this intimate moment will likely fade once the song ends. Ishiguro deliberately utilises the short-story format to ensure that the characters' nostalgic returns are brief and fleeting, highlighting nostalgia's elusive nature. While this is not as sustained a meditation on a theme as compared to a number of his novels, there is evidence here of a critical perspective concerning nostalgia despite some of the limitations of the short-story format.

A reflective and critical nostalgia

Ishiguro has in the past lamented the common 'pejorative' understanding of nostalgia as a form of escapism and 'political and historical' evasion (Shaffer, 2008: 166). He prefers to view the 'pure emotion' of nostalgia as something that can positively influence people to imagine and pursue a better future, drawing inspirational forms from childhood memories (Shaffer, 2008: 166–167). However, even within Ishiguro's fiction there seems to be a tension between both evasive and inspirational forms of nostalgia, and this includes the stories within *Nocturnes*. For example, in *When We Were Orphans*, Banks's naive attempt at restoring peace during the Japanese invasion of Shanghai leaves him with not only further complications concerning his family's past but also the realisation that it was finally time for him to leave his long-held childhood idealism behind (*WWWO*: 277). The excruciatingly long wait for Ryder's piano recital in *The Unconsoled* ultimately leads to the disappointment of an almost empty auditorium (*U*: 519), and the regret of not being able to fulfil a long-standing wish for his parents to attend one of his major concerts (*U*: 512). Ishiguro's characters' yearning for the past in *Nocturnes* appears on the surface to be initiated by pejorative forms of nostalgia that leave them shackled to the past, unable to move forward with their lives. Many of the stories tell of music being used as a tool to revisit past happiness and old glories, with mostly inconclusive outcomes. The form of the short-story collection employed here certainly aids in representing the elusive quality of nostalgia and memory. One might ask if this is indeed the thematic conclusion to reading *Nocturnes*, that, in spite of the occasional utopian spaces found in these stories, the positive aspect of nostalgia as something that can inspire a better world is an elusive quality and one that is ultimately undermined by the narrative. If the story cycle is concerned only with the wistful and elusive nature of nostalgia, signposted through allusions to the era of the Great American Songbook (with the exception of 'Malvern Hills'), then one might be inclined to see *Nocturnes* as a less fulfilling read. Delving further into the complexities of nostalgic experiences in the stories reveals a more reflective and critical element at play.

Charlie's longing for home, represented by his appeal to Ray to 'make everything okay again' with his struggling marriage in 'Come Rain or Come Shine' (N: 44), is a wish that is likely to be impossible to fulfil, as such a wish does not take into account the irretrievable nature of the past and the changes that people undergo throughout their lifetimes. Rather than accepting the changes to their individual lives and relationship and finding a way forward, Charlie is desperate for a return to the past as how he remembers it, a time of stability between him and Emily as though 'the last two months haven't happened' (N: 44). In 'Crooner', Tony Gardner's plans to romantically serenade his wife Lindy, in spite of the impending end to their marriage, are an attempt at recapturing the sense of romance that dates back to their visits to Venice and London twenty-seven years ago. Given that Tony and Lindy plan to separate after their holiday, this trip to Venice and the performance bookend their marriage. As Tony discusses the plans for serenading Lindy with Janeck, his thoughts turn to the current state of his relationship with Lindy and the happier times they have had over the years. When he has finished recounting the story of the significance of the song 'I Fall in Love Too Easily' to the early memories of their marriage, Janeck observes Tony 'wiping away tears' (N: 23). For Janeck, however, his encounter with Tony revives his memories of his late mother and her love of Tony Gardner's music. Unlike for Tony, that night's performance does not herald an end for Janeck, but rather it helps rekindle and restore the memory of his mother. Upon first hearing Tony's voice in front of him in the gondola during their practice of 'By the Time I Get to Phoenix', Janeck is transported back to being 'a boy again, back in that apartment' where his tired mother is sitting on the sofa listening to one of Tony's records (N: 14–15). The song, 'full of travelling and goodbye', is a poignant reminder of his mother's inability to leave her sadness behind her (N: 27). For both characters these American jazz and pop standards trigger memories of happier times with their loved ones. The past, however, appears to have a hold on these two characters. Even with the looming separation, there seem to be unspoken intimacies and intense feelings both Tony and Lindy have for each other that remain unresolved at the crossroads, and, while Tony's nostalgic longings indicate the presence of old memories of their relationship, there is no impetus to try to come to an alternative solution. Janeck seems to be partially tied to a child's point of view. After witnessing Tony's tears as described above, he tries to comfort and reassure him by recalling how much his music helped his mother during times of sadness and relationship crises. Janeck's words to Tony start off in a mature and hopeful voice, but it gradually descends into a naive optimism where he declares that, if Tony's music could help 'millions of others', it should be capable of helping him too (N: 24). Ishiguro's narrative creates a confrontation between Janeck's childhood view of the trials and tribulations of finding love with Tony's adult world of ruthless pragmatism and celebrity consciousness.

Moments like the ones discussed above are examples of the more pejorative impression of nostalgia that Ishiguro is wary of, one that is indicative of 'escapism of a bad sort', or something that 'impedes people from doing things properly' (Shaffer, 2008: 166). However, by taking a slightly different view of the stories and investigating the nostalgic qualities of the music that are sought after by a number of characters, and considering some of the links between the theme of music and the form of the collection, we can observe a more reflective and critical nostalgia at work. We first begin by considering the bittersweet nature of the longings associated with nostalgia. There is a palpable sense of desire, even addiction in some instances, for these nostalgic emotions by characters in the stories. Music in *Nocturnes* encapsulates the bittersweet memories of an inaccessible past. Nostalgia's power and appeal is dependent on the 'irrecoverable' nature of the past (Hutcheon, 2000: 19–20), intensifying that sense of yearning for what has been lost for ever, whether it be a person, a place or a feeling. The quest for these bittersweet experiences through music, embarked upon by both performers and listeners, is exemplified in most of the stories, beginning with American pop and jazz standards in 'Crooner'. As Janeck begins playing an introduction on his guitar for 'By the Time I Get to Phoenix', he tries to make it sound 'like America, sad roadside bars, big long highways' (N: 27). The sense of sadness, isolation and loneliness experienced by the singing subject accompanies many of the songs from the Great American Songbook. In the opening pages of 'Come Rain or Come Shine', Ray recalls the early days of his friendship with Emily and their mutual appreciation for American jazz standards. He remembers a particular instance when they discover a recording of 'Come Rain or Come Shine' by Ray Charles, where, as he describes it, 'the words themselves were happy, but the interpretation was pure heartbreak' (*N*: 38). The space of heartbreak opened up by these songs makes accessible the previously inaccessible past. Returning to the concept of home, standing for a happy, ordered and simpler (idealised) past, these songs allow for the weary soul to return home momentarily while distancing themselves from the troubles of the present. Steve, the jazz saxophonist in 'Nocturne', recovering from the facial plastic surgery that is hoped would revive his music career, has a series of encounters and meetings with Lindy Gardner (from 'Crooner' and who has also had facial surgery) in the Beverly Hills hotel they are both recovering in. Lindy asks to listen to Steve's music, and when he plays her his signature track on the CD player 'The Nearness of You', Steve extols to the reader the unique interpretation of this jazz standard by his band and his saxophone playing. He claims that 'there are colors there, longings and regrets' at certain moments in the track (*N*: 154). We observe here that once again nostalgic emotions of yearning, wistfulness and sadness are channelled through the music. As described earlier, Eloise in 'Cellists' explains to Tibor a quality concerning his musicianship that speaks of 'desertion, abandonment', and the memory of the joy of love (*N*: 205). These quests to experience the bittersweet emotions that accompany music-based triggers of memories point to a more active form of engagement for the remembering subject. John J. Su argues that nostalgia provides a way of 'imagining more fully what has been and continues to be absent' (2005: 9). These experiences force characters to confront and engage with loss in imaginative ways, and to perhaps reach a point where they are more capable of acknowledging the complex origins of their regret or longing. The creation of an imagined and more idealised version of the past 'merges with a dissatisfaction with the present' in these nostalgic moments (Hutcheon, 2000: 20), allowing for a momentary but profound sense of release that is coveted by the remembering subject.

While there is indeed evidence of a more profound meditation of nostalgia in the story cycle beyond a generalised impression of evasion and escapism, as with many of Ishiguro's characters from his novels, there is no conclusive sense of what the remembering subject does at the conclusion of the stories, or if these nostalgic experiences relate to any subsequent life-altering decisions. Some of this is due to the brevity and form of the 'interrelated short story collection' used by Ishiguro (Whitehead, 2021: 37). The Gardners' marriage in 'Crooner' ends in a divorce as planned, and one assumes that Janeck is still an itinerant musician among the piazza café orchestras at the end. While Ray and Emily share an intimate moment dancing on the terrace, there is a palpable sense of inevitability that their friendship will revert back to the way it was in the earlier part of 'Come Rain or Come Shine'. Tibor's summer-long encounter with Eloise in 'Cellist' comes to an abrupt end when Peter, who had been trying to win her affections, arrives in the city to find her. When the narrator sees Tibor again, it is seven years later back in the same city, with no conclusive information regarding his status as a musician. As in 'Crooner', a marriage break-up paves the way for an attempt at rejuvenating a professional music career in 'Nocturne', with no further indication of how successful this next phase will be for Steve. 'Malvern Hills' is slightly different from the other stories in the cycle, not only because of its countryside setting but due to its focus on an older couple, Tilo and Sonja, who are both musicians and who perform together. Examining the nature of what keeps a relationship together, Ishiguro asks the question of what happens when a couple struggle to find things that they have in common, even in music. Similarly to 'Crooner' and 'Cellists', there is a younger aspiring musician, who also narrates the story, with whom the older characters form a temporary bond. There are a few hints at the theme of nostalgia in this story: the protagonist who remembers as a child not being keen to go for walks in the hills with his family, but now, with his parents divorced and the family home sold, feels 'affection, even nostalgia' for the area (N: 94). When Tilo describes to the protagonist the music he and Sonja play as part of their act, the mention of bands like The Beatles, The Carpenters and ABBA evokes a sense of nostalgia for 1970s popular music. The ending, like the other stories, is inconclusive as the protagonist watches Tilo walking in the distance, having recently had a falling out with Sonja.

Ishiguro's meditations on nostalgia examine not only its utopian and reflective qualities but its elusive and fleeting nature as well. The attraction of the wistful and bittersweet experience of nostalgic spaces is often contrasted with a pervading sense of loss once the moment has passed. This eventually leads to an addiction for more of such moments, a longing to return to these stable, ordered and idealised versions of the past. In doing so, Ishiguro's writing in *Nocturnes* considers a third possibility in conceptualising nostalgia, beyond the more traditionally polarising options of nostalgia as either evasion or reflection. Through his utilisation of the short-story form and the theme of music, Ishiguro's narrative confronts the reader with the contradictory nature of nostalgia as a (transient) source of hope for the future. It can be a timely reminder to the remembering subject of long-forgotten passions and goals that fell by the wayside, while its fleeting and elusive nature means that the subject is always left having to reconcile their longings with the realities of present circumstances, finding a way forward that allows them to fulfil their dreams.

Ishiguro's use of form

This collection of stories is ultimately about dreams and dreamers, and the difficulties of holding on to one's dreams and initial optimism for the future. There are moments when a character's dissatisfaction with circumstances in the present can trigger a nostalgic yearning. In the case of these dreamers, nostalgia becomes the means by which they are reminded of what is absent in their lives, while also being a useful, critical tool that brings to mind one's original goals and the circumstances that inspired them. Apart from the characters and their encounters with the past, the story cycle's form and internal structure exemplify aspects of the nature of nostalgia highlighted by Ishiguro.

The interrelated short-story collection facilitates a loose thematic link across the five stories, comprising tales of hurt, disappointment and longing. Two of those stories, 'Crooner' and 'Malvern Hills', depict encounters between musicians from different generations. There is also present a more specific theme, one that is evident in each story, of the struggles that couples face at different stages of their relationships. The question about what happens when the number of things that a couple have in common begin to dwindle, and when there is a growing sense of estrangement within the relationship, is one that Ishiguro examines in his writing. These uncertainties come up again in his 2015 novel *The Buried Giant*, a profound meditation of the tenuous bond of memory and forgetting that keeps a couple together. Such thematic links help foster a sense of the communal nature of nostalgic experience between the different characters in *Nocturnes*, even if their specific narratives do not overlap (with the exception of Lindy Gardner's appearance in both 'Crooner' and 'Nocturne'). The short-story form enables the portrayal of a small ensemble of characters who are at different turning points in their relationships and careers, creating the setting for Ishiguro's examination of the act of remembering, and utilising a critical form of nostalgia to highlight the difficulties that arise for the characters who cling on to memories that are idealised.

Music has been a medium by which Ishiguro inscribes utopian spaces in his fiction, and this practice is limited to music not as a theme but also as form. His successful musical collaboration with Stacey Kent and Jim Tomlinson across several of Kent's albums from 2007 to the present is evidence of Ishiguro's continued interest in jazz and how his fictional narratives have another creative outlet through its musical form. Through his songwriting on the 2007 Kent songs 'The Ice Hotel', 'I Wish I Could Go Travelling Again' and 'So Romantic' there is a continuation of his themes of longing, regret and nostalgia (Teo, 2014: 87), while his lyrics to Kent's 'Breakfast on the Morning Tram' from the same album is also a place to explore themes of utopian spaces initially portrayed at the end of *The Unconsoled* (Teo, 2014: 123). In *Nocturnes* Ishiguro continues to inscribe utopian spaces within his fictional worlds through a number of musical genres including songs from the Great American Songbook, popular jazz and classical music. These spaces as described above provide a unique meditation of nostalgia's power, manifested in both its transformative potential to overcome loss and its equally formidable efficacy in keeping an individual ensnared in the past. But what is also intriguing here is that Ishiguro channels the musical form and themes of popular jazz standards in depicting these stories, where a powerful sense of yearning for the past is depicted together with the inconclusive endings to each story, akin to the endings of songs on an album, lending an elusive quality to the reminiscences. There are elements of improvisation to a number of stories that yield a comedic effect, such as the risky attempt at returning the stolen Jazz Musician of the Year trophy in 'Nocturne', or the ill-advised mission of staging a home invasion by a neighbour's dog in order to cover up Ray's crime of vandalising Emily's diary in 'Come Rain or Come Shine'. These moments do not last, however, as the narrative ultimately returns to some form of stability through the first-person narrative voice, avoiding what Ray dismisses as 'endless improvisations' that ignore the precision of the 'beautifully crafted songs' found in jazz standards (N: 37). The musical form of the collection informs the critical aspects of nostalgia that are being deployed in the story cycle.

There are admittedly some issues with the musical reference points featured in the collection, namely the utilisation of American music and culture from the 1920s to the 1960s. No doubt Ishiguro's affection for the Great American Songbook and American jazz standards permeates this collection; however, such a narrative strategy ultimately limits the scope of an otherwise engaging inquiry on memory, heartbreak and nostalgic longing. In 'Cellists' even a conversation about performing the work of Russian composer Sergei Rachmaninov is led by an American (N: 204). While a critique of how *Nocturnes* examines twentieth-century American cultural hegemony goes beyond the scope of this discussion, it should be noted that the forms of nostalgic experiences depicted in the three jazz-themed stories are inflected by mid-twentieth-century American popular music. Despite these influences, the function of *Nocturnes* as a text embodies, in both form and thematic content, the fleeting and elusive qualities of nostalgia. The collection functions as a 'musical text', weaving together 'a web of images, references and locutions' between the stories, as noted by Gerry Smyth (2011: 151–152). In his study of Ishiguro's musical imagination in *The Unconsoled* and *Nocturnes* Smyth writes about the 'formative influence' that popular music has had on Ishiguro's generation of late twentieth-century British writers, and how music as a 'salient cultural form' can be utilised in a powerful way to understand the world and our relationship with it (2011: 145). Through his deployment of a range of musical references and connections, Ishiguro's musical text encourages the reader to be an 'active agent in the creation of meaning' (Smyth, 2011: 151). In doing so, Ishiguro creates narrative spaces where the active reader's music-inflected memories may be triggered by the characters' range of nostalgic responses across the stories.

Conclusion: hope for the future

In *Nocturnes* Ishiguro utilises the concept of the short-story collection as a critical form of nostalgia, one that acknowledges different ways of remembering the past as well as the complications that accompany the longing to cling on to cherished memories. These memories are often related to imagined, fictive pasts that have more of a bearing on present difficulties and disappointments than they do to past events. Characters yearn for imaginary homelands that are not necessarily tied to an exact place of origin but are instead indicative of homes in their minds that often relate to childhood memories of a more innocent, stable and safer time. Through the collection Ishiguro creates what Boym calls an 'imagined community of dreaming strangers' (2001: 256), a utopian environment where characters both long for home and long to be away from home. The characters' lives are encased in a unique story cycle and musical text in which the form and internal structure constitute a depiction of various facets of nostalgic experience that generates meaning for the active reader.

While spaces of nostalgic longing are capable of sustaining the remembering subject, Ishiguro, being wary of nostalgia's historical links with escapism and evasion, advocates for a more critical and reflective form of nostalgia, one that acknowledges its shortcomings as well as its potential to inspire positive change. This collection of stories portrays the lives of a community of dreamers, and the challenges they face of holding on to their dreams and hopes for the future. Nostalgia, Ishiguro contends in *Nocturnes*, is a (transient) source of hope for the future, one that comes as a timely reminder to the remembering subject of long-forgotten dreams, while its fleeting nature challenges the subject to face up to their present circumstances.

Notes

1 Anne Whitehead's insightful essay on *Nocturnes* helpfully considers the collection as an 'interrelated short story collection', placed in 'the interstices between short story and novel' and 'between literary fiction and musical album' (2021: 37).
2 This experience is described by Boym as being 'homesick' while also being 'sick of being at home' (Boym, 2011).

References

Boym, Svetlana (2001). *The Future of Nostalgia* (New York: Basic Books).
—. (2011). 'Nostalgia', in *Atlas of Transformation*, http://monumenttotransformation.org/atlas-of-transformation/html/n/nostalgia/nostalgia-svetlana-boym.html (accessed August 2021).
Hutcheon, Linda (2000). 'Irony, Nostalgia, and the Postmodern: A Dialogue (with Mario J. Valdés)', *Poligrafías*, 3, 18–41.
Ishiguro, Kazuo. (1986). *An Artist of the Floating World* (London: Faber and Faber)
—. (2000a). 'Author Q & A: A Conversation with Kazuo Ishiguro about His New Novel *When We Were Orphans*', Knopf Publishing, www.penguinrandomhouse.com/books/85614/when-we-were-orphans-by-kazuo-ishiguro/9780375724404 (accessed August 2021).
—. (2000b). *When We Were Orphans* (London: Faber and Faber).
—. (2005). *Never Let Me Go* (London: Faber and Faber).
—. (2009). *Nocturnes* (London: Faber).
Pickering, Michael and Emily Keightley (2006). 'The Modalities of Nostalgia', *Current Sociology*, 54:6, 919–941.
Rushdie, Salman (1991). *Imaginary Homelands: Essays and Criticism 1981–1991* (London: Granta).
Shaffer, Brian W. (2008). 'An Interview with Kazuo Ishiguro', in Brian W. Shaffer and Cynthia F. Wong (eds), *Conversations with Kazuo Ishiguro* (Jackson: University Press of Mississippi), 161–173.
Smyth, Gerry (2011). '"Waiting for the Performance to Begin": Kazuo Ishiguro's Musical Imagination in *The Unconsoled* and *Nocturnes*', in Sebastian Groes and Barry Lewis (eds), *Kazuo Ishiguro: New Critical Visions of the Novels* (Basingstoke: Palgrave Macmillan), 144–156.
Su, John J. (2005). *Ethics and Nostalgia in the Contemporary Novel* (Cambridge: Cambridge University Press).
Teo, Yugin (2014). *Kazuo Ishiguro and Memory* (Basingstoke: Palgrave Macmillan).
Waugh, Patricia (2011). 'Kazuo Ishiguro's Not-Too-Late Modernism', in Sebastian Groes and Barry Lewis (eds), *Kazuo Ishiguro: New Critical Visions of the Novels* (Basingstoke: Palgrave Macmillan), 13–30.
Whitehead, Anne (2011). 'Writing with Care: Kazuo Ishiguro's "Never Let Me Go"', *Contemporary Literature*, 52: 1 (Spring), 54–83.
Wong, Cynthia F. (2019). *Kazuo Ishiguro* (Liverpool: Liverpool University Press, on behalf of Northcote House, 3rd edn).

9

Disinterring the English sublime: haunted atmospherics in *The Buried Giant*

Kristian Shaw

Ishiguro has proved himself to be a remarkably prescient author. Although he is not considered a particularly political figure – avoiding the polemical stance of fellow authors such as Jonathan Coe or Ian McEwan – his body of work does contain a sustained interrogation of major cultural events to comment on the politics of national identity, memory and trauma. Further, Ishiguro has recently been uncharacteristically outspoken on the disastrous approach taken by British politicians in post-Brexit negotiations. Following the EU referendum result, he placed himself alongside the pro-Remain majority of artists and intellectuals in questioning this symbolic retreat from Europe, voicing a fear that a postwar Europe which had been transformed 'from a slaughterhouse of total war and totalitarian regimes to a much-envied region of liberal democracies living in near-borderless friendship – should now be so profoundly undermined by such a myopic process' (Ishiguro, 2016). His 1989 novel *The Remains of the Day* anticipated some of the key catalysts that laid the groundwork for the Leave vote, detailing how the lingering power of nostalgic regression is manipulated for political purposes, as well as the societal temptation to whitewash the national past or retreat into the simplifying logic of populist rhetoric rather than actively confront the decline of English culture. Lord Darlington's arrogant denunciation of greater political representation, for example, rejecting the assertion that 'the will of the people being the wisest arbitrator' (*RD*: 197), assumes greater significance in light of the events of 2016.

Although his 2015 novel *The Buried Giant* was conceived and published before the fateful EU referendum vote it speaks to urgent political debates defining contemporary Britain. Literary critics and journalists were initially unsure what to make of Ishiguro's foray into fantasy literature – how could a novel populated by ogres, pixies and dragons provide some perspective on our moment of political rupture? – but the novel has been reappraised in the post-Brexit period. Weaving together the quotidian and the fantastic, Ishiguro returns to his core theme of the fallibility of memory to question mythic conceptions of nationhood. This chapter will argue that *The Buried Giant* holds a clear anticipatory logic in channelling the cyclical nature of national violence, unearthing suppressed historical memories, and deconstructing mythical constructions of Englishness. After all, when discussing King Arthur and the *Britons*, it is a narrower Englishness under inspection. As Alan MacColl explains, the land inhabited by the Britons often equates to 'England and Wales, or simply England itself' (1999: 8), often referring to lands south of the Humber.[1] Though Englishness and Britishness are often used interchangeably in popular discourse, it will be argued the amnesiac anxieties of the novel are more reflective of the English identity crisis in particular (a primary factor in driving Britain's Leave vote), with the chapter drawing clear parallels between Ishiguro's post-Arthurian landscape and the fractious landscape of twenty-first-century society.[2] Ishiguro's Nobel Prize win in 2017, awarded during a fraught period of Brexit negotiations, reinforced the perception that his body of work contains a clear ethico-political message in gesturing to cultural divisions which continue to plague the present; according to the committee, Ishiguro possesses a unique ability to 'uncover the abyss beneath our illusory sense of connection with the world' (Ishiguro, 2017). By interrogating the elusive origins of nationhood, at a time when the parameters of cultural belonging are increasingly illusory and up for debate, *The Buried Giant* acquires a hauntological edge, pointing to the spectral influence of our national past.

Speaking in 2009, Ishiguro communicated his ongoing fascination with the politics of memory, voicing an authorial desire to move beyond personal recollections towards collective and national forms of remembrance: 'communities and countries remember and forget their own history. There are perhaps times when a nation *should* forget and when you *can* cover things up and leave things unresolved because it would stir things up' (Matthews, 2009: 118 – emphasis in original). Acknowledging that his novels 'have concentrated on countries going through big social changes on the one hand, or individual memories on the other hand', he concedes 'I've never been able to put these two things together' (quoted in Moore and Sontheimer, 2005).[3] *The Buried Giant* marks a purposeful attempt to marry these two disparate processes. The novel also signals a departure from Ishiguro's usual approach to narrative perspective, oscillating between first-person narrators and an omniscient narrator, a Charon-like boatman figure, whose personal thoughts open the novel. This dynamic interplay between several homo-diegetic narrators and an extra-diegetic narrator should unsettle and decentre the narrative; however, Ishiguro's first-person narrators contribute to his postmodern provocation of the assumed objective certainties of national history. As Jane Hu notes, the multi-narrator structure also complements Ishiguro's thematic attempt to capture the wider implications of collective memory: 'Rather than narrate Britain's national origins as one emergent storyline, the novel's multiple conflicting voices unfold a highly contingent and speculative process of uneven narrative development' to capture a historical moment in which 'the Anglophone empire is not yet guaranteed' (2021: 145).

Ishiguro's unreliable first-person protagonists, deceiving themselves about their own shadowy pasts, mark an authorial desire to return to traumas which lie 'somewhere just beneath the surface of things' (Ishiguro, 1981: 21). As Cynthia F. Wong points out, Ishiguro's narrators across his body of work undertake a universal 'quest for consolation' (2000: 5) from which the reader is partially excluded. In *The Buried Giant* past events are occluded from the narrative, recollections are tenuous and narrators conflate personal and collective memories to construct flawed personal accounts marked by repression and self-delusion. The omniscient narrator seemingly speaks from a contemporary perspective, yet one that is still difficult to precisely locate and a temporal divide is established: 'We did not yet have the hedgerows that so pleasantly divide the countryside today into field, lane and meadow' (*BG*: 30). His use of 'we' includes himself as a member of this unbroken national community. By suggesting the view of the landscape Axl and Beatrice enjoy on their journey 'may not have differed so greatly from one to be had from the high windows of an English country house today' (*BG*: 87), Ishiguro subtly derides the notion of a timeless English culture and the persistence of a cherished mythopoeia which persists to the present day; a mythopoeia he goes on to gradually deconstruct. The opening statement by the extra-diegetic narrator forces the contemporary reader to cast aside timeless images of Englishness housed in the cultural imaginary and consider the nation's slumbering origins, 'You would have searched a long time for the sort of winding lane or tranquil meadow for which England later became celebrated. There were instead miles of desolate, uncultivated land'; he strikes an almost apologetic tone in his depiction of the nation: 'I am sorry to paint such a picture of our country at that time, but there you are' (*BG*: 3; 5). Indeed, post-Arthurian England is described as a 'featureless landscape' – an empty space yet to be filled with the sacred signifiers of quintessential Englishness (*BG*: 30). Ishiguro has elucidated on his decision to utilise the post-Arthurian period for this very purpose, stating that the era represents a 'blank period' of history about which little is known, enabling him to play with mythic constructions of nationhood and heritage (quoted in Alter, 2015).[4]

Across his body of work Ishiguro has intimated how closely Englishness clings to its national heritage. *The Remains of the Day* indicates the ways by which heritagisation is employed to hold the cultural imaginary in stasis and resist cultural or demographic developments to the nation. He considers his earlier novel to be 'more English than English' via its invocation of 'a harmless nostalgia for a time that didn't exist. The other side of this, however, is that it is used as a political tool [...] It's used as a way of bashing anybody who tries to spoil this "Garden of Eden"' (Vorda and Herzinger, 2008: 74). For Ishiguro the English people are complicit in purposely sustaining the mythical construction of Englishness, taking succour from historical moments which suggest that ethnic homogeneity and cultural dominance are deeply rooted qualities of their national past: 'It seems to me a nation's myth is the way a country dreams. It is partly of the country's fabulized memory and it seems to me to be a very valid task for artist to try to figure out what that myth is and if they should actually rework or undermine that myth' (Vorda and Herzinger, 2008: 74–75). England itself is 'a mythical place' with its citizens possessing 'that myth of what England is like', its outlines 'already present in the imaginations of many people around the world, including those who had never visited the country' (Ishiguro, 2017). It is, therefore, not surprising that *The Buried Giant* marks a return to the idea of 'mythic England [...] the kind of England that is often used by the heritage or nostalgia industry to sell tablecloths or teacups', at a moment when the English national identity seems to be entering another period of crisis (quoted in Watchel, 1996: 26). A discussion of nationhood further expounds Ishiguro's decision to set his narrative in a post-Arthurian Britain. Though little is known and much is contested about this period, it is still regarded as 'the mythological root of British sovereignty', marking the 'fulcrum point' at which the 'restive minority population' is threatening the well-being and sanctity of the nation (Vernon and Miller, 2018: 70). By engaging with the root of English nationhood and folklore, Arthur, Ishiguro utilises fantasy to deconstruct the mythical genealogy of England and challenge preconceived notions of nationhood. Ishiguro may confront the idea of England as a sentimental fantasy, an artificial construct that evades empirical fact, yet he also avoids a simple postmodern parody of Englishness by indicating the value and merit of national culture and its narrative role in grounding personal and collective experience.

The English sublime

Set in a mythologised, late fifth- or early sixth-century post-Arthurian Britain, in which the east of England is threatened by Saxon occupation, *The Buried Giant* follows an elderly couple named Axl and Beatrice whose village suffers from a form of collective amnesia. As the narrator explains, 'in this community the past was rarely discussed. I do not mean that it was taboo. I mean that it had somehow faded into a mist as dense as that which hung over the marshes. It simply did not occur to these villagers to think about the past – even the recent one' (*BG*: 7). As Axl and Beatrice set off to visit their son in a neighbouring village, they soon realise that the amnesia is a national pandemic and find themselves embroiled in a quest to determine the source of this condition: an amnesia which veils the shadows of our national origins and historical atrocities. The couple are joined on their travels by Wistan, a Saxon warrior from the eastern fenland; Sir Gawain, the renowned nephew of King Arthur and protagonist of the late fourteenth-century chivalric romance *Sir Gawain and the Green Knight*; and Edwin, a young Saxon boy under Wistan's protection who is thought to carry a dragon bite.

It is revealed the melancholic mist of forgetfulness is produced by the breath of a dragon, Querig; following the genocide of colonising Saxons by Arthur's forces, the dragon is imprisoned and bewitched by Merlin in order to enforce a false peace on the nation and erase the memories of Arthur's ethnic cleansing campaign.

It is, perhaps, understandable why Ishiguro has chosen King Arthur for his discussion of collective memory and national history. The mythical history of Arthur, a fabled leader who masterminded the defence of Britain against Saxon invaders in the late fifth and early sixth centuries, encapsulates the heart of what I term the 'English sublime': 'a nationalist fable founded on a haunting and destructive jingoism which aggressively mourns the illustrious past, offers redemptive traces of former imperial glories and laments the cultural heterogeneities of the inferior present' (Shaw, 2021: 72). As a central figure in the repository of national memory, Arthur almost functions as the master-signifier to encapsulate an intangible English identity, resurfacing across historical periods when the legitimacy of the nation is threatened. For Lauren Berlant, 'cultural expression of national fantasy is crucial for the political legitimacy of the nation' (1991: 21), accentuating the role played by historical figures in shaping the national imaginary and the public's diachronic engagement with these hallowed signifiers. Though Englishness remains an elusive, if historically weighted concept, resistant to socio-cultural developments, the practice of nostalgic historicisation conceals the constructed nature of nationhood. Arthur's own shadowy personal history, which can only be gleaned from sparse references in the *Annales Cambriae* and *Historia Brittonum*, complements the tenebrous origins of English national identity. The genocide to which Wistan refers, suggested to be the Battle of Badon which delayed the encroachment of Saxon settlers in this period, is itself shrouded in the shadows of history and subject to ongoing revision, with academics unable to pin down the exact date, location or outcome of the fighting. In this sense the genocide is ideally positioned for Ishiguro's fictional revision of the post-Arthurian period: a moment in which national origins and cultural co-ordinates could not be more contested or inconclusive.

Despite his death years earlier, Arthur still haunts the narrative; his manipulation of Querig symbolises how political regimes and governments control the production of memory and dictate which historical events and cultural symbols are permitted to enter into the national imaginary. As Maurice Halbwachs explains, it is 'individuals who remember, not groups or institutions, but these individuals, being located in a specific group context, draw on that context to remember or recreate the past' (1992: 22), indicating the ways by which individuals are influenced by wider collective forms of cultural memory to interpret the past. The promotion of a commemorated history – often shaped by ruling powers or political elites – attains a certain *authenticity* and it becomes difficult or unpatriotic for citizens to reinterpret the past or question deeds undertaken in the name of nationalism. Querig's mist operates as a poignant allegory for the ways in which individual trauma is often effaced from official histories and public discourses, while also pointing to how communities decide to suppress those wartime memories which hinder the progression of the nation state. The mist seems to act as an atmospheric phenomenon, often appearing as a denser fog clouding the landscape, but also functions on a figurative level to allude to the difficulty in recalling individual or collective forms of memory. As Ivor comments, 'ah, the mist. A good name for it' (*BG*: 70). Indeed, Ishiguro's hauntological narrative itself, much like his fictional post-Arthurian Britain, seems to exist in a sea of mist and it is difficult to recall notable events of the novel without repeated readings.

In a discussion of Ishiguro's earlier novels, Yugin Teo notes that memory is a central theme of his work, particularly 'the effort of the individual to mediate with their past through the processes of forgetting, remembering, and the releasing of painful memories in order to break cycles of regret and retribution' (2014: 10). Rather like Etsuko in *A Pale View of Hills* or Ono in *An Artist of the Floating World*, Axl and Beatrice constantly reassess the reliability of flawed recollections in a process of continual modification to consider their personal impact on past crises. The evasion of marital grievances becomes more apparent (and highly selective) the closer they come to Querig's lair as the gradual accumulation of disparate and overlapping memories – little more than figurative disjecta membra – force the couple to confront painful truths. The reader comes to understand the lives of the characters through what is omitted or absent from the narrative as meaning is consistently camouflaged and truth must be inferred from conflicting perspectives. However, Ishiguro's complementary attention to the conceptualisation of national memory intimates how our understanding of our collective past influences the perception of our personal histories and shapes our reading of contemporary developments to society. Wulf Kansteiner argues that collective memory is unstable, unreliable and malleable, being 'as much a result of conscious manipulation as unconscious absorption and it is always mediated' (2002: 180). The politics of national memory is a difficult and contested process; communities are forced to decide which elements or individuals become immortalised as symbols of coherent nationhood and which should be expunged from the historical record due to their failure to project a unified vision of cultural identity. Duncan Bell reaches a similar conclusion in perceiving national mythopoeias to function as a 'story that simplifies, dramatises and selectively narrates the story of a nation's past and its place in the world, its historical eschatology: a story that elucidates its contemporary meaning through (re)constructing the past' (2003: 75). The hallowed narrative of nation is thus rooted in the past and struggles to incorporate cultural developments in the present.

The events of the narrative feed directly into Ishiguro's interest in the manipulative political power of collective remembrance; Ishiguro (2017) utilised his Nobel Prize speech to debate whether such cultural amnesia is a viable preventative measure in curbing recurrent patterns of civil war and bloodshed, questioning 'Are there times when forgetting is the only way to stop cycles of violence, or to stop a society disintegrating into chaos and war? On the other hand, can stable, free nations really be built on foundations of wilful amnesia?'[5] The ethical fulcrum upon which the narrative uneasily rests thus becomes apparent: exterminating Querig will result in the mist dissipating and personal and collective memories being restored but such remembrance will also revive the dormant underlying animosity between Britons and Saxons, with potentially disastrous consequences for Axl and Beatrice. Even this historical animosity bears contemporary significance, gesturing to contemporary debates surrounding issues of nationhood and the desire to mark certain ethnic groups as foreigners polluting the supposed purity of British sovereignty.

Querig functions as a fictional device for Ishiguro to question the limits and trappings of collective remembrance: 'Does a nation remember and forget in much the same way as an individual does?

[...] What exactly are the memories of a nation? Where are they kept? How are they shaped and controlled?' (Ishiguro, 2017). Carmen Borbely recognises the unique interpretative role Querig plays in the narrative, condensing 'threats of aggressive dissolution levelled at the body politic and at its collective memory', emerging as a 'beneficent figure of containment that protects, preserves and endlessly defers the assignation of sense to this collective memory' (2016: 23). Though Arthur and his knights justify their actions by pointing to the tentative armistice that has been established, dampening further bloodshed between Briton and Saxon settlements, Querig remains a mendacious and dangerous form of national defence installed to prevent retribution for acts of genocide. Enmity is not translated into conciliation and healing; rather, a comprised peace emerges which fails to remedy cultural divides. Querig's haunting presence intensifies latent feelings that the Saxons have been deceived or betrayed by the tentative accord. Arthur's violation of the truce also reintroduces the notion of a perfidious Albion, resorting to duplicity and treachery in order to pursue England's self-interests. Reading the novel against Ishiguro's recent comments on the European Union, the legacy of the Second World War and the impact of Brexit, clear cosmo-political parallels can be drawn between the novel's post-Arthurian landscape and twenty-first-century Britain. Like Arthur's truce, the postwar European project (from the 1951 Treaty of Paris onwards) was designed to stabilise war-torn nations, prevent further nationalist violence and produce integrative communities. The dismantling of supranational accords, like the removal of Querig, poses a threat to the well-being of communities, risks the resumption of ethnic hostilities and reopens old internal wounds riven deep into national psyches. James Meek notes how politicians often drew on Arthurian rhetoric to frame an exit from the EU in a similar light. The fateful referendum vote was sold to the British electorate as a patriotic form of national *awakening*, 'a swordthrust in the dragon's heart that would end the suffering of 'all good people', without any mature consideration of 'its unexamined effect on the intricate, fragile fabric of peace, regulation and exchange the British live in' (Meek, 2019: 9).

Querig's death is, rather appropriately, anti-climactic; she has become a pathetic, emaciated victim of Arthur and Merlin's manipulation of collective memory, seemingly unaware of her impending death at Wistan's hand: 'it was hardly clear at first she was alive. [...] it took a moment to ascertain this was a dragon at all' (*BG*: 310). Like the distorted memory of Arthur's rule, Querig's 'menace comes less from her own actions than from the fact of her continuing presence' in the national consciousness (*BG*: 69). Gawain may provide a direct link to Arthur and the mythical foundations of nationhood, yet his supposed duty to exterminate Querig is predicated on a dangerous falsehood; not only is he secretly the protector of the dragon, and thus the defender of the English sublime via his maintenance of Arthur's cultural legacy, but his belief in the tentative accord established between Britons and Saxons reveals his post-Arthurian nation to be little more than a tenuous imagined community united only by deceit and historical concealment. As Nick Bentley notes, if we follow Benedict Anderson in accepting national identities to be artificial constructs grounded in a melancholic nostalgia for the past, then this naturally ensures that 'they can be manipulated by interested parties (cultural, aesthetic and political) to support particular versions, each with their own implied and modelled ideologies' (2015: 69). Arthur's and Merlin's plan fails because it simply sublimates collective memory in the minds of the populace rather than creating a viable alternative; national belonging struggles to develop in the process and citizens are left unsure of their own pasts or connections to their fellow compatriots with the act of forgetting retarding any hope of reconciliation. A nation without any memory of its national past is no nation at all.

According to Cillian McGrattan and Stephen Hopkins, collective memory has long been considered 'an essential component within ethno-national belonging', establishing a sense of historical continuity and contributing to the formation of group identification; in the process, however, exclusionary practices can occur, as other memories and experiences are 'muted, displaced or deferred' (2017: 488). As Ed Cairns and Michael Roe note, such cultural erasure leaves minority groups with 'a sense of victimhood that stems from unacknowledged and unreconciled historic losses. These in turn present a powerful barrier to traditional methods of peacemaking and diplomacy and create new senses of wrong and injustice thus creating the potential for future conflict' (2003: 4–5). The term collective memory itself begins to unravel in the face of dissonant historical subjectivities and power imbalances and has to be understood in relation to the organising logics of cultural authority. It is especially important to challenge the notion of collective memory in relation to nationhood, as governing mythologies of the dominant group hold a privileged position. The formation of collective memory, then, 'may be seen not simply as a battle between remembering/ remembrance and forgetting; but rather as a very political process involving contestations over meaning, articulation and inscription', particularly in relation to traumatic events 'which provoke struggles over ownership, authorisation and, ultimately, political (de)legitimacy' (McGrattan and Hopkins, 2017: 490). As Wistan asks, 'How can old wounds heal while maggots linger so richly? Or peace hold for ever built on slaughter and a magician's trickery?' (*BG*: 311–312). Ishiguro thus indicates the crucial role played by collective memory, as well as customs, laws and values, in shaping individual memories and cultural identities.

With this in mind, Axl and Beatrice's desire for Wistan to succeed in his mission, if at the cost of their own lives and the revival of a vicious cycle of sectarian vengeance, suggests that nations must move beyond their historical amnesia and suppression of trauma to heal lingering psychological wounds and grievances within disparate communities. And yet, as Gawain reminds the couple, the development of the English nation has been defined by this practice of historical erasure, elision and denial; cultural imaginaries are dependent upon the obscuration of truths which diminish the quixotic notion of nationhood and destabilise the body politic. Having escaped from duplicitous inhabitants of the monastery through underground passages, the characters encounter a tunnel littered with bones. Gawain utilises the burial chamber to force his companions to contemplate the dark underbelly of England's historical development: 'I dare say, sir, our whole country is this way. A fine green valley [...] [But] Dig its soil, and not far beneath the daises and buttercups [...] lie the remains of old slaughter' (*BG*: 186). The chamber is representative of the nubilous terrain of Ishiguro's narrative more generally; the ground is all memoranda and signatures – a palimpsestic landscape bearing the marks of ethnic conflict and scars of historical traumas. The monastery itself becomes a contested site which bears the scars of past conflict and discord as various factions are drawn into the process of maintaining the national myth; as Wistan explains, the monastery was once a hillfort, its walls whispering 'of days gone by' (*BG*: 153), reinforcing Gawain's assessment that the blanketing of traumatic memories is a widespread practice in concealing suppressed histories that unsettle national unity. The monks are internally divided on their contribution to maintaining Arthur's lie; while certain monks feed Querig in order to perpetuate the dispersion of the mist, locking themselves in a cage exposed to carrion birds in order to assuage their guilt for past crimes committed in the country, others accentuate the need for ethical accountability: 'we must uncover what's been hidden and face the past' (*BG*: 166).

Ishiguro's resurrection of Gawain to further this argument on historical accountability – a mythological literary figure integral to the national imaginary – is rather appropriate in this regard, as is the authorial decision to retreat into myth and work within the fantasy genre rather than his initial impulse to draw on more recent ethnic conflicts or cleansing campaigns such as the Bosnian war or Rwandan genocide. As Meek argues, myth functions as 'a story that can be retold by anyone, with infinite variation, and still be recognisable as itself [...] It's an instrument by which people simplify, rationalise and retell social complexities. It's a means to haul the abstract, the global and the relative into the realm of the concrete, the local and the absolute. It's a way to lay claim to faith in certain values' (2019: 8). Gawain is no longer the proud and virile warrior of his original chivalric romance – a representation of the nation's strength and vigour – having become a Pythonesque parody of his former glory. Once a formidable adversary and central figure on Arthur's round table, Ishiguro paints Gawain as an elderly patriarch of national decline, a haunting reminder of the Arthur's once-great realm: 'His armour was frayed and rusted, though no doubt he had done all he could to preserve it. His tunic, once white, showed repeated mending [...] a sorry sight' (*BG:* 113). Ishiguro's comedic depiction of Gawain aligns with his authorial attempt to disrupt the English sublime, deconstructing the mythical foundations of national origins and peeling away the quixotic façade of Arthur's rule, signified by the tattered condition of Gawain's 'once white' tunic. By taking solace in a fabricated national mythology and sustaining an illusion of grandeur rather than seeking restitution for past transgressions, Gawain is unable to accept his diminished position in the evolving cultural imaginary, remaining deeply invested in the false, essentialist constructedness of his role as national protector. Yet despite his acknowledgement of the shadowy nature of national origins – applying Blakean rhetoric to consider the 'pleasant green carpet' (*BG*: 311) covering England's battle-scarred landscape – Gawain enjoys a surprisingly self-deluded interpretation of his role in national events and adopts a circumlocutory manner when evading personal liability in Arthur's genocide. The ageing knight almost comes to believe his own lies regarding his quest to destroy Querig: a *willed* amnesia to maintain both the illusion of superiority and a deeply held personal belief that he is part of a great cultural tradition. Ishiguro thus exposes the shameful apertures that often exist in narratives of monocultural nationhood, concealed by patriotic discourses and imperial ideologies. Just as Stevens in *The Remains of the Day* comes to believe that the fate of the nation is predicated on the professional completion of his duties, Gawain believes Querig is the only means of preserving the status quo, neglecting the Saxon invasions which threaten to overwhelm Britain regardless of the dragon's survival. Further, the Saxons on the eastern fenlands, situated away from the locus of Querig's power, still recall some aspects of the broken accord; even Britons recall the prior period of hostilities, harbouring a reluctance to live alongside migrant Saxons. Wistan points out, in attempting to find a new home for Edwin, 'When the elders asked me to take the boy to a distant village, they meant no doubt a *Saxon* village' (*BG*: 89 – emphasis in original). Axl's village, too, is left tending towards localism rather than any inclusive nationalism which transcends the Briton-Saxon divide. As Catherine Charlwood recognises, Ishiguro's nation is an imaginary construct 'precisely because it has been falsely united through amnesia' (2018: 28). Rather than openly acknowledge his personal accountability in the systematic extermination of Saxon peoples, then, Gawain instead constructs an elaborate alternative history, nursing a misplaced trust in Querig's mist and painting a picture of a benevolent Arthur acting for the greater good against the incursion of Saxon invaders.

'Gawain's First Reverie', a flashback which elucidates on the broken truce which led to the slaughter of Saxon peoples, delves more closely into the rhetoric of nationalist ideology and develops stronger reflections on contemporary forms of popular sovereignty.

For Gawain there can be no solace in the truths of the past; his defence of Arthur's grand deception equates to a patriotic defence of national sovereignty and the need to protect English national identity in the face of foreign influence: 'isn't it our duty still to wear his crest with pride for all to see?' (*BG*: 120). It is easy to draw analogies between Gawain's image of Arthur seemingly protecting his 'island' from Saxon invasion and the defence of the nation against continental incursions up to the present moment. This struggle to determine who belongs and who does not, who is a neighbour and who is a foreigner, has always been riven deep into the nation's history. Arthur, then, retains his paradoxical position as a historical war hero, as well as a mythical protector of the nation. Gawain's plea to Wistan, 'Leave this country to rest in forgetfulness' (*BG*: 311), is equally a plea for an integrative period of Arthurian dominance – free of cultural division – to remain a central myth in the national imaginary. In resisting the closure of Arthur's legacy, Gawain takes psychological refuge in the traditions and rituals of the past, nostalgically venerating an instinctual and essentialist form of nationhood suspended in cultural stasis.

Mythscapes and imaginaries

As Homi Bhabha reminds us, 'writing the nation as narration' involves this veneration of 'historical objects' (1990: 305) to sustain a unified nationalist pedagogy. The potential extermination of Querig, then, equates to the defenestration of Arthur's legacy from cultural memory and a subsequent reshaping of the national narrative which negates the role of Britons in defying foreign invasion. As Axl explains, 'the she-dragon's no more, and Arthur's shadow will fade with her' (*BG*: 324). Further, Arthur was later 'appropriated by the descendants of their Saxons conquerors and incorporated into the history of the English' (MacColl, 1999: 7), weakening persistent claims for a monocultural Englishness which has come to underpin political motivations to re-establish England as a distinct entity from the rest of the UK. The battle over Arthur's memory thus recalls Bell's notion of a 'mythscape': 'the temporally and spatially extended discursive realm wherein the struggle for control of people's memories and the formation of nationalist myths is debated, contested and subverted incessantly' (2003: 66). While for Gawain the dragon ensures the protection of his people's status and security, for Wistan and his Saxon leaders Querig's removal enables their colonisation of the British landscape. The dragon is thus not only a corrupted national symbol of Arthur's enduring legacy but a political instrument employed to delay changes to the ethnic make-up of Britain. Gawain's willingness to comply with Arthur's demands and partake in Merlin's act of national delusion, taking comfort in his role as the last surviving protector of the English sublime, alludes to the extent to which nations can refuse to face contemporary developments and remain in stubborn denial about the atrocities written into their historical pasts.

During the EU referendum campaign, Brexiteers relied on similar political storytelling tactics in order to frame a range of heterogeneous issues as a matter of national defence and sovereignty; by valorising an inauthentic (and asynchronous) English past and drawing on English military victories, the Vote Leave and Leave.EU campaigns succeeded in rousing a misplaced sense of patriotism in voters and galvanising support for the Eurosceptic cause. A *vampiric* Englishness emerged, which bore no relation to the contemporary moment and served as a hollow reminder of the nation's ailing potency, but sustained itself by feeding off the glories, insecurities and misconceptions of the past. In doing so it was believed that nationalist discourses and policies would serve as a bulwark against cosmopolitan incursions into the cultural imaginary, exploiting the psychological urge for a cohesive grand narrative that secured the *authenticity* of the English identity. Manipulation of the collective memory of war, as evident in the Brexit referendum, persuades a cultural group that they share a common heritage, shared goals and similar socio-cultural values, while simultaneously fostering a synergistic hostility for those perceived to exist outside of this group or residing in neighbouring nations. Leave supporters often referred to Brexit as a *crusade* to regain Britain's independent sovereignty and protect its cultural heritage, neglecting the European influence on the nation's medieval history.

Matthew Eatough notes chivalric rhetoric has long been 'internalized within far-right nationalist discourse' (2021: 56) and right-wing populism while nationalist political parties in the UK often employ medieval symbolism and terminology to point towards the idea of ethnic homogeneity. For Eatough, by undermining the myths of national consensus and ethnic homogeneity, Ishiguro not only 'erases the distance' between post-Arthurian England and 'present day ethno-nationalism' (2021: 59) but creates parallels between the chivalric language employed by Gawain and Wistan and political rhetoric utilised in anti-immigration campaigns. This ideological subversion of Arthur, and the related production of outdated fantasies to confront constitutional realities, have been a feature of English political rhetoric for generations, but recent years have witnessed nationalist groups subverting Arthur's shadowy history to their own ends. For Andrew B.R. Elliott (2017) the use of medieval imagery by the English Defence League and British National Party, political groups that overwhelming supported a Leave vote in the EU referendum, marked an attempt to 'construct a heritage for themselves within an imaginary, exclusionist white history'. Ishiguro's remarks on a divided Britain in the wake of the EU referendum buttresses the reading of his medieval novel as a commentary on the present:

> anger will make a treacherous guide in our current situation, and it is imperative we think and act coolly [...] I believe, in fact, that in the coming weeks, what we face is a fight for the very soul of Britain. If I were a strategist for the far right, I would today be rubbing my hands with excitement: never has there been a better opportunity, at least not since the 1930s, of pushing Little England xenophobia into neo-Nazi racism. All of us who don't wish to see such a development must now do all we can to unite a sharply divided, bewildered, anxious, leaderless nation around its essentially decent heart. (Ishiguro, 2016)

By positioning the Saxon as the foreign invader, threatening England's (elusive and intangible) mythological origins, the novel communicates the temptation to obscure the ethno-political past in order to justify the repudiation of undesirable cultural changes in the present. Though Querig's breath plagues the land, robbing the populace of their memories, Axl and Beatrice hope that Wistan defeats their fellow countryman Gawain in combat, even if this outcome reawakens the metaphorical buried giant and disinters suppressed memories of past wars, resulting in potentially disastrous consequences for Britons via further acts of Saxon invasion. As Matthew Vernon and Margaret A. Miller note, lines of loyalty in the novel 'do not form across neat and obvious lines of division, whether geographic or nationalistic' (2018: 84), strengthening Ishiguro's critique of nativist modes of affiliation. In chronicling Wistan's victory over the fabled knight – a victory for collective remembrance of past atrocities over the manipulation of historical records – Ishiguro ruptures the sanctity of the English sublime and critiques the valorisation of national origins.

Drawing parallels with the contemporary moment, Ishiguro acknowledges that, although the Britons were 'an indigenous people' struggling to withstand an influx of 'migrants who were in increasing numbers taking over parts of the island', it is often forgotten that the (Anglo-) Saxons 'later became the English; they basically took over the whole country' (quoted in Rukeyser, 2015). As Inga Bryden reminds us, 'one of the most powerful myths of the origin of English national identity is Anglo-Saxonism'; a myth which relies on cultural fictions and 'the assumption of a uniform, or at least integrated, society' (2016: 33). Such mythic genealogy, and the parameters of Arthur's 'empire', seem to exist outside of geographical boundaries, with Arthur himself unbound by temporal limits, existing eternally as a floating signifier in the English national imaginary. Ishiguro's textual representation of Arthur, as a character long dead before the events of the narrative, indicates his immeasurable position as both a historical figure of the past and an intangible essence of the English sublime, existing in a kind of deep time that evades concrete representation. The ethno-symbolism of Arthur conveys the image of prelapsarian golden age in which members of the nation were secure in their cultural identity and could locate their cohesive collectivity in a resonant shared history. Mythical figures such as Arthur serve as routes into memory, no matter how tenuous or fabricated those representations are, and become the means of structuring cultural identification and prescribing what is expected of the national experience. Such acts of remembrance establish clear boundaries between that which is national and that which is foreign or other; the resulting mythopoeic manipulation transmigrates across historical periods and is employed to tackle emergent threats to the nation. Gawain's death at the hands of Wistan in personal combat marks the passing of an outdated mode of Englishness – one grounded in a mythical cultural imaginary – that has somehow survived and mutated throughout historical periods but is unable to confront recent cultural changes and struggles to move beyond an island mentality.

Wistan serves as Ishiguro's devil's advocate, arguing that the urge to forget may be a natural cultural response to historical atrocity, but ignoring or concealing such events impacts a national community on personal and collective levels, haunting future generations and breeding new monsters in the process. Lord Brennus's aim to conquer Britain in Arthur's wake, and drive all Saxons from the land, proves a legitimate motivation for Wistan's quest; none the less; Wistan's desire for retributive justice is flawed. In seeking vengeance against all Britons regardless of their involvement in the genocide of his fellow Saxons, he indicates how victims can become perpetrators and the impact of deep-rooted ethno-nationalism in exacerbating, as opposed to ameliorating, ethnic hostilities. His manipulation of Edwin, as a potential agent to continue his vengeful enterprise, is likely to be just as destructive as Gawain's participation in engendering a national amnesia, repeating the error of drawing on the grievances and scars of the past to create new conflicts. Civil war, of course, is far more likely to stoke the fires of nationalism and tribalism and exacerbate hostilities between Britons and Saxons, as well as fear of further demographic change. Wistan also fails to acknowledge that atrocities were committed by both sides during the civil war, such as Gawain's example of a young female Briton who joins the battle to seek vengeance against a Saxon lord for his treatment of her mother and sisters. Ishiguro's description of the girl tormenting the lord with her gardening tool, bringing 'the hoe down not with a swing, but a small prod, then another', as if meditatively 'searching for potatoes in the soil' (*BG*: 230), alludes to the limitations of retributive justice in righting the wrongs of the past.

In his commentary on the troubled terrain of post-conflict resolution, Ishiguro instead communicates the need for cosmopolitan empathy and a process of healing to emerge which marks the tentative stirrings of a shared narrative that transcends cultural divides, encapsulated by Axl and Beatrice's caring bond for Edwin. A narrative of reconciliation based on dialogue and mutual understanding does not appear in the novel; instead, a narrative of grievance continues to dictate relations across the scarred landscape – a narrative that bleeds and informs the present. Though the titular buried giant signifies the potential collective violence and slaughter that could re-occur across the nation in revenge for Arthur's act of duplicity, it also gestures to a more individual desire for retribution as a painful response to suppressed trauma. Wistan warns the small company that he will be personally involved in seeking further vengeance now the mist has dissipated: 'The giant, once well buried, now stirs [...] this will become a new land, a Saxon land, with no more trace of your people's time here than a flock or two of sheep wandering the hills untended' (*BG*: 324). Arthur's resistance movement, then, has only postponed the continental invasion. While Ishiguro chooses not to narrate the subsequent fallout or confirm whether the quest is an act of national self-harm, the closing scenes of the novel hint towards the cultural and ethnic divides already re-emerging based on simple suspicion and distrust. A potential Saxon assault, their forces reinvigorated by Querig's removal, represents the re-emergence of a rudderless divided kingdom, vulnerable not only to further invasions but to fresh mythologising by Britons unwilling to accept their post-Arthurian decline.

The past thus haunts and stalks the narrative. Axl resists Gawain's attempts to implicate him in his nation's traumatic wars, imploring Gawain to 'Remind me no more' (*BG*: 298). For Axl the act of remembering is intimately tied to his own traumatic involvement in brokering the fateful truce and suspension of hostilities as the so-called Knight of Peace. While Axl is not a conspirator in the manufacturing of cultural deceit, registering an animosity towards the memory of Arthur for breaking the tentative armistice, his desire for a peaceful future is predicated on an acceptance of his role in past conflicts. In an amnesiac society disturbed by the struggle for collective remembrance, Axl's attempt to open up the troubled process of accountability marks an attempt to forge with Wistan and Edwin what Aleida Assmann would term 'dialogic memory'. According to Assmann, as memory can be 'double edged. It can both serve as medium for reconciliation, peacemaking and coexistence on the one hand and for rekindling conflicts by refueling hatred and revenge on the other' (2015: 199), two countries can overcome traumatic histories of national violence by engaging in a constructive dialogic memory which mutually acknowledges the suffering they have inflicted on each other.

And yet, as Ivan Stacy identifies, the titular buried giant 'does not lend itself to such a straightforward allegorical reading' because Wistan makes his speech at 'the site of a cairn [...] a cultural marker of memory' (2021: 122) employed to commemorate its passing, rather than the giant's grave itself.[6] On the one hand, it is possible to concur with James Wood (2015) in perceiving Ishiguro's allegory to be 'at once too literal and too vague', with the fantastical elements of the narrative weakening parallels that can be drawn with peace-building and post-conflict recovery efforts in the postwar era. Nevertheless, his claim that *The Buried Giant* 'points everywhere but at us […] its fictional setting is feeble, mythically remote, generic, and pressureless', fails to appreciate why Ishiguro has employed fantastical elements in his consideration of real-world myth and folklore. Fantasy, after all, is 'a way of making our metaphors concrete, and it shades into myth in one direction, allegory in another' (Gaiman, 2015), enabling Ishiguro to exaggerate the question of cultural memory and its impact on a populace. Moreover, Wood's analysis not only ignores how the novel articulates emergent divisions within English society – and imparts a bleak warning on our uncertain moment of political rupture – but indicates how the same organising logics of remembrance and commemoration reverberate across national history. As the extra-diegetic boatman reminds the reader, 'Some of you will have fine monuments by which the living may remember the evil done to you […] You are in any case part of an ancient procession' (*BG*: 291). Any potential reconciliation or forgiveness between the opposing communities, then, can only be achieved 'by combining a respect for the content of memory with the recognition that meaning is built around that content in the form of narratives that are malleable, flawed and self-interested' (Stacy, 2021: 126), with ethnic divides likely to deepen due to the propagation of fabricated histories by splintered factions. As Axl contemplates following Querig's demise, 'who knows what old hatreds will loosen across the land now? We must hope God yet finds a way to preserve the bonds between our peoples, yet customs and suspicion have always divided us. Who knows what will come when quick-tongued men make ancient grievances rhyme with fresh desire for land and conquest' (*BG*: 323).

Conclusion

Ishiguro's purposeful allusion to 'quick-tongued men' at the close of the narrative forges a clear parallel with the nationalist debate in contemporary British politics and reinforces his authorial critique – evident throughout the novel – on the ways by which political discourse draws on outdated ethnic symbols and national myths to influence debates surrounding affiliation, belonging and cultural protectionism. While acts of cosmopolitan hospitality punctuate the novel, nationalist affiliations hold firm and the couple's kindness is unlikely to alleviate entrenched ethnic hostilities, allay sectarian attitudes or overcome impediments to integrative memory. Though Edwin begins to question Wistan's blind hatred of all Britons, regardless of their innocence in past atrocities, 'Must I hate a Briton who shares with me his bread? Or saves me from a foe as lately did the good Sir Gawain?' (*BG*: 264), the denouement suggests he will continue Wistan's legacy and dampen the possibility of rapprochement, truth recovery or transitional justice. Edwin even interprets Axl's parting gesture, 'raising a hand into the air', to carry questionable motives and he remains doubtful of allegiances built across cultural lines: 'Was it in farewell or an attempt to detain him?' (*BG*: 328). The denouement thus registers Ishiguro's (2017) own anxieties – communicated in his Nobel Prize speech – about the proliferation of 'tribal nationalisms' and Little Englander racism 'once again on the rise, stirring beneath our civilised streets like a buried monster awakening'.

The inability of contemporary nations to come to terms with their troubled historical legacies certainly augments the haunted atmospherics of the novel. In registering the memories of historical abuse from the individual level to the broader national frame, Ishiguro suggests the ways by which we remember the past influence how we conceptualise the present and warns that nostalgic efforts to recover or replicate the past in order to 'take back control' are doomed to fail. Reading *The Buried Giant* against recent geopolitical developments, Ishiguro dramatises how the myopic violence of nation states, as well as the manipulation of collective memory, can destabilise post-conflict reconciliation and unravel cross-cultural ties. Through the guise of fantasy he works to unravel and disparage the supposed factual basis of historical modes of knowing, exposing how the mythopoeia of national identity reveals truths that continue to infect the present. By anticipating the debates and discourses that would come to define the EU referendum campaign and post-Brexit period, *The Buried Giant* forces us to consider the internal ailments affecting the body politic as we seek to establish new borders and thresholds for our sceptred isle.

Notes

1 Wynkyn de Worde's 1529 edition of Sir Thomas Malory's *Le Morte Darthur* identifies Arthur as the 'somtyme kyng of grete Brytayne now called Englande' (Malory, 1529).
2 A 2013 IPPR report, 'England and its Two Unions', anticipated that Brexit would be a decidedly English revolt, stating 'It is English, rather than British, hackles that rise in response to Europe' (Wyn Jones et al., 2013: 22).
3 As Sara Upstone suggests in Chapter 4 above, one could argue that *The Remains of the Day* marks an early attempt to do just that.
4 Ishiguro considered setting his novel in a range of other historical periods and locations, but medieval Britain won out over other societies faced with the troubled prospect of post-conflict reconciliation, including 'Bosnia, America and post-second world war Japan and France' (quoted in Cain, 2015).
5 This is not the first time Ishiguro has addressed collective amnesia. As Teo notes, in *When We Were Orphans* Ishiguro 'lays bare the human capacity for a more sinister form of collective forgetting, one that distances itself from accountability and believes in its own alternate vision of history' (2014: 59). *The Unconsoled* arguably reinforces this authorial fascination with wider forms of collective memory, documenting the attempt by an unnamed community to forgot and move beyond its troubled past.
6 Axl and Beatrice encounter the giant's burial mound at the beginning of the novel; it lies unrecognised in the landscape, yet the couple choose to circumnavigate its perimeter for fear of reawakening its symbolic menace.

References

Alter, Alexandra (2015). 'For Kazuo Ishiguro, *The Buried Giant* Is a Departure', *The New York Times*, 19 February, www.nytimes.com/2015/02/20/books/for-kazuo-ishiguro-the-buried-giant-is-a-departure.html (accessed June 2021).
Assmann, Aleida (2015). 'Dialogic Memory', in Paul Mendes Flohr (ed.), *Dialogue as a Trans-disciplinary Concept* (Berlin: De Gruyter), 199–214.
Bell, Duncan S.A. (2003). 'Mythscapes: Memory, Mythology, and National Identity, *British Journal of Sociology*, 54:1, 63–81.
Bentley, Nick (2015). 'Rewriting National Identities in 1990s British Fiction', in Nick Hubble, Philip Tew and Leigh Wilson (eds), *The 1990s: A Decade of Contemporary British Fiction* (London: Bloomsbury), 67–94.

Berlant, Lauren (1991). *The Anatomy of National Fantasy: Hawthorn, Utopia, and Everyday Life* (Chicago: University of Chicago Press).
Bhabha, Homi K. (1990). 'DisseminNation: Time, Narrative, and the Margins of the Modern Nation', in Homi K. Bhabha (ed.), *Nation and Narration* (London: Routledge), 291–322.
Borbely, Carmen-Victoria (2016). 'The Monster as a Placeholder of the Memory/Oblivion Divide in Ishiguro's *The Buried Giant*', in *Petronia Petrar and Amelia Precup* (eds), *Constructions of Identity VIII* (Cluj-Napoca: Presa Universitara Clujeana), 23–32.
Bryden, Inga (2016). *Reinventing King Arthur* (Abingdon: Routledge).
Cain, Sian (2015). 'Writer's Indignation: Kazuo Ishiguro Rejects Claims of Genre Snobbery', *The Guardian*, 8 March,
Cairns, Ed and Michael Roe (2003). 'Introduction: Why Memories in Conflict?', in Ed Cairns and Michael Roe (eds), *The Role of Memory in Ethnic Conflict* (Basingstoke: Palgrave Macmillan), 3–8.
Charlwood, Catherine (2018). 'National Identities, Personal Crises: Amnesia in Kazuo Ishiguro's *The Buried Giant*', *Open Cultural Studies*, 2, 25–38.
Eatough, Matthew (2021). '"Are They Going to Say This Is Fantasy?": Kazuo Ishiguro, Untimely Genres, and the Making of Literary Prestige', *Modern Fiction Studies*, 67:1, 40–67.
Elliott, Andrew B.R. (2017). 'A Vile Love Affair: Right Wing Nationalism and the Middle Ages', *The Public Medievalist*, 14 February.
Gaiman, Neil (2015). Kazuo Ishiguro's *The Buried Giant*', *The New York Times*, 25 February, www.nytimes.com/2015/03/01/books/review/kazuo-ishiguros-the-buried-giant.html (accessed June 2021).
Halbwachs, Maurice (1992). *On Collective Memory* (Chicago: University of Chicago Press).
Hu, Jane (2021). 'Typical Japanese: Kazuo Ishiguro and the Asian Anglophone Historical Novel', *Modern Fiction Studies*, 67:1, 123–148.
Ishiguro, Kazuo (1981). 'A Strange and Sometimes Sadness', in *Introduction 7: Stories by New Writers* (London: Faber and Faber), 13–27.
—. (1989). *The Remains of the Day* (London: Faber and Faber).
—. (2015). *The Buried Giant* (London: Faber and Faber).
—. (2016). 'Kazuo Ishiguro on His Fears for Britain After Brexit', *Financial Times*, 1 July, www.ft.com/content/7877a0a6–3e11–11e6–9f2c-36b487ebd80a (accessed June 2021).
—. (2017). 'My Twentieth Century Evening – and Other Small Breakthroughs', 7 December. *The Nobel Foundation* 2017, www.nobelprize.org/uploads/2018/06/ishiguro-lecture_en-1.pdf (accessed June 2022).
Kansteiner, Wulf (2002). 'Finding Meaning in Memory: A Methodological Critique of Collective Memory Studies', *History and Theory*, 41:2, 179–197.

MacColl, Alan (1999). 'King Arthur and the Making of an English Britain', *History Today*, 49, 7–13.
Malory, Thomas (1529). *Le Morte Darthur*, London.
Matthews, Sean (2009). '"I'm Sorry I Can't Say More": An Interview with Kazuo Ishiguro', in Sean Matthews and Sebastian Groes (eds), *Kazuo Ishiguro: Contemporary Critical Perspectives* (London: Continuum), 114–125.
McGrattan, Cillian and Stephen Hopkins (2017). 'Memory in Post-conflict Societies: From Contention to Integration?', *Ethnopolitics*, 16:5, 488–499.
Meek, James (2019). *Dreams of Leaving and Remaining* (London: Verso).
Moore, Michael Scott and Michael Sontheimer (2005). 'I Remain Fascinated by Memory', *Spiegel Online*, 5 October, www.spiegel.de/international/spiegel-interview-with-kazuo-ishiguro-i-remain-fascinated-by-memory-a-378173.html (accessed June 2021).
Rukeyser, Rebecca (2015). 'Kazuo Ishiguro: Mythic Retreat', *Guernica*, 1 May.
Shaw, Kristian (2021). *Brexlit: British Literature and the European Project* (London: Bloomsbury).
Stacy, Ivan (2021). 'Looking Out into the Fog: Narrative, Historical Responsibility, and the Problem of Freedom in Kazuo Ishiguro's *The Buried Giant*', *Textual Practice*, 35:1, 109–122.
Teo, Yugin (2014). *Kazuo Ishiguro and Memory* (Basingstoke: Palgrave Macmillan).
Vernon, Matthew and Margaret A. Miller (2018). 'Navigating Wonder: The Medieval Geographies of Kazuo Ishiguro's *The Buried Giant*', *Arthuriana*, 28:4, 68–89.
Vorda, Allan and Kim Herzinger (2008). 'An Interview with Kazuo Ishiguro', in Brian W. Shaffer and Cynthia Wong (eds), *Conversations with Kazuo Ishiguro* (Jackson: University Press of Mississippi), 66–88.
Watchel, Eleanor (1996). *More Writers and Company* (Toronto: Alfred A. Knopf).
Wong, Cynthia F. (2000). *Kazuo Ishiguro* (Tavistock: Northcote House).
Wood, James (2015). 'The Uses of Oblivion: Kazuo Ishiguro's *The Buried Giant*', *The New Yorker*, 23 March, www.newyorker.com/magazine/2015/03/23/the-uses-of-oblivion (accessed June 2021).
Wyn Jones, Richard, et al. (2013). 'England and Its Two Unions: The Anatomy of a Nation and Its Discontents', London: Institute for Public Policy Research, www.ippr.org/publications/england-and-its-two-unions-the-anatomy-of-a-nation-and-its-discontents(accessed June 2021).

10

Klara and the humans: agency, Hannah Arendt and forgiveness

Robert Eaglestone

Questions about agency and its attendant problems are at the heart of Ishiguro's fiction: knowing or not knowing how to act; the ability or inability to act; the impact of actions from the past on the present; the involvement, willing or not, in the mass-actions of others (in nationalist movements, or anti-Semitism, for example). These problems of agency are usually seen through their impact on the agent, even if the agent does not seem to recognise them, which is the source of much of the pathos (in *The Remains of the Day* or *Never Let Me Go*) or irony (*When We Were Orphans*) or unsettling humour (*The Unconsoled*) in his work.

Two visions of agency

Klara and the Sun marks a development in what we might call the 'novelistic thinking' about agency in Ishiguro's work. Not only are there many agents – there are more plots and subplots than in most of Ishiguro's other novels– but, at its core, the novel contrasts two visions of, or ideas about, agency: a machinic or technological vision of agency against a more 'human' one. Significantly, as this chapter will demonstrate, machine thinking is not limited to machines, and humans have problems with 'human' thinking. The novel plays out and so illuminates the differences between these visions, which, as the chapter argues, tells us something about our world. More, and more importantly in the context of Ishiguro's work, what I term the 'human' vision of agency offers a way out of an intellectual impasse which characterises much of Ishiguro's fiction.

These two visions of agency, this contrast between a vision of life as technological or as human, do not simply stem from the fact that Klara is a machine or that Josie is 'lifted' (that is, in the world of the novel, genetically enhanced) or from some notional humanity of the other characters. This contrast is much older and originates in the West from classical antiquity in the philosophy of Plato and Aristotle. I turn to their work to interpret this novel, first and foremost, because they make up the foundational matrix of Western thought, which deals with the same fundamental questions as *Klara and the Sun*: who or what are we? How are we different, or not, from animals and other thinking creatures? Is our thinking at root technical or somehow something else? How are agency and knowledge linked? What role does transcendence play in our lives and in relation to reason? Second, because one strand of this thinking, in the work of Martin Heidegger and Hannah Arendt, has led to some of the most interesting work on AI, machine thinking, agency and its importance. This is also, incidentally, an answer to those attacks on Ishiguro by those in the science-fiction community, like Iain Banks (2011), who see him as appropriating science fiction tropes to write about 'new things' – AI, genetic modification – the *novum* often taken to be at the core of the genre. In fact Ishiguro is using these to talk about *very old* things.

Klara and the Cave

The first vision of how agency works in the novel is Klara's: a model of agency from the point of view of a product. Perhaps, at first sight, we might think that this is heart-warming: It (I am not going to call it 'she') is a product designed to be an Artificial Friend (AF), of course, so It sounds almost friendly. But we note It is only as good as Its programming. It follows Its pre-programmed hierarchies and ultimately obeys Its owner, Josie's Mother. For example, the Mother orders Klara to accompany her to the waterfall without Josie, against Josie's wishes, and Klara obeys, rationalising (using the metaphor of sight) that, since 'Mother and Josie had now expressed the view' that It should go, 'I could see how likely it was […] that I would gain new, perhaps crucial insights concerning Josie's situation' (*KS*: 96). More chillingly, It obeys Its owner's commands even when these seem to threaten Josie: instructed by the mother to replace Josie, it says until 'just now' that it 'believed it was my duty [i.e. programming] to save Josie, to make her well. But perhaps this is a better way' (*KS*: 214). Klara's programming means It also notes only 'black-skinned people' as exceptions. Josie Gill (2020: 65) notes a similar trope in *Never Let Me Go* as Kathy has 'quite a good look' at George 'the big Nigerian man' (*NLMG*: 251) but fails to see Miss Emily. Even the moment that looks most like an action beginning in Its own free agency, Its act of worship at the Sun's barn, stems from a logical series of inferences concerning Josie's health: Klara brings 'several speculations together' until the 'idea came into my mind' (*KS*: 115). Perhaps this oddly passive construction is an articulation of programming, not thinking. This is because in the question echoed in its model number, 'B2' (*KS*: 42), It is not 2B.

Klara can only follow Its programming in matters of agency: It does, however, acquire something that at least looks like knowledge. In fact, this acquisition closely parallels the most famous story about knowledge in Western culture, Plato's allegory of the Cave. At the centre of *The Republic*, at the start of Book VII, the allegory's protagonist begins in the depth of the dark cave, chained in fetters with others. The talk is of the images they can all see, but as the protagonist breaks free, these are revealed to be shadows on the wall cast by puppets. The protagonist is wrenched up and out of the cave into the daylight where, slowly adjusting to the world outside, he begins to see and then to understand the real, true, beautiful world illuminated by the light of the sun. Descending back into the cave, the protagonist discovers that the former prisoners now despise him and resent his strange talk of the real world and would murder him if they could. It is a journey which parallels the rising and sinking of the sun: rising from our painful, shared human time, in which things change, into the peak of the eternal realm, in which things are for ever true and unchanging, and then back down to darkness. In Plato knowledge and agency are bound together: one reading of Plato is that through reason, through knowledge, his work is trying to give us agency, to make us free from convention, free from others, free even from our own bodily desires, to achieve the 'inner freedom of the soul' (Williams, 2008: 154).

Klara begins in a shop, a cave, imprisoned with others, even though It 'always longed to see more of the outside' (*KS*: 6). Rosa and the other AFs talk about frivolities or tease each other: Klara is keen to learn. Even though It gets sent to the darkness at the back of the shop, It is eventually bought and leaves the shop/cave for Josie's house. From there It goes outside and makes Its way to the Sun's barn, where It communes with the real world, has an insight or illusion of mystical knowledge. Having communed with the Sun, It takes Its lessons back to the world. In the end Klara goes back into a cave, the little utility room, and then finally to a yard where, although It can turn its head (*KS*: 303), It is unable to move (like the cave). It suffers a 'slow fade' (*KS*: 298) (and not 'reverse engineering', being taken apart, at the hands of Mr Capaldi).

Klara's model of knowledge, like Plato's, is of seeing: 'to *see* more of the outside' (*KS*: 6). Others echo this continually: 'All right Klara, just you wait and see' (*KS*: 27) says AF Rex; Manager praises Its 'extraordinary observational ability' (*KS*: 44); It 'notices things no one else does and stores them away' (*KS*: 77); '"Maybe", Josie says, "you can see things the rest of us can't"' (*KS*: 108). Its sense of knowledge-as-seeing extends to calculating what goes on inside people: Manager notes Its 'unusual insight' (*KS*: 304). Again, Gill notes this trope in Kathy, who '"sees" in order to understand the thoughts of others' (2020: 70). Klara also segments space – the waterfall is described as 'filling eight boxes' (*KS*: 100); and time – Rick's visits 'fell into three phases' (*KS*: 118). The geometrical shapes It constantly describes are not only the result of its perception system being overwhelmed (nor only, as one of my students insightfully realised, its memory systems running down in the yard in the time of the narration) but also insight into the Platonic nature of reality: echoes, as in the dialogue *Meno*, of the ideal forms.

Klara may acquire something that looks like knowledge, as the philosopher does in Plato, escaping from the cave, but it can never acquire that 'inner freedom of the soul' because it is a programmed machine. Indeed it illustrates what Heidegger sees as a monumental but subtle shift in Plato's allegory. While the Sun is the revelation of the true, the beautiful and the good, the philosopher does not bring back the Sun and its revealing light: instead, they bring the *images* of what is illuminated. In the cave what is seen is not truth-as-revelation but instead *truth-as-accuracy*, right-or-wrong, standards. The cave-dwellers compare their shadows on the wall with the now-shadowy images brought back from above. That is to say,

'Cave-thinking' cannot understand these 'beyond moments' and can only comprehend them in its own, limited idiom (see Heidegger, 1998). This is what computers do: they are accurate, they are not truthful. That is, your laptop can spellcheck 'I love you' but can never mean it.

This is all relevant because one reading of Plato is to see his world as the world of products dominated by technical thinking. Alexander Nehamas writes that the

> fundamental assumption on which Plato's system depends is an image of living a life as practicing a craft, as a process that proceeds by definitive rules and whose product depends on how well its rules are applied. To put the point bluntly, just as we are willing to take the advice of shoemakers on the most appropriate shoes, so, he believes, we should be willing to take the advice of philosophers on what life is best for us. (1999: 327)

This is a *product's* way of seeing the world. Like a computer program or algorithm, it works by applying the right knowledge, the right rules, to get the right outcome. This is true even in Klara's interaction with the Sun. Klara believes that if It enters the right information in the right way, and undertakes the right actions, It will get the right result: a childish view of religion. The novel shows us that this grounding belief is false. The Sun does not bring the homeless man back to life, for example, nor is it angry that Klara fails in Its chimerical mission to prevent pollution: the Sun is just the sun.

One could object that Klara's seemingly religious vision of the Sun is not rational or a result of craft, of technological thinking. This seems flawed in three ways. First, to be rational is not necessarily to be materialist or atheist (this conflation of views, that rationalism is the same as materialism is the same as atheism is a contemporary 'New Atheist' view). That is to say: Klara's apparent religion is not irrational. Indeed, second, Klara's thought process, given Its view of the Sun, is entirely rational: whether the starting point – the near-omnipotence and omniscience of the Sun – is correct is an issue beyond rationality: it is neither a rational or irrational decision and cannot be measured in those terms. Third, and perhaps most important, is the 'argument by design' for God which assumes that the universe is designed, just as a watch must have a watchmaker. For us humans this argument is flawed as an argument (not least because evolution can be understood to achieve the same end) and it begs an array of the deepest religious and existential questions. But this is not the case for Klara. Klara *is* a watch, a machine, and unquestionably does have a maker; so it is hardly a surprise that Its view of the universe is 'by design', teleological and algorithmic and that the Sun, Its energy source, is the 'designer' and repairer of things broken in the world. Moreover, bearing in mind that It is programmed to see and draw empirical inferences from Its vision, we see that the story of the 'resurrection' of Beggar man and his dog by the Sun ('a special kind of nourishment from the Sun had saved them') underlies the development of Its rational (if incorrect) beliefs (*KS*: 37). From this belief in the creator/preserver God of the Sun, all Klara's deductions follow a rational process.

Klara, then, has the illusion of agency but without agency. This does not mean that It cannot do things: Jane Bennett writes that vibrant matter is 'a creative not-quite-human force capable of producing the new' (2010: 118). Bennett is referring to nature, to non-human matter, which applies as well to Klara. A watch, or a robot, does something, but may not have agency. It might be suggested that Klara does display agency: take, for example, Its desire to go outside. Klara has 'estimated' (a mathematical word) that Josie has drawn a picture for Rick and offers to take it to his house to help repair the rift between them: AFs, Josie notes, 'go on errands all the time'; Klara adds that it 'would be good for me to explore the outside' and that Rick might forgive Josie 'and be her best friend again' (*KS*: 135). This latter is Its motivation but this is clearly a programmed desire, to make the object of Its programming happy (through observations Klara can access 'quite comprehensively all of Josie's impulses and desires' (*KS*: 210), just as Google can many of ours). Very significantly, as the chapter will suggest below, Its lack of real understanding is shown immediately. Josie crossly says that it is 'for *me* to forgive *him*' and Klara has to admit that It does not understand 'yet the rules about forgiveness' (*KS*: 135). It never will because forgiveness has no rules, and, without rules, Klara cannot grasp anything. As Jacques Derrida argued, 'forgiveness is not, it *should not be*, normal, normative, normalising. It should remain exceptional and extraordinary [...] as if it interrupted the ordinary course of historical temporality' (2001: 32 – emphasis in original). If there were rules to forgiveness, it would simply be an exchange, one for another, an algorithm. By contrast, he points out that, for thinkers like Arendt, forgiveness is 'a human possibility' (2001: 37).

A human possibility: *action* and agency

Klara and the Sun offers another vision of agency based not on 'product' or 'technological' thinking but on a vision illuminated usefully by Arendt and in which forgiveness, one of the themes of the novel, is understood anew. In *The Human Condition* (1998), Arendt outlines three modes in which we humans live. The first is *labour*, repetitive work undertaken to keep the body alive (think: the cyclical sowing and harvesting of crops; cleaning the home; or even the daily brushing of teeth).

The second, and especially relevant to Klara, is *work*, making things. This is the task of the *homo faber*, the mode of being of humans-as-makers, as humans-as-machines (and, in the case of Klara, machines-as-humans). Work is algorithmic, it follows a pattern or a blueprint, and in following a blueprint arrives at a pre-planned end. It uses the resources of the world: material (a tree becomes a table) but also, we can add to Arendt, less material: the smile and 'have a nice day!' phrasing of a customer service agent is work, as are Klara's addresses to the Sun, which aim to achieve what It is programmed to do. Klara is simply a more sophisticated version of the robot machines that, say, make cars. As I have suggested, Klara both works and is a *work*, a made-object: Its function as an AF to make a world, a more pleasant world for Its teenager.

Arendt's third mode is *action*. This is widely seen as Arendt's most innovative idea from *The Human Condition*. Action, for Arendt, 'alone is the exclusive prerogative of man; neither a beast nor a god is capable of it, and only action is entirely dependent upon the constant presence of others' (1998: 22–23): this is why action is the source of politics, our being together. Action stems from the fact of human plurality, that we are always in society with others, and that we act with others. It is unlike the making that work is, because, while making has an end in mind, for action the end is unclear: the doing itself is the point, and, in that doing, you express who you are. For example, we do not know what the consequence will be from going on a political demonstration: we may hope or intend a certain consequence, but in taking the action together we are only expressing ourselves and hoping for the result we desire. By contrast, screwing the legs to the tabletop, as per the blueprint, inevitably makes a table if you do it properly. Actions establish relationships but can also end them. Action, as the demonstration example suggests, is unpredictable and irreversible: you can disassemble a table but you cannot 'take back' an action, and any action sets off a chain of further consequences and actions. When the Mother 'lifted' her first daughter Sal, and then Josie, she took an action. The consequences and damages are unforeseen. The chain of actions lead first to Sal's death, and seems as if it will lead to Josie's too. These kinds of chains of events are a central theme of Ishiguro's fiction: a decision taken often years before (to become a painter for the Japanese nationalist movement; to teach nationalism; to choose not to ask someone to marry you; to aid commitment of a genocide) begins a series of events forging a link in a chain which remains unbroken.

These chains of actions, one following unpredictably on from another, are broken only by forgiveness, Arendt argues. It is forgiveness that prevents endless bitterness and anger and is the resolution to the problem of the unpredictable consequences of sequences of action. Arendt writes that the 'discoverer of the role of forgiveness in the realm of human affairs was Jesus of Nazareth. The fact that he made this discovery in a religious context and articulated it in religious language is no reason to take it any less seriously in a strictly secular sense' (1998: 238). Arendt means: we do not have to be theists to take forgiveness seriously: 'forgiveness may be the necessary corrective for the inevitable damages resulting from action' (1998: 239). In *Klara and the Sun* these two models of agency come to meet and contrast most clearly in the central moment of forgiveness in the novel. It is this moment, too, which marks the novel out as different from other Ishiguro fictions and, heard most fully, shows a development in the thought of his work: as I will go on to suggest, it answers, in part, questions posed in his previous works.

Forgiveness

Before focussing in detail on the most important moment of forgiveness, and in order to stress how important forgiveness is in *Klara and the Sun*, I want to look at three examples in the novel: one is fake, one is not forgiveness (despite the appearance of it) and one is real. First, a fake, totally instrumental non-apology, from Miss Helen to Vance. Rick and his mother meet Vance, her lover from twenty-seven years before, in order to persuade him to offer Rick a scholarship to the Atlas Brookings College. Vance takes the chance to attack Helen, he 'changed the mood so suddenly I almost let a surprised sound escape me' (*KS*: 250). She apologises, badly, 'I often wish I could line up all the people [...] I've treated shabbily [...] the way a monarch might [...] look each one in the eye and say, I'm so sorry' (*KS*: 252–253) and then, more abjectly in response to particular wrongs: 'that evening at Miles Martin's house [...] That voicemail' (*KS*: 254). Vance, knowing full well the apology is designed as an exchange (an apology for a scholarship), clearly declines it. Immediately afterwards, Miss Helen affirms its instrumental nature, 'I'm wondering if that was enough. If that will satisfy him' (*KS*: 256). This is not an apology, it is a simple exchange, almost an exercise in ritual humiliation, and certainly a kind of economic exchange (a submission for a favour).

A second kind of 'non-apology' occurs towards the end of the novel. Like her comparable counterpart Jessie from *Toy Story 2*, Klara is more or less thrown away by Josie as Josie grows older. For a while It is stored in the little utility room and eventually sent to the junkyard. In this period Rick is concerned for It: 'Are you going to be OK?' he asks, and It replies that 'The mother is always very kind to me' (*KS*: 292). Josie's farewell is not much: 'I guess you may not be here when I get back. You've been just great Klara' (*KS*: 301). But Klara is nether bitter nor forgiving, because – as a machine – It can be neither. Indeed it may be that 'all humans are lonely. At least potentially' (*KS*: 260) but Klara is not, because It is not human. Klara has no capacity for 'being with', only a programme to look as if it has, and so no need to ask, or be offered, forgiveness.

A third, real act of forgiveness occurs between Rick and Josie. Not only is their teenage relationship full of acts of forgiveness and making up, but their growth into an adult relationship, as friends, is as well. They change and grow, and 'now we're no longer kids, we have to wish each the best and go our different ways' (*KS*: 292). They are friends and have, as it were, forgiven and freed each other from each other, and remain fond: a positive way to come to be with former lovers. This kind of positive view of a former relationship is almost unique in Ishiguro's work and is a sign that there is something important in that act of forgiveness. These three examples serve only to build or reflect on the core moment of forgiveness in the novel.

That's some message

The crucial scene in the novel is based around forgiveness and draws on the metaphorical field of light/dark, sun and vision. It brings into stark contrast the technological, machinic work-world and the plural human shared sense of action with all its fallibilities. Josie is ill, possibly dying like her sister, from 'being lifted'. The Mother, bitter and in despair, lashes out at Rick: does he feel like the winner, even though he was not 'lifted'? All he has is the 'dark sky' (*KS*: 280) that she gestures at as she 'waved her hand at the window' (*KS*: 281). Something 'ignited' (*KS*: 281) in Rick's face. He passes on a message from Josie; the Mother's eyes are 'filled with fear' (*KS*: 281) in apprehension, in case Josie is going to condemn her, as her actions seem to have risked killing Josie. But, in fact, the message is one of love and of forgiveness. Josie loves her Mother and was happy to be lifted despite the seeming real risk of her death: 'she'd do exactly what you did and you'll always be the best mother she could have' (*KS*: 282). The Mother replies:

> 'That's some message', she said finally.
> 'Excuse me', I said.
> 'Jesus', the Mother said and sighed quietly. 'That's some message'.
> 'Excuse me!'. This time I'd almost shouted [...] 'I'm sorry to interrupt. But there's something occurring outside. The Sun's coming out!'
> (*KS*: 282)

The Mother means 'Jesus' as a kind of expletive but we do not have to hear it that way: instead, following Arendt, we can hear it as noting the power of forgiveness. Klara is interrupting because the Sun is appearing (and we can note: the humans are concerned with what they can *hear*, the robot with what it can *see*). It demands: 'we must go upstairs', to Josie. Klara and Rick, 'coming to some intuitive conclusion' (*KS*: 283), throw open the window, 'the Sun had broken through the dark clouds, and all at once – as if each of us in the room had received a secret message – we turned to look at Josie' (*KS*: 284). She wants to drink water. This scene is a quasi-miracle ('quasi' in the sense of 'as if'): it seems like a marvellous, redemptive event.

From the machinic, technological point of view Klara's plea to the Sun and the Sun's coming out are linked: if the proper steps are followed in the algorithm, if the ritual is performed in the correct way, the Sun will respond. But we know not only from our common sense but also from the novel itself that this is not the case. The Sun is not a divinity in the novel, nor is it like a reliable 'piece of technology' that can be switched on by the right actions (like a child's version of the Christian God): it is Klara's product-vision of agency which has created this idea for it. But from the other view of agency, of human action, a different kind of event has occurred. Josie's act of forgiveness (and of love) has broken the chain of events. It is this breaking of the chain that, as it were, *is* the miracle. Josie is the victim of her Mother's choices, and her life is in danger. But once she has forgiven her Mother, the burden of the past is thrown off (are there other examples of this 'throwing off' in Ishiguro's wider body of work? It is hard to think of any, and none so obvious: even Axl's forgiveness of Beatrice's affair in *The Buried Giant* is combined with anger and long-held grudges). Josie's recovery may not stem from her forgiveness, but the physical recovery is almost secondary to the psychic one: the Sun breaking through the clouds is metaphor for the breaking of the chain of events, perhaps ('Josie and the sun'. 'Josie and the son'), and the secret message is that all is forgiven and can begin afresh.

In the novel this moment undoes all the knots and plots: Josie is free to live on; Rick is freed from his obligations to Josie and so any sense that he needs to be 'lifted'; the sinister plan with Mr Capaldi will come to nothing; even Josie's need for Klara, which stemmed in no small part from her sickness and her Mother's concern, begins to wane. The forgiveness begins the happy ending of the novel. It is even more significant, perhaps, for the change it marks in Ishiguro's fiction. I began this chapter noting that Ishiguro's fiction is about the ways in which our past choices, whether made or unmade, whether free or not, trap us and how they then shape our present and future. Masuji Ono trapped by his nationalist past in *An Artist of the Floating World*; Stevens led to loneliness through dignity in *The Remains of the Day*; Kathy's 'choiceless choice' of passivity in the genocidal world of *Never Let Me Go*; Banks trapped in an adult version of his childhood trauma in *When We Were Orphans*. These characters live with but cannot escape the way they are trapped by the actions of their past: Ryder simply tries to leave the city at the end of *The Unconsoled*. In the novel immediately before *Klara and the Sun*, this 'entrappedness' is given its full significance, namely Wistan's vision of the retributive genocide and atrocity in *The Buried Giant*: 'Men will burn their neighbour's houses by night. Hang children from trees at dawn. The rivers will stink of corpses bloated from their days of voyaging' (*BG*: 324). In that novel, as in the Ishiguro's earlier works, there is no way out from the choices of the past, and simply living with them (by learning to banter, say, and enjoying the remains of the day) is not enough to avoid the catastrophe that the past brings to the future: Kathy is both a collaborator with and will be a murdered victim of genocide; Wistan's allies will commit retributive atrocities. All these are examples of Klara's algorithmic, 'machine' way of thinking, its product vision of agency. One move leads inexorably to another and then to another: there can be no escape.

But as we saw in Arendt, and in Rick's message from Josie, there is a way to end this chain, there is a kind of reply to Wistan. That is forgiveness which breaks the chains of action. Now a slightly wild claim: *Klara and the Sun* retrospectively imagines this forgiveness across Ishiguro's canon. The novel is full of conscious, powerful echoes from Ishiguro's earlier works: significantly, in *Klara*, each one is case redeemed. Who are Coffee Cup Lady, 'I estimated sixty-seven years old', and her Raincoat Man, 'I estimated seventy-one years old' (*KS*: 19) but Beatrice and Axl, once sundered and now reunited: 'at special moments like that, people feel a pain alongside their happiness' (*KS*: 21). They are referred to again at the close of the novel (*KS*: 293). They may also be Miss Kenton and Mr Stevens, spending the remaining hours of the sunny day together, 'She and the man were holding each other so tightly they were like one large person, and the Sun, noticing, was pouring his nourishment on them' (*KS*: 20): this image of two united as one, each having found 'their other half', is taken, of course, from *The Symposium*. The Mother and Miss Helen are echoes of Etsuko and Sachiko from *A Pale View of Hills*, right down to the suggestion of a potential murder plot and the uncertainty about their degrees of mental stability: but, unlike the earlier novel, nothing wicked this way comes. The Mother, too, with her 'Sal' doll (and potentially her Josie doll) hints at Kathy's dance in *Never Let Me Go*: but Mother *does have* a child. Josie and Rick parallel Kathy and Tommy, a couple who hope that their love will allow them something special. Rick, like Tommy, is kind of a failure (he has not been 'lifted') but has something special to show (his mechanical birds which will be used for surveillance, of what is past or passing or to come). Yet both grow out of their love in a healthy and human way (that is, they are not murdered for their organs). Klara itself is also like Kathy, with her naivety and her keen observation of others, but with her blindnesses, too: but Klara (unlike Kathy) is simply a machine. Klara is also like Stevens, with views on good household management and, much more significantly, abetting something wicked or questionable because it is told to by an authority: but it sacks no Jewish maids, nor does the plot for It to replace Josie come to anything. It is also teased by Josie's cronies in a way that clearly recalls Stevens's interrogation by Lord Darlington and his friends, in which Stevens has to act the role of 'the man on the street' (itself a rewriting of Tolstoy's scene between Lavrushka the Cossack and Napoleon in *War and Peace*): but Klara does not feel shame, nor does it need to dissimulate. Even in terms of the style, the novel has sections which echo the mysterious oneiric quality of *The Unconsoled* (why, for example, are the shop's shelves complete with coffee cups seen in the barn?).

However, in contrast to Ishiguro's earlier novel we even see one of these scenes 'from the inside' (*KS*: 306) where we and Klara understand what it means (the meaning is redeemed, as it were), while the interlocutor, Manager, does not: there is a version of the same bravura prose trick earlier in the novel too, in a conversation between Rick and Klara (*KS*: 159). All this is to say that Ishiguro has gone some way towards answering the challenge made by Wistan in *The Buried Giant*: he has found, for an individual at least, a way of breaking the chains that lead from action to retribution. That is: forgiveness. However, in order to do this, he has had to present a different model of agency, one in which forgiveness is possible. As Mother puts it in *Klara and the Sun*: 'That's some message' (*KS*: 282). He has achieved this by using a machine to draw our attention to the limits of 'machine thinking' and so to the possibilities of 'human thinking'.

Conclusion

In a review of *Never Let Me Go*, Louis Menand (2005) writes that there is 'something animatronic' about Ishiguro's characters: they are 'simulators of humanness, figures engineered to pass as "real". What it means to be really human is always a problem for them. Can you just copy other people? Would that take care of it?' (2005). This is why, Menand writes of that novel, genetic engineering 'the idea of human beings as products programmed to pick up "personhood skills" – is a perfect vehicle for a writer like Ishiguro'. I am not sure I agree completely with this assessment: in my reading, Menand is picking up on the way that Ishiguro's characters seem often to accept a 'machine' version of human agency (2005). However, it is the case that in *Klara and the Sun* the 'simulator of humanness', Klara, is what leads us to see (or, better, to hear) through Its own limitations; what is not 'animatronic', what is really human in the other characters.

In this chapter I have argued that agency is a central issue in all of Ishiguro's fiction, and that *Klara and the Sun* offers two visions of agency. The first is Klara's: a vision of agency about production from a product, in which one event follows – is made – by another in programmable, predictable steps. This sense of agency corresponded to one way of understanding a Platonic vision of the world, that living life is the same as practicing a craft. The other is more profoundly free and more profoundly human vision: the sense of agency involved not with production but with action that Arendt describes. In this vision of our human condition, forgiveness is what breaks the potentially endless chain of actions. In *Klara and the Sun* it is Josie's forgiveness of her mother that breaks this chain and resolves the plots of the novel. The possibility of personal (though not communal) forgiveness and the sense of agency it implies marks a movement beyond his previous novels.

References

Arendt, Hannah (1998). *The Human Condition* (Chicago: University of Chicago Press, 2nd edn).
Banks, Iain M. (2011). 'Science Fiction Is No Place for Dabblers', *The Guardian*, 13 May.
Bennett, Jane (2010). *Vibrant Matter: A Political Ecology of Things* (Durham, NC: Duke University Press).
Derrida, Jacques (2001). *On Cosmopolitanism and Forgiveness* (London: Routledge).
Gill, Josie (2020). *Biofictions; Race, Genetics and the Contemporary Novel* (London: Bloomsbury).
Heidegger, Martin (1998). 'Plato's Doctrine of Truth', translated by Thomas Sheenhan, in William McNeill (ed.), *Pathmarks* (Cambridge: Cambridge University Press), 155–182
Ishiguro, Kazuo (2015). *The Buried Giant* (London: Faber and Faber).
—. (2021). *Klara and the Sun* (London: Faber and Faber).
Menand, Louis (2005). 'Something About Kathy', *New Yorker*, 28 March.
Nehamas, Alexander (1999). *Virtues of Authenticity* (Princeton: Princeton University Press).
Williams, Bernard (2008). *Shame and Necessity* (Princeton: Princeton University Press).

11

Kazuo Ishiguro's film and television scriptwriting

Anni Shen

From 1978 to 2005 Kazuo Ishiguro proposed fourteen screenplays, with four being successfully produced. Being a full-time novelist, Ishiguro still writes screenplays as a self-proclaimed 'enthusiastic amateur'. However, at the beginning of his career, Ishiguro tested the waters with writing screenplays along with short stories. In 1978 Ishiguro wrote his first radio play, 'Potatoes and Lovers', which got him accepted into the MA creative writing programme at the University of East Anglia. With piano music set instructions bracketed as the introduction, the play tells a love story about two shy cross-eyed people and how their love fails as they struggle to identify themselves being at odds with 'the idealized stereotypes of romance, and indeed sex, and how they finally succumb to social pressures' (Archive 47.2).[1]

Writing screenplays for radio, television and cinema comes naturally for Ishiguro for at least two reasons. First, Ishiguro finds short-story writing and scriptwriting similar. 'Films, in story terms, are usually shorter things and so the model of the typical film is much closer to the two-hundred pages novel' (Archive 26.1). Second, as a young writer, unsure of himself as either a screenwriter or novelist, Ishiguro experimented with ideas by writing novels and screenplays simultaneously. Ishiguro was also well aware of the differences and similarities between these two forms, remarking that '[a] key difference between writing for cinema and writing novels is that in cinema, the story is told principally through images and music – the words are a kind of supplement. In a novel, words are all you have. But the two forms have many things in common, of course, and I think you can learn much about one from the other' (Archive 62.5).

Ishiguro knew from the start that novels would not be able to compete with television and cinema unless novelists took advantage of the strengths of its linguistic medium (Archive 62.5). He was also alert to the danger that his scriptwriting posed to his novel writing. 'Looking back,' says Ishiguro, 'my first novel, *A Pale View of Hills*, looks to me very close to a screenplay in technique. It moves forward scene by scene with pared-down dialogue, little set descriptions and stage directions' (Archive 62.5). Ishiguro's scriptwriting experience led him to search for a way to make his novels 'unfilmable', which means two things. First, Ishiguro wishes to write books that can offer an experience completely different from what the audience gets in front of the screen. Second, he wants his novel to work uniquely as a novel, and his screenplay uniquely as a film (Archive 62.5). As I will show, Ishiguro achieves that goal and develops his inimitable style through scriptwriting experimentation that blends into his novel-writing process.

Most scholars read Ishiguro's screenplays as a subfield that the author unfurls to revisit the themes or plots that originate in his novelistic artistry. I venture to upset this line of interpretation that dictates, by default, the origin of the author's novel writing over scriptwriting by claiming instead that scriptwriting serves as a crucial foundation for Ishiguro's novels. On the basis of archival research on the Ishiguro Papers housed in the Harry Ransom Center at the University of Texas at Austin, I demonstrate that Ishiguro articulates his ideas, at both the narrative and thematic levels, through film and television plays before finalising them in novels.

The dynamic interplay between fiction and film in Ishiguro's works can be categorised in two parts. I call the first part 'the novelistic output to cinema', and the second 'the cinematic input to novel'. The former includes the adaptations of Ishiguro's fictions for the screen and the works of the visual media in which Ishiguro participates in a variety of roles (such as playwright, film critic and film producer); the latter includes the influence of specific films or cinematic genres on Ishiguro's writing, as is evident in intertexts, allusions and references, and the influence of Ishiguro's television and film scripts on his own fiction. Partly due to the bias of seeing novels as the primary medium of contemporary culture, literary scholars tend to approach the relation between fiction and film by prioritising novelists' linguistic output to cinema. Therefore the majority of scholarship on fiction and film falls into the category of adaptation studies. A limited number of essays on Ishiguro's screenplays reflect such a view.[2]

Among these essays Lisa Fluet points to Ishiguro's stylistic propensity for reiteration and thematic concern about authenticity. Using *The White Countess* (2005) as an example, she notes that Ishiguro's screenplay 'invites experienced Ishiguro readers' to revisit 'characters, events, crises and conclusions' that echo his previous novels, thus exhibiting 'a curious inauthenticity' (2007: 207–208). Sebastian Groes and Paul-Daniel Veyret also claim that 'Ishiguro's screenwriting addresses many of the topics and themes that characterize his fiction, but is often marked by a more overtly political stance' (2010: 32). For Groes and Veyret, Ishiguro articulates through *The Gourmet* (1984) his 'fierce criticism of the corrosive effects of Thatcherism on the socio-cultural fabric of Britain', whereas through *The Saddest Music in the World* (2003) and *The White Countess* Ishiguro makes tentative 'explorations of the possibility of creating a utopia' where harmony and conflict between nations coexist (2010: 32). Chu-Chueh Cheng, rather, reads the repetition from Ishiguro's novels to the screenplays as the author's adaptation of his own prose, a 'tactic of reframing and re-significance' mingled with the inspirations that he took from other novelists (2019: 384).

Contrary to the conventional interpretations that believe screenwriting to be a peripheral site that Ishiguro develops to rework the ideas that originate in his novels, I argue that Ishiguro often starts thinking through narrative voices, themes, characters and settings in his film and television plays and then later develops these thoughts in his novels. I support this argument first by exploiting the development of Ishiguro's famous butler character. The butler was introduced by Ishiguro in both television film scripts and short stories before the character's maturation in *The Remains of the Day* (1989). By tracing Ishiguro's choice of narrative voice and point of view in butler-related television-film script experiments, I demonstrate how Ishiguro expands the self-deception theme from the personal level to the national level. Next, I focus on Ishiguro's unpublished adaptation of Jun'ichiro Tanizaki's novel *Diary of a Mad Old Man* (1961) and explore how its character relation, plot and theme intertwine with Ishiguro's *The White Countess*, *The Gourmet* and *An Artist of the Floating World* (1986). Furthermore I investigate how Ishiguro's early drafts of *The Saddest Music in the World* helped him articulate two key themes that continue to inform his later novels, namely *When We Were Orphans* (2000), *Never Let Me Go* (2005) and *The Buried Giant* (2015).

A Profile of Arthur J. Mason and the gestation of 'the butler'

As the first film script that Ishiguro wrote, *A Profile of Arthur J. Mason* marks the birth of the butler, Stevens. The writing of this 1984 television film was essential in the evolution of Ishiguro's Booker Prize-winning novel *The Remains of the Day*, not only because it was Ishiguro's first 'outing with a butler character' but also because the actor of the film provides the prototype for Stevens: 'As I later began to work on *Remains*, I remember I saw in my mind for Stevens the face and manner of Bernard Hepton, the actor who portrayed Arthur Mason [the butler] in that film' (Archive 16.4). The Ishiguro archive includes several unpublished works that the novelist refers to as 'run-up' to his celebrated third novel.[3] Three out of five of the precursors are television film scripts, and they are also the first three times that Ishiguro attempted to capture the butler character. The archive reveals that the novelist made trial runs of the butler story, changing it back and forth between the film script and prose, before he found the proper narrative voice.

Commissioned by Britain's Channel 4, *A Profile of Arthur J. Mason* was directed by Michael Whyte, starring Bernard Hepton, Cherie Lunghi and Charles Gray. It won the Golden Plaque for 'Best Short Film' at the Chicago Film Festival of 1984. Ishiguro was asked by BBC4 to write the script in 1982, the same year his first full-length novel *A Pale View of Hills* was published. The fact that the film's actualisation took time obscures the fact that Ishiguro's English butler and Japanese mother Etsuko were created around the same time but for two different media.

Ishiguro's script and *The Remains of the Day* have a lot in common. The former is also about a butler's wasted life as follows:

> Arthur Mason, 64 years old, has been a butler all his life to the family of his present employer, Sir James Reid. Twenty-two years ago, Arthur completed a novel which remained unpublished. The novel has now been discovered, championed by notable literary figures. Over the years, Arthur has disciplined himself against further flickers of literary

ambition to the extent that he has avoided reading novels entirely. Until recently, he had convinced himself he was happy doing what he was, that his way of life was as meaningful as any other. Clearly, the belated recognition of his book has implications Arthur prefers not to think through. To all appearances, he cares little about it, and about its belated acclaim. Therefore, he has turned down lucrative advances, refuses to recognize his newly-won status and continues to give priority to his duties as butler. (Archive 16.5)

Arthur resembles Stevens, as they both take their butler profession so seriously to the extent that it hinders the romantic aspect of their lives. Arthur's wife left with his child twenty years ago, while Stevens's beloved Miss Kenton left and married another man. Similarly to Stevens, Arthur lives alone in a stark bedroom in his master's house, refusing to socialise with others. He has a habit of making car models at his leisure, indulging a fantasy of travelling and going outside of his world. In *The Remains of the Day* Steven does not own a vehicle but borrows his master's car to travel across England for the first time in his life.

Other than the character type that Ishiguro migrates from the film to novel, he develops, through this screenwriting experience, one of his crowning techniques that allows him to show meaning beneath the surface. Ishiguro wrote in the script synopsis: 'The TV play has all the appearance of a documentary profile, comprising of a series of interviews with the subject and people around him' (Archive 16.5), namely, Arthur's employer, Sir James – a prototype for Lord Darlington – and literary critics who reveal a narrative that is different from Arthur's own. Cumulatively, this butler-focused documentary drama indicates that Arthur's recognition is due to the literary climate at the moment that lauds the meteoric ascent of solitary working-class genius instead of his actual literary merit – 'Arthur is, in fact, quite talentless'. The play thus presents 'a television profile of a fictional character' (Archive 16.5). This use of the objective documentary tone with several third-person accounts on the same subject to bring out the theme of self-deception was to be modified by Ishiguro later, in favour of using the first-person limited point of view in prose.

Hindsight allows us to see that Ishiguro's preference for the first-person narrative in prose is exactly what distinguishes his novel writing from his scriptwriting, possibly because the novelist sees that the unreliable first-person voice is exclusively associated with novels that are meant to be 'unfilmable'. Although there are a few memorable films that attempt to frame stories entirely from the first-person perspective, cinema in general uses the first-person perspective intermediately with the third-person omniscient. Nevertheless, at the early stage in the novelist's career, he certainly felt unsafe with the first-person voice and experimented together with the third-person voice, trying to determine which worked best for his butler story.

Ishiguro's exploration of the third-person perspective is visible in his portrayal of *A Profile of Arthur J. Mason*'s female interviewer who hides behind the documentary camera and guides the spectator's point of view. Ishiguro specifies the tone for this outside narrator along with detailed camera directions in the film synopsis. The 'highly educated' interviewer named Anna 'comes to Sir James' house with a TV crew to film a documentary profile of Arthur Mason for arts program'. She is nothing but a quiet observer and cannot help but step into the scene at times to share her opinions. 'Hostile to [the] feudal set-up of the household and prejudiced against Sir James on account of his background', she is 'eager to express respect for Arthur on account of his being an artist', commenting on the new Marxist perspective on British class rivals that Arthur's book brings to the literary scene, which Arthur himself is unconsciously doing. She is also 'exasperated that Arthur should fail to acknowledge this respect and persist in subservient role of butler' (Archive 16.5). Ishiguro decisively takes the outsider point of view to set up the scene, concerning the camera position, as is evident in the scene in which Arthur is reading his diary to the camera and the interviewer.

However, Ishiguro was not satisfied with the delivery of target themes for the butler film. As he noted looking back, 'the political themes were still underdeveloped, focusing rather crudely on traditional class issues rather than on the small man's relationship to big power, as it was in *Remains*' (Archive 16.4). Additionally, there are two themes that Ishiguro has not yet introduced to the butler story: the first theme is 'what appeared to be good turns out to be evil', and the second theme is 'a mythical version of England and Englishness created for nostalgia and the consumption of foreign Anglophiles'. The former is found in Ishiguro's second portrayal of the butler.

The butler character appears for the second time in the unfinished short story called *The Patron* (1984). It is about a butler working in a prestigious household for Sir Arnold, a man who loves to fund people who excel in their field – chemistry, poetry, philosophy and, most recently, charity in the church, which is to be revealed as a sham. For this piece Ishiguro brings forth many aspects evident in his third novel. The script is written in the first person from the butler's viewpoint with a restrained and detached tone that resembles that of Stevens. Further, it is an earlier version of the Stevens–Darlington relationship, although 'the master here involves himself naively in domestic politics' instead of foreign affairs. Also, through the master – an early version of Lord Darlington – Ishiguro attempts again to convey the idea that people wish to leave something behind, large and fine, but fail terribly. To continue this thought, as pointed out by Ishiguro, 'the passage in which Sir Arnold falls on the steps, and is observed later going up and down the same steps also goes into *Remains*' (Archive 16.8). *The Patron* is, however, unfinished because Ishiguro had writer's block, as he was unaccustomed to and unsatisfied with the switch from the third person to the first person. He eventually abandoned the draft, leaving a note that says: 'the dialogue scenes should be in third person with the description in first person by the butler, and this could be a good film script' (Archive 16.8). During 1984 and 1986, he did precisely that, changing the butler story back to a film script under the same title.

In 1987, almost immediately after the publication of his second novel, Ishiguro rewrote the butler story through another film script called *Service in Japan*, featuring the butler for the third time. This film script tells a story of an English butler who must pretend to be his missing master to give a political speech in Japan during the American occupation. *The Remains of the Day* mimics this idea where Stevens enters a local pub on his way to the country and pretends to be a lord, discussing world politics with the locals (*RD*: 186–188). During the misplacing crisis the butler in *Service in Japan* befriended a Japanese translator whose idealism misled him during the Second World War. The Japanese translator, therefore, sees the butler as his younger self. Ishiguro's film script, to some extent, mixes elements from his second and third novels.

In writing *The Patron* and *Service in Japan* screenplays, Ishiguro struggled among three choices of narrative perspectives (Archive

17.1). The first option is to have two protagonists telling the story in turn as narrators in the first person, 'both ramble and drift', presenting a feeling of travel writing. The second option is to have the butler's wife telling the story in the first/third person. The third is to have the story told through an anonymous third/first person. The terms first/third and third/first that Ishiguro uses need annotation here. The left side of the slash indicates the narrative voice, while the right side indicates the point of view. The first/third, therefore, equals the first-person extra-diegetic narrative in the literary term, in which the narrator tells the story in the first person but is excluded from the story being told. The narrative, in such a case, takes an outsider point of view, whereas the third/first refers to an anonymous third-person narrative that can shift perspectives among characters. It is also known in literary studies as free indirect discourse. Ishiguro is experienced with the first/third person in his scriptwriting – as *A Profile of Arthur J. Mason* was told as a reportage by a reporter in the first/third person. Nevertheless, the third/first person voice (free indirect discourse) has a special appeal to the novelist because he thought that it can better frame an individual in conflict with his surrounding culture. In a note written in 1984 Ishiguro pondered:

> In the last two novels, we've used the 1st person in a fairly sophisticated way. But for novel 3 [*The Remains of the Day*], we're contemplating linking personal self-deception to a national (or British) self-deception. The traditional way to do this is to have a central character who is symbolically British. But this is unsatisfactory – it goes against idea of individuals – people don't represent whole cultures. Besides, I am interested in the tension between an individual and his background. Therefore, the 3rd/1st person may be the answer. The anonymous 1st person is perhaps ideally suited to representing a culture. The cultural character could be followed about in a myth-making way. This requires novelty of a rather difficult balance of the 1st and 3rd person. (Archive 17.1)

Ishiguro's interests in the technical operation of free indirect speech are rooted in his scriptwriting practices. The legendary Italian film director and scholar Pier Paolo Pasolini points to the fact that, even though free indirect speech is commonly seen in literature, not every writer consciously harnesses its poetic potential to express an implied thematic meaning. In its extension Pasolini distilled the characteristics of all third-person retrospective discourse: 'the author [narrator] cannot abstract from re-lived discourses a certain sociological consciousness of the milieu he is evoking: the social condition of a character determines his language' (1976: 548). Interestingly, Ishiguro's assessment of free indirect speech stands as a counter-argument against Pasolini's idea and states instead that an individual cannot represent the entire culture. For Ishiguro at that time an anonymous first-person narrator that potentially passes for the third person is better suited for the representation of a culture, precisely because of the mythical quality that it evokes. The choice of third-person narration for his 2005 novel *The Buried Giant* later justifies this early point from the novelist's notes. At the end of the novel the anonymous third-person narrator switches to the first-person ferryman who resembles the mythological Charon. In this way Ishiguro urges readers to reflect on how knowledge about their own reality and history is retold and controlled.

The film-inspired ambiguous third-person voice that comes across as the first person also manifested in *The Unconsoled* (1995). There is a scene in which the protagonist Ryder, from his position in a parked car, impossibly records the conversation between Stephan and Miss Collins in a back room of her house (*U*: 56). The critic Robert Lemon argues that Ryder's 'uncanny ability to eavesdrop on the internal thought of other character' and his 'godlike omniscience regarding events that take place out of sight and earshot' cannot be simply categorised as 'the oneiric realism' that most critics regard the narrative mode to be (2011: 217). Lemon rather considers it to be a 'heterodiegetic manoeuvre', which obliges Ryder 'to straddle the gulf between an unreliable narrator and an omniscient narratorial voice', a typical Kafkaesque technique to conceal the narrator's viewpoint. However, as I have shown, Ishiguro's third-person narrative method is not entirely Kafkan but also filmic.

Ishiguro's career as a novelist begins as he attempts to fill this urge to write a novel that is 'unfilmable' (Archive 17.1). The dynamic interplay between fiction and film, therefore, remains at the centre of Ishiguro's art, not only because, as novelist, he is consciously under the influence of cinema in terms of narrative technique, structure, plot and theme but also because, as a storyteller, he divides his energy, especially at the beginning of his career, almost equally between these two media. Through this process of switching back and forth between print and film formats, between the third- and first-person voices, *The Remains of the Day* is born.

The White Countess, The Gourmet and the adaptation of the Tanizaki novel

Three of Ishiguro's novels and one screenplay are set in Japan and China. Early critical responses explain the novelist's stylistic and thematic choices by analysing his oriental signatures. 'Japanese readings', encompassing subjects of psychology, architecture and visual art, dominate in such studies. Relevant to this section's discussion is the Japanese critic Takayuki Shonaka's study which compares *A Family Supper* (1980) and *A Pale View of Hills* with Yasunari Kawabata's *Yama no oto* (*The Sound of the Mountain*, 1954) regarding the stage settings, characters, structures and narrative strategies. Furthermore, it examined the style and theme of *The Remains of the Day* referring to Jun'ichiro Tanizaki's *Bunsho dokuhon* (*A Guide to Literary Style*, 1934). Shonaka claims that, even though it is not certain whether Ishiguro has read Tanizaki, the novelist has inherited some essence of Japanese quality that is beautifully defined in Tanizaki's book, possibly through Japanese films and novels he has seen and read (2011: 10–11). On the basis of my archival research I argue instead that, in Ishiguro's case, these two Japanese influences on Ishiguro are warranted rather by cinema. It is more likely that Ishiguro knew *The Sound of the Mountain* from Mikio Naruse's 1954 adaptation of the novel rather than as the literary text itself, given that Ishiguro is a self-proclaimed cinephile of 1950s Japanese cinema and knows Naruse's works well, as is evident in the multiple mentions of Naruse's films in Ishiguro's notebooks (Archive 49.12). Moreover, and as essential as it is little known, is the fact that Tanizaki's influence on Ishiguro manifests through the novelist's screenwriting and in specific connection to Ishiguro's own film adaptation attempt of Tanizaki's *Futen rojin nikki* (*Diary of a Mad Old Man*, 1961). I focus on the discussion of the latter next and demonstrate how Ishiguro repeats the literary process of 'blending' for characters, settings and themes that first appear in his and others' screenplays.

After the successful film adaptation of *The Remains of the Day* in 1993, Merchant and Ivory Production commissioned Ishiguro again to write an adaptation for Jun'ichiro Tanizaki's 1961 novel *Diary of a Mad Old Man*. During 1992 and 1994, Ishiguro composed three treatments along with two drafts of the film, only to abandon it at the end and replace it with an original screenplay later known as *The White Countess*: the original screenplay and Ishiguro's adaptation of Tanizaki are, therefore, intertwined.

Tanizaki's novel is told through the protagonist Utsugi's first-person voice in the form of a journal. He is a 77-year-old man with refined tastes whose body is decaying. Nevertheless, his sexual interest is unintentionally sparked and occasionally satisfied by the kind attention of his daughter-in-law Satsuko, who, by implication, used to work at a Geisha house. To Ishiguro 'the novel deals with the old man's desire to cling to life and youth against the inevitable eroding of the body. To do so, it focuses on the man's sexual obsession towards his daughter-in-law, which seems to be rooted in things that are to do with what he had found vital and fulfilling in life.' Ishiguro thinks that the failure of the Tanizaki novel lies in that the man's 'obsession does not quite reverberate enough as echoes of his earlier life' (Archive 39.2). Therefore, in adapting the novel, Ishiguro kept only the third part of the original plot and spent most of his script building a new richer link between the protagonist's sexual deviation and his nostalgia for the past.

One of Ishiguro's major revisions of Tanizaki's work is to change the nationality of the protagonist and the setting from Japan to America. Ishiguro's protagonist, Norton Andrews, is an American art collector travelling between East and West in the post-Vietnam war era. He used to be a gourmet in Japan and, as a middle-aged man, established himself as an aesthete who brought art from Japan to America, squandering his inherited wealth. This, he believes, is 'the role of his older, cultured New England families, to lead through civilizing' the nation of the United States (Archive 39.6). However, 'it is very difficult to gain civilization because values of art keep changing' – a recurring theme in Ishiguro's works. Norton's eye for Japanese art, much praised in the early days during the Second World War, turns questionable years later when he decides to sell his art collections in America. At the character's professional level,

Ishiguro's version combines Ono from *An Artist of the Floating World* and Manley from the 1984 television film script *The Gourmet*.

At the character's personal level, on the other hand, Ishiguro was also adapting his former model of Charles Manley in *The Gourmet*. Spending his life travelling around the world, Manley searches for various cuisines to retain his international declared ambition to 'taste things man has never tasted before' (Archive 48.8). He visits a London church at a time of economic recession that left many people homeless, and his target is a ghost that haunts the church. Manley manages to kill and devour the ghost, but the irony is that the thing appears to be a homeless man who came to seek shelter from the street. Ishiguro intends to present London and, by implication, 'Britain as a strange almost surreal place, [a] blending of extreme wealth and poverty', by 'focusing on the motifs of eating' – both as survival and as perverted gratification (Archive 48.8).

The protagonist in Ishiguro's adaptation is also someone who has always had an insatiable appetite for pleasures. Norton in his early days of Japan searches for the cause of this. It is revealed to be a surface symptom in disguise of a deeper self-defeating homosexuality after he sleeps with a Japanese *onnagata* (a male actor who plays women's roles in Japanese Kabuki theatre) – this being one significant detail that Ishiguro took from the Tanizaki original (Tanizaki, 1971: 8). Later in a post-stroke state and unwilling to leave both his art and his sexual desire unfulfilled, Norton directs his frustrated sexual desire to an alternative forbidden thing in his life – his daughter-in-law, Satsuko. Ishiguro's mad old man is latently gay, 'in which came his lusting after Satsu's feet may well be to do with a memory of the onnagata' (Archive 39.4). Ishiguro sees that his adaptation is, at its core, about a man going about his last chance in a sense that he is similar to the hero played by Clint Eastwood in *In the Line of Fire* (1993). 'Late in life for both men, an opportunity comes that makes a life that seems a failure at both professional and personal level glorious' (Archive 49.5).

Ishiguro's adaptation of the father and daughter-in-law relationship is also a perverted version of the relationship between Etsuko and Ogata-san in *A Pale View of Hills*. The daughters-in-law, Etsuko and Satsuko, perform as intermediaries between the estranged fathers and sons. In Ishiguro's adaptation the father (Norton) and son (Charles) have become distant since the mother died. Satsuko cares for the old man on behalf of her husband Charles. The relationship between Satsuko and Norton moves 'from hostility, to acceptance, to fondness, and to dangerous sexual obsession' (Archive 39.6). Different from Tanizaki's manipulative and unfaithful daughter-in-law, Ishiguro's Satsuko is as good and innocent as Etsuko appears to be. She eventually reminds the old man of his need for familial love and companionship, and the story ends with Norton's acceptance of his son.

Another new aspect that Ishiguro introduces to the Tanizaki original is the protagonist's friendship with the Japanese Matsuda. Ishiguro adds an East–West relationship that resembles, in his own words, '*Colonel Blimp* crossed with [*An*] *Artist of the Floating World*' (Archive 39.3). 'Colonel Blimp' here refers to Michael Powell's 1943 British war film *The Life and Death of Colonel Blimp*. The film centres on the developing friendship between two men – a German and an Englishman – in a three-part narrative encompassing the Boer Wars and the two world wars. Borrowing Ishiguro's 1997 comments on the similar Aziz–Fielding friendship in E.M. Forster's novel *A Passage to India* (1924), the film frames an 'emotionally charged' friendship that is 'necessarily desexualized' so that 'it can be made to stand much better as a symbolic relationship' between two rival countries 'in a way that a male-female relationship would not have done' (Archive 49.5). *Colonel Blimp*'s narrative structure and character-relationship have a huge appeal to Ishiguro in that the novelist had been considering this idea to incorporate a symbolic relationship between two countries since his composition of *The Remains of the Day*, and he attempted to illustrate it at that moment with his hedonistic American art collector Norton and Japanese artist friend Masuda, who introduced Norton to Japanese woodblock art and the lustrous nightlife of Japan.[4]

The Matsuda friendship is more convincingly conveyed in Ishiguro's later screenplay *The White Countess*. Quite similar to the Matsuda in Tanizaki's novel, Ishiguro's Matsuda is a mysterious Japanese man who appears to share the protagonist Jackson's aesthetics and secretly assists his project to his own aim. Matsuda, in both cases, stands for the inactivator of Ishiguro's protagonists' idealistic fantasy that gradually derails them from the real world. The former American diplomat Jackson who has literally lost his sight and languishes in

Shanghai's gentlemen's clubs in *The White Countess* has a lot in common with Tanizaki's dying old man whose obsession with the feet of the Japanese girl reveals his last effort to cling to his disillusioned aesthetic ideal. Notably, the working title of Ishiguro's 1995 script was 'The Aesthete' – referring to the old man Norton's profession. This makes sense given the fact that Ishiguro abandoned his Tanizaki project mid-way to hand over, instead, an original play to James Ivory. For *The White Countess* Ishiguro shifts *A Diary of a Mad Old Man*'s time and setting to late 1930s prewar Shanghai. The choice is made partly because of Ishiguro's personal relation with Shanghai of the 1930s – both his grandfather and his father worked in Shanghai during the international occupation. Additionally, China, as an exotic location to the West, had not yet been overly exploited as Japan had been, especially after Alain Resnais's film *Hiroshima mon amour* (1959) (Archive ISK0009).

The similarity between Ishiguro's two scripts is visible not only in the working title of *The White Countess* script but also in the protagonist's problematic idealistic pursuit. Norton and Jackson are both connoisseurs of decadence, retreating into a smaller and more controllable world that harbours an ambition that they had always secretly nurtured. For Jackson it is to create in Shanghai's pleasure district the 'perfect sleazy bar', with Sofia – the exiled Russian countess – as the centrepiece (Archive 46.6). For Norton it is to regain his passion for beauty through fantasised lust for the sleazy Japanese daughter-in-law, which estranges his wife and son in real life. The Japanese girl and the Russian countess, thereby, symbolise the fallen grandeur of things, the beauty that Ishiguro's protagonists once believed in and that now falls out of date.

Chu-Chueh Cheng also reads *The White Countess* as a liberal cinematic 'adaptation' of *Diary of a Mad Old Man*. Although Cheng's instinct to connect the two is right, he uses 'adaptation' in a figurative sense rather than in the literal sense that I have discussed in this chapter. Claiming that 'imprints of Tanizaki's writing, though elusive, are detectible' (2019: 385) in Ishiguro's script, on the basis of a comparative reading of style, Cheng brings to focus that Ishiguro's 'each new work evinces his attempt to revisit an earlier theme' and 'Matsuda in *Countess* exemplifies Ishiguro's repetition in variation' (2019: 384). However, a sense of 'non-relation' between Ishiguro's script and Tanizaki's novel is conveyed, as Cheng notes, 'Matsuda in the *Countess* does not resemble any character in Tanizaki's novel', and the core idea of *Countess* originates from Ishiguro's earlier novels. I generally endorse that *Diary* is a hidden text that Ishiguro integrates into his screenplay of *The White Countess*, but characters like Matsuda together with the themes and settings, as I have shown through Ishiguro's 'real' adaptation script of Tanizaki's novel, are things Ishiguro 'transplants' from his earlier screenplays rather than entirely from his own novels.

The Saddest Music in the World and Ishiguro's other writings

Ishiguro's fourth original film script, *The Saddest Music in the World*, was successfully adapted to screen by the Canadian filmmaker Guy Maddin in 2003. The script is, surprisingly, among the early writings of the novelist, which not only blends in themes of his previous screenplay but also shapes his later novels. Ishiguro started working on the screenplay in 1987 and finished the first draft in 1990. The film then went through a hard period, passing by several directors – Atom Egoyan, Don Mackellar – in the 1990s, during which Ishiguro kept revising the script under the commission of Paramount Pictures until he finished the second draft in 1998. The waiting continued until Rhombus Media Production and the experimental film director Guy Maddin took the project in 2002. Guy Maddin and his collaborator George Toles made drastic changes to Ishiguro's script to the extent that they felt certain that Ishiguro would reject their adaptation proposal. Maddin and Toles disclosed in an interview that they only kept 'the title, the premise and the contest – to determine which country's music was the saddest', and rewrote all its characters and plots on the basis of their own 'notion of sadness as an entity' (Ball and Navratil, 2004). Having his script truncated and remoulded by Maddin was not an easy decision for Ishiguro to make. However, trusting Maddin's talent, Ishiguro eventually softened and let Maddin take the project.

First shown at the Toronto International Film Festival in September 2003, the film adaptation won six film festival awards, including 'The Best Adapted Screenplay'. Jonathan Rosenbaum proclaimed the film a masterpiece and wrote in his 2004 *Chicago Reader* review that 'the grief expressed in the story is too keenly felt to be a target of derision; the facts may be cruel and monstrous, but the laughter provoked by them is almost always sympathetic and tender'. Isabella Rossellini plays Lady Port-Huntly in the Maddin adaptation, a legless beer baroness who organises a large-prize contest to discover the saddest music in the world of the 1930s Depression era. She believes that the musicians gathering at Winnipeg will promote her business. It almost works. However, during the competition, a love triangle and a family feud slowly brew into a Maddinesque melodrama.

Different from Maddin's musical, which involves repressed sadness, brutal amputation and love rivalry between father and son, Ishiguro's *The Saddest Music in the World*, like all his works, exhibits a rigorous refusal to sensationalise. In the 1987 script synopsis Ishiguro noted that much of the texture of the film derives from documentary coverage of the performance of the artists itself 'to capture them preparing, performing and talking about their music' (Archive 40.11). Ishiguro's music competition is set in London of the 1980s and is sponsored instead by a soft drinks company in order to determine, around the globe, whose history is more tragic on a national level. 'Behind the music', Ishiguro wrote, 'lie stories of wars, exile, oppression; of small nations swallowed up and vanished from the map; of refugees cruelly tossed by the tides of history' (Archive 40.11). At the centre of this 'massive lament on the tragedies of human history' is a triangular relationship among three characters – Geraldine, Pieter and Mario. Geraldine is an American former pianist who sacrificed her promising music career for a failed marriage. One thing that has sustained her throughout her life of sorrow is Mario Cesar's music, through which Geraldine has found a reflection of her own pain and frustration. She follows Mario to this competition. However, Mario is under the conviction that an authentic artist such as himself should make music out of the tragedies of his people – the Peruvian Indians – wherein lies his music's meaning. He, therefore, considers Geraldine's equation of her trivial life frustration with his nation's tragedy 'a disgraceful misunderstanding of his art'. Mario's belief is to be changed as he realises that 'the international appeal of his art very much depends on such misinterpretations' (Archive 40.11).

As the life of an individual and the destinies of a civilisation are always intertwined in Ishiguro's work, the matter of personal sadness is linked with the great national tragedies of history by the love affair of Geraldine and Pieter during the music contest. Pieter Myrdal is an Estonian musician in rivalry with Mario on both artistic and romantic aspects. He plays the traditional music of his people to 'keep alive the memory of his forgotten nation' (Archive 40.11), but he also fabricated his past experience under the regime of the Nazis and Stalinism to 'give himself a false authenticity'. Geraldine, on the other hand, has only personal sadness. It is the only way she accesses meaning, through which she misinterprets music with grand motives as embodiment of her divorce, bereavement and estrangement from her child. Pieter finds in Geraldine the genuine individual expression of tragedy that his music lacks. Thereby their love builds.

Ishiguro composed two versions of scripts (1987 and 1999) for *The Saddest Music in the World* within seventeen years, aiming to bring on two themes that set forth his later novels. The initial theme is to answer 'the question of whether tragedies of a person's life have any meaning next to the huge tragic events of history' (Archive 43.2). This intersection between personal and national grief develops into *The Buried Giant*, in which Ishiguro focuses on the love of an old Christian couple and the Britons' tragedy. Interestingly, the Britons' tragedy is also briefly glimpsed in Ishiguro's 1987 version of *The Saddest Music in the World* screenplay. Among the Depression-era musicians who sob away at what they deem to be the world's saddest tunes are the Celtic lamenters from Ireland. *The Buried Giant* repeats this Celtic-history theme, but it is expressed not through music but through the ferryman storyteller. He tells a tale about an old Briton couple's bereavement of their son, their estrangement from their people and their final separation, along with the tale of the pre-Anglo-Saxon Britannia in the similar predicament but on a larger scale. The implied readers addressed by the mythical ferryman in the third-person narration were supposed to be 'the ghosts of children who have been slaughtered in the past war' (Georgesco and Ishiguro, 2017). Telling the story for the amusement of his underworld audience through the ferryman, Ishiguro suggests that the Saxons' vengeful massacre of the Britons in history represents the re-emergence of the suppressed within the Christianised realm. *The Saddest Music in the World* can thus be read as a precursor of Ishiguro's novel because they both ponder on what Ishiguro phrases, 'the paradox that the human suffering can be turned into art for the sublime enjoyment of others' (Archive 40.11).

The second theme that Ishiguro's screenplay ponders is 'the limit to which art can convey the sorrows of one people to another', and in its extension, 'the extent to which people can share and sympathize with each other's sorrows' (Archive 40.11). *The Saddest Music in the World* expresses it through Geraldine's misplaced admiration for Mario through music. This theme was first voiced in Ishiguro's second screenplay, *The Gourmet*, written three years earlier in 1984; its protagonist literally consumes for pleasure the flesh of the dead, upon which he builds a prestigious artistic career.

Empathy for sadness is further developed in Ishiguro's 2000 novel *When We Were Orphans* as a logic of association for its first-person narrator Christopher Banks. In a 1996 note Ishiguro comments that in this detective novel he intends to build upon the idea that 'Banks takes on cases not because they parallel his own parents' case, but rather that he is driven to a less precise emotional thing – a sadness, a loneliness, a let-down-ness about some future or person in the case. He is lured as though to a piece of music, by the melancholy, ineffable pull which echoes with something in his own spirit' (Archive 26.6). Later, in Ishiguro's 2005 novel *Never Let Me Go*, the theme of the limit of emotional empathy returns again through the vessel of music, as Madame sees Kathy playing the song 'Never Let Me Go' and holding her imaginary baby. Madame is brought to tears because she misinterprets it as clones' plea for mercy towards humans, whereas what truly troubles Kathy at the moment is of a much smaller scale – that is, to hold on and never let go of the precious thing that she imagines that she is having, 'a baby', which embodies hope for the future (*NLMG*: 70). Therefore, the quilting point between the personal sadness of Kathy and the mass grief of her kind is first shown to the readers through chance, by a misunderstanding, and without the first-person narrator's recognition, through which Ishiguro conveys the poignancy and inconsolability of the story.

Conclusion

Kazuo Ishiguro has an important relationship with television and film that has been considered peripheral in the past, but 'any critical account of his work must consider the nature of this lifelong engagement with visual arts' (Groes and Veyret, 2010: 32). As this chapter has shown, Ishiguro is a writer who has taken cinema inside his prose, and his scriptwriting provides an essential platform for Ishiguro to test and integrate ideas in-between the two media. To support this claim I have examined his published and unpublished television and film plays in relation to his major novels. My aim has been to shed light on the overlooked influence of Ishiguro's own scriptwriting on his novel writing by showing that some crucial themes, narrative techniques and character relationships in Ishiguro's fictions occur in his early screenplays and that almost every Ishiguro novel reprises an earlier theme from his film scripts.

Ishiguro's scriptwriting continues to this day. During the COVID-19 pandemic lockdown Ishiguro finished his second adaptation script to date, entitled *Living*. It is an adaptation from Akira Kurosawa's 1952 original screenplay *Ikiru*. Ishiguro moves the setting from Japan to England in 1952 and tells the story of a veteran civil servant William's quest for the meaning of his monotonous life after learning that illness will soon take him. William finds meaning by befriending a young woman who exemplifies what life and living should have been for him. Inspired, he uses his remaining days to work through a project to help the poor children of London (Wiseman, 2020). Ishiguro's *Ikiru* reinterpretation seems, once again, a reiteration of the dying old man Norman in his adaptation of *Diary of a Mad Old Man*, who ponders over death and attempts to seize the day, intrigued by a young woman. Nevertheless, 'the inner story' of the new adaptation, as Ishiguro puts it, lies in that 'it's the responsibility of each of us to bring meaning and satisfaction to our life. That even against the odds, we should try to find a way to be proud of, and happy with, the lives we lead' (quoted in Wiseman, 2020).

Funding/acknowledgment

This research is supported by the National Social Science Foundation of China under project No. 22BWW039; and Harry Ransom Center, The University of Texas at Austin (Alfred A. and Blanche W. Knopf Fellowship 2020).

Notes

1 In this work I indicate all of the citations of the Kazuo Ishiguro papers in the Harry Ransom Center with 'Archive' in addition to the box-file-page number or video number.
2 For further guidance on adaptation studies in relation to Ishiguro, see Göçmen and Akdoğan (2021); Williams (2020) and Shang (2017).
3 The precursors of *The Remains of the Day* include *A Profile of Arthur J. Mason* (1982), *England in October* (1983), *The Patron* (1984), *The Great East and West Novel* (1986) and *Service in Japan* (1987).
4 Ishiguro attempted to replicate the British–German relationship in his 1989 draft for *The Great East and West Novel* and *Butler in England* script – both are unfinished precursors for *The Remains of the Day*.

References

Ball, Jonathan and David Navratil (2004). 'Guy Maddin and George Toles Interviewed about Writing *The Saddest Music in the World*', *Scri(i)pt Magazine*.
Cheng, Chu-Chueh (2019). 'Reframing Ishiguro's Oeuvre through the Japanese Militarist in *The White Countess*'. *Orbis Litterarum*, 74, 381–391.
Fluet, Lisa (2007). 'Antisocial Goods', *Novel: A Forum on Fiction*, 40:3, 207–215.
Georgesco, Florent and Kazuo Ishiguro (2017). 'Kazuo Ishiguro, Nobel Prize for Literature 2017', 8 October, www.youtube.com/watch?v=hQ18swkKaVA (accessed June 2021).
Göçmen, Gülşah and Özlem Özmen Akdoğan (2021). 'Nostalgic (Re)Visions of Englishness in Merchant Ivory's Adaptation of Kazuo Ishiguro's *The Remains of the Day*', *Journal of Language, Literature and Culture*, 68:1: 49–63.
Groes, Sebastian and Paul-Daniel Veyret (2010). 'Like the Gateway to Another World: Kazuo Ishiguro's Screenwriting', in Sean Matthews and Sebastian Groes (eds), *Kazuo Ishiguro: Contemporary Critical Perspectives* (London: Bloomsbury), 32–44.
Ishiguro, Kazuo (1984). *A Profile of Arthur J. Mason*, Channel 4, 18 October, directed M. Whyte.
—. (1986). *The Gourmet*, Channel 4, 8 May, directed M. Whyte.
—. (1989). *The Remains of the Day* (London: Faber and Faber).
—. (1995). *The Unconsoled* (London: Faber and Faber).
—. (2003). *The Saddest Music in the World*, IFC, 24 October, directed Guy Maddin.

—. (2005). *Never Let Me Go* (London: Faber and Faber).
—. (2005). *The White Countess*, Sony, 21 December, directed James Ivory.
Lemon, Robert (2011). 'The Comfort of Strangeness: Correlating the Kafkaesque and the Kafkan in Kazuo Ishiguro's *The Unconsoled*', in Stanley Corngold and Ruth V. Gross (eds), *Kafka for the Twenty-First Century* (Rochester, NY: Camden House), 207–221.
Pasolini, Pier Paolo (1976). 'The Cinema of Poetry', in Bill Nichols (ed.), *Movies and Methods* (Berkeley: University of California Press), 542–558.
Rosenbaum, Jonathan (2004). 'The Saddest Music in the World', *Chicago Reader*, 14 May.
Shang, Wu (2017). 'Articulations in Translation at the Intersection of World Literature and Popular Culture: Film and TV Adaptations of Ishiguro's *Never Let Me Go*', *Canadian Review of Comparative Literature*, 44:3, 553–564.
Shonaka, Takayuki (2011). *Kazuo Ishiguro: Nihon to Igirisu no aida kara* (Tokyo: Shunpusha).
Tanizaki, Jun'ichiro (1971). *Diary of a Mad Old Man*, translated by Howard Hibbett (Berkeley: Berkeley Publishing Corporation).
Williams, Chanda (2020). 'Abject Adaptations: Disability in Clone Culture and Adaptation of Kazuo Ishiguro's *Never Let Me Go*', *The Midwest Quarterly*, 61:2, 274–288.
Wiseman, Andreas (2020). 'Living Deadline', *Deadline*, 15 October, https://deadline.com/2020/10/living-bill-nighy-aimee-lou-wood-to-star-in-kazuo-ishiguro-adaptation-of-kurosawas-ikiru-for-carol-producer-number-9-rocket-science-afm-1234597919/ (accessed June 2021).

Index

agency 77, 80, 212–214, 217, 218, 219, 222, 225
AI *see* posthumanism
Arendt, Hannah 13, 89, 213, 218–219, 221, 223, 225
Armstrong, Nancy 149, 167

Baudrillard, Jean 152, 154, 155
Bennett, Andrew 11, 82 n.13
Bhabha, Homi K. 18, 93, 201
biotechnology 150–151
Boym, Svetlana 171–173, 175, 177, 186, 186 n.2
Brexit 10, 13, 87, 94–95, 97, 98, 99, 102, 188, 189, 196, 202, 209 n.2

Cheng, Chu-Chueh 46, 48, 229, 240–241
childhood 49, 51, 52, 57, 76, 84, 131, 132, 139, 141–142 n.3, 156, 170, 173, 175, 177, 178, 180, 186, 223
Cold War 19, 28, 34, 154, 173
cosmopolitanism 5, 6, 11, 95, 101, 109, 115, 116, 118, 122, 124, 142 n.7, 202, 205, 208
hospitality 10, 86, 90, 91, 93, 99, 110, 208

Derrida, Jacques 10, 86–87, 90, 91, 92, 93, 94, 95, 96, 98, 101, 102, 104, 217–218

domesticity 9, 24, 26, 28, 33, 45, 137

Eaglestone, Robert 6, 13
Eckert, Ken 23, 25, 43, 44–45
empathy 2, 9, 11, 40, 51, 57, 146, 148, 149, 151, 156, 157, 158, 159, 160, 162, 164, 165, 166, 167, 205, 244
England 2, 13, 19, 20, 26, 28, 30, 33, 34, 44, 55, 56, 78, 86, 93, 110, 111, 112, 129, 136, 142 n.10, 167 n.1, 170, 189, 191–192, 196, 198, 200, 201, 203, 208, 209 n.1, 209 n.2, 231, 232, 245
Englishness 13, 68, 189, 191, 192, 193, 201, 202, 204
English sublime 6, 12, 13, 192–201, 202, 204
Europe 4, 87, 95, 96, 100, 102, 114, 118, 188, 196, 202, 209 n.2
European Union 86, 87, 94–95, 97, 103, 188, 196, 202, 209 n.2

family 6, 9, 10, 24, 33, 45–51, 52, 53, 56, 58 n.3, 58 n.5, 68, 109, 121, 131, 132, 137, 155, 163, 173, 182, 242

Index

Finney, Brian 128, 130, 135, 141 n.3
forgiveness 6, 13, 217–218, 219–220, 221–225
Fukuyama, Francis 149, 150

Gill, Josie 214, 215
grief 7–8, 28, 42, 43, 47, 50, 116, 242, 243, 244
Groes, Sebastian 229, 245
guilt 8, 20, 21, 22, 25, 26, 28, 33, 34, 35, 42, 43, 44, 45, 47, 48, 64, 67, 158, 199

Heidegger, Martin 13, 213, 215, 216
Herzinger, Kim 41, 85, 191
Horton, Emily 8
Hutcheon, Linda 174–175, 180, 181
Huxley, Aldous 152
   Brave New World 11, 148, 151–152, 156, 160

immigration 17, 49, 94, 129, 142 n.7, 203
imperialism 7, 8, 20, 22–23, 27, 34, 36, 64, 65, 70, 89, 94, 131, 138, 140, 141 n.2, 156, 193, 200
Ishiguro, Kazuo
   An Artist of the Floating World 2, 3, 8–9, 21, 40–58, 61–82, 155, 156, 177, 194, 223, 229, 238, 239
   The Buried Giant 6, 7, 10, 12–13, 49, 81 n.1, 86, 109, 110, 124 n.1, 129, 184, 188–209, 222, 223, 224, 230, 235, 243
   childhood 2, 20, 49, 85, 170
   A Family Supper 63–64, 236
   The Gourmet 14, 14 n.2, 229, 236, 238, 244
   The Great East and West Novel 246 n.3, 246 n.4

   Klara and the Sun 1, 6, 7, 12, 13, 58 n.3, 103, 107–108, 110, 148, 212–225
   Living 14, 245
   Never Let Me Go 1, 5, 6, 7, 11–12, 13, 86, 89–90, 101, 103, 108, 146–168, 170, 171, 212, 214, 223, 224, 225, 230, 244
   Nobel Prize 1, 4, 22, 144 n.17, 189, 195, 208
   Nocturnes 7, 12, 170–186
   A Pale View of Hills 2, 3, 8, 17–37, 40–41, 48, 51–58, 63, 64, 69, 74–75, 194, 224, 228, 230, 236, 238
   The Patron 233, 246 n.3
   Potatoes and Lovers 227
   A Profile of Arthur J. Mason 14, 14 n.2, 230, 232, 234, 246 n.3
   The Remains of the Day 1, 2, 3, 7, 10, 14 n.2, 47, 64, 68, 75, 84–104, 108, 109, 116, 123, 155, 156, 188, 191, 200, 209 n.3, 212, 223, 229, 230, 231, 232, 233, 234, 236, 237, 239, 246 n.3, 246 n.4
   The Saddest Music in the World 14, 229–230, 241–244
   Service in Japan 233, 246 n.3
   The Unconsoled 3, 10–11, 58 n.3, 108–125, 126, 142 n.4, 155, 178, 184, 185, 209 n.5, 212, 223, 224, 235
   When We Were Orphans 2, 11, 68, 82 n.13, 126–144, 170, 178, 209 n.5, 212, 223, 230, 244
   The White Countess 14, 15 n.4, 131, 141, 143 n.15, 229, 236, 237–241
Japan 2, 3–4, 6, 8, 9, 14 n.2, 18, 19, 20–22, 27, 28, 29, 30,

31, 32, 34, 35, 36, 40, 42, 47, 49, 55, 56, 57, 58 n.4, 61, 62, 63, 64, 65, 68, 73, 81 n.4, 81 n.5, 131, 133, 136, 138, 139, 143 n.15, 156, 178, 209 n.4, 219, 230, 233, 236, 237, 238, 239, 240, 245
Nagasaki 2–3, 4, 23, 24, 29, 31, 33, 40, 49, 84
  see also Second World War

Karni, Rebecca 4, 9, 11, 45, 49, 142 n.6, 142 n.9
Keen, Suzanne 11, 148, 158–159, 160, 161, 162, 166

Lewis, Barry 4, 23, 25, 36 n.1, 42, 58 n.3
London 3, 14 n.2, 51–52, 127, 173, 179, 238, 242, 245

Mason, Gregory 3, 4, 20, 21, 28, 44, 63, 81 n.5, 81 n.6
Matek, Ljubica 21–22, 43, 45, 56
memory 2, 5, 6, 7, 8, 12, 17–18, 21, 25, 36, 42, 43, 44, 46, 49, 57, 58 n.6, 71, 109, 129, 130, 133, 155, 156, 170, 171, 172, 174, 175, 176, 178, 179, 181, 184, 185, 188–191, 193–198, 201, 202, 204, 206, 207, 208, 209 n.5, 215, 238, 243
  collective 6, 189–190, 192, 193, 194, 195–196, 197–198, 202, 204, 205, 206, 208, 209 n.5
  see also trauma
migration 2, 8, 17–18, 19, 20, 21–22, 26, 28, 29, 30, 34, 35, 45, 49, 55, 56, 58 n.5
  diaspora 8, 17–23, 25, 27, 29, 31, 34, 36, 36 n.1
modernism 4, 5

Molino, Michael 43–44
motherhood 19, 25–27, 32, 33

nationalism 8, 10, 13, 19, 20, 34, 36, 40, 49, 53, 71, 95, 127, 193–194, 196, 200, 201–203, 205, 207–208, 212, 219, 223
  populism 7, 13, 188, 202
neo-humanism 149, 167
neo-imperialism 19, 23, 29, 31, 34, 35
nostalgia 7, 12, 18, 21, 47, 49, 94, 170–187, 191, 192, 197, 232, 237
Nussbaum, Martha 11, 149, 159–162, 166, 167

Orientalism 8, 9, 20, 23, 29, 30–31, 34–36, 37 n.1, 61, 81 n.4

Plato 13, 87, 213, 214, 215–216, 225
posthumanism 10, 11, 12, 13, 58 n.3, 107, 117, 146–147, 148, 149–152, 157, 158, 159, 161, 162, 164, 165, 167, 213
postmodernism 4–5, 7, 35, 57 n.1, 74, 85, 103, 147, 190, 192
pregnancy 23, 24, 25, 27, 42, 56, 58 n.5
presentational realism 9, 62–64, 67–68, 69, 74–76, 80–81
Puccini, Giacomo 8
  Madama Butterfly 8, 20, 28, 29, 31, 34–35

racism 13, 19, 127, 138, 143 n.13, 203, 208
responsibility 9–10, 33, 48, 85–104, 137, 245
Robbins, Bruce 6, 10–11, 76
Rushdie, Salman 21, 22, 172

Second World War 2, 6, 34, 64, 65, 84, 103, 104, 126, 128, 133, 136, 196, 209 n.4, 233, 237
Sergeant, Harriet 136–140, 143 n.12, 143 n.13, 143 n.14, 143 n.15
Shanghai 138–139, 143 n.16
Shanghai 126, 128, 129, 131, 132, 133, 135, 136, 137–138, 139, 140, 142 n.5, 142 n.7, 143 n.11, 143 n.15, 170, 178, 239–240
Shaffer, Brian 21, 41, 126, 127, 136, 141 n.1, 142 n.3, 142 n.9, 143 n.11, 144 n.17, 155, 178, 180
Shaw, Kristian 6, 10, 12–13, 94–95
Shelley, Mary 150
  Frankenstein 11, 148, 150–151, 152, 154, 167
Shen, Anni 13–14, 57
Sloane, Peter 5, 11–12, 14 n.1, 41–42
spectrality 7, 8, 24, 25, 31, 33, 34, 46, 52, 55, 140, 172, 189, 193–194, 196, 199, 205, 206, 208, 238, 243

Tanizaki, Jun'ichiro 4, 236
  A Diary of a Mad Old Man 15 n.4, 229, 236, 237, 239, 240–241

Teo, Yugin 12, 44, 194, 209 n.5
Thatcher, Margaret 29, 34, 94, 103, 229
Tokyo 32, 49, 50, 64
transglossic 6, 104
trauma 7, 8, 17–18, 20, 21, 22–23, 24, 25–27, 28, 29, 31, 32, 33, 40, 43, 45, 52, 56, 156, 188, 190, 194, 198–199, 206, 223

Upstone, Sara 6, 9–10, 209 n.3

Veyret, Paul-Daniel *see* Groes, Sebastian
Vorda, Allan *see* Herzinger, Kim

Walkowitz, Rebecca 5, 6, 19, 42, 43, 49, 78
Waugh, Patricia 171, 175
Whitehead, Anne 11, 146, 159, 160, 161, 162, 165, 166, 182, 186 n.1
Wilhelm, Kate 152
  Where Late the Sweet Birds Sang 11, 148, 152–153, 154, 162
Wong, Cynthia 3, 8–9, 80, 126–127, 135–136, 141 n.1, 141 n.3, 142 n.9, 143 n.11, 144 n.17, 155, 170, 190

Yentob, Alan 84, 88, 97, 101, 104

EU authorised representative for GPSR:
Easy Access System Europe, Mustamäe tee 50,
10621 Tallinn, Estonia
gpsr.requests@easproject.com

www.ingramcontent.com/pod-product-compliance
Lightning Source LLC
Chambersburg PA
CBHW051608230426
43668CB00013B/2021